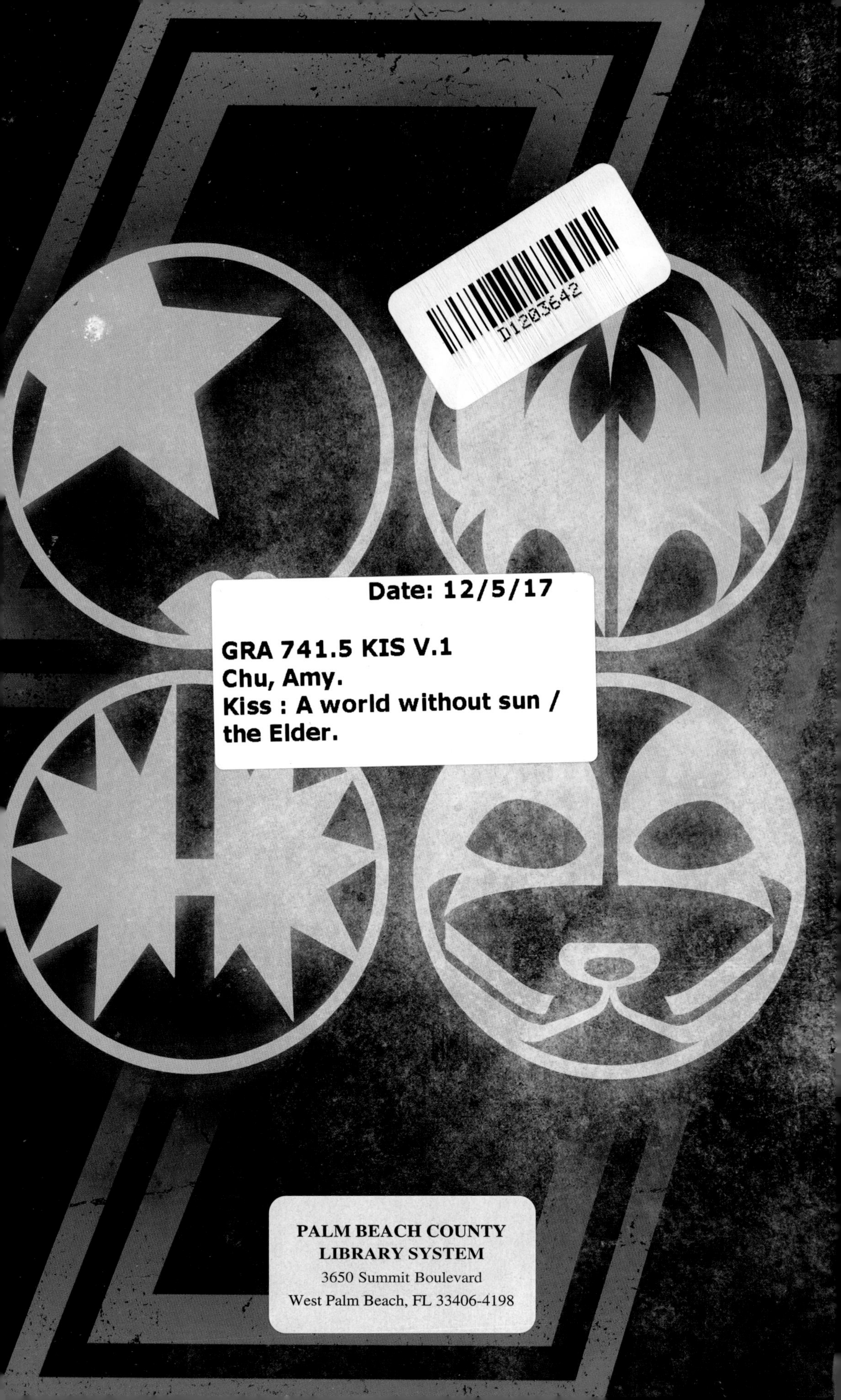

KISS®: THE ELDER

WRITTEN BY
AMY CHU

ART BY
KEWBER BAAL

LETTERING BY
TROY PETERI

COLOR BY
SCHIMERYS BAAL

VOLUME I: A WORLD WITHOUT SUN

COLLECTION COVER BY
**NICK BRADSHAW
& PETE PANTAZIS**

EDITS BY
**ANTHONY MARQUES
& JOSEPH RYBANDT**

COLLECTION DESIGN BY
CATHLEEN HEARD

DYNAMITE®

Online at www.DYNAMITE.com
On Facebook /Dynamitecomics
On Instagram /Dynamitecomics
On Tumblr dynamitecomics.tumblr.com
On Twitter @dynamitecomics
On YouTube /Dynamitecomics

Nick Barrucci, CEO / Publishe
Juan Collado, President / CO

Joe Rybandt, Executive Edito
Matt Idelson, Senior Edito
Anthony Marques, Associate Edito
Kevin Ketner, Editorial Assistar

Jason Ullmeyer, Art Directo
Geoff Harkins, Senior Graphic Designe
Cathleen Heard, Senior Graphic Designe
Alexis Persson, Production Artis

Chris Caniano, Digital Associat
Rachel Kilbury, Digital Assistar

Brandon Dante Primavera, V.P. of IT and Operation
Rich Young, Director of Business Developmen

Alan Payne, V.P. of Sales and Marketin
Keith Davidsen, Marketing Directo
Pat O'Connell, Sales Manage

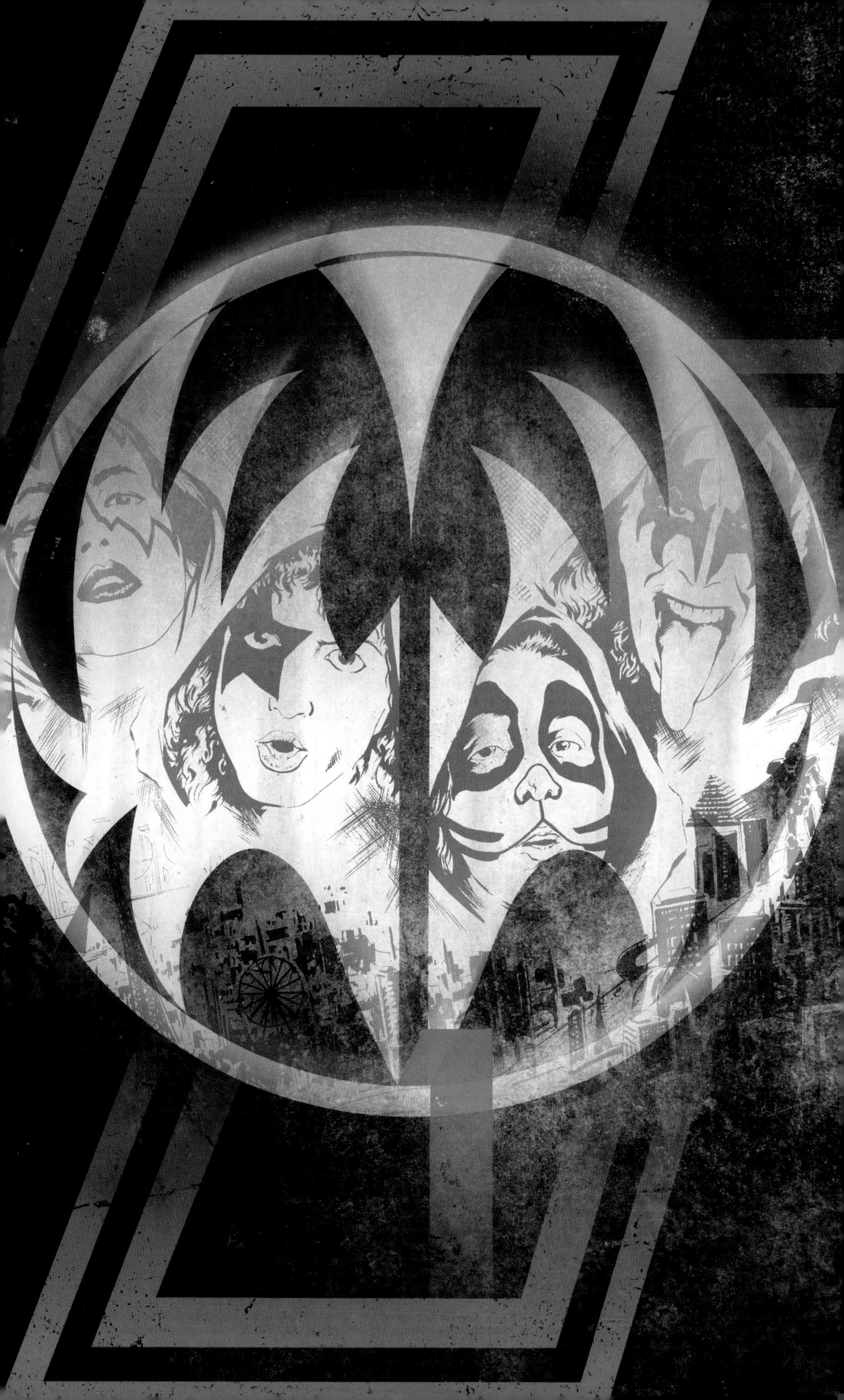

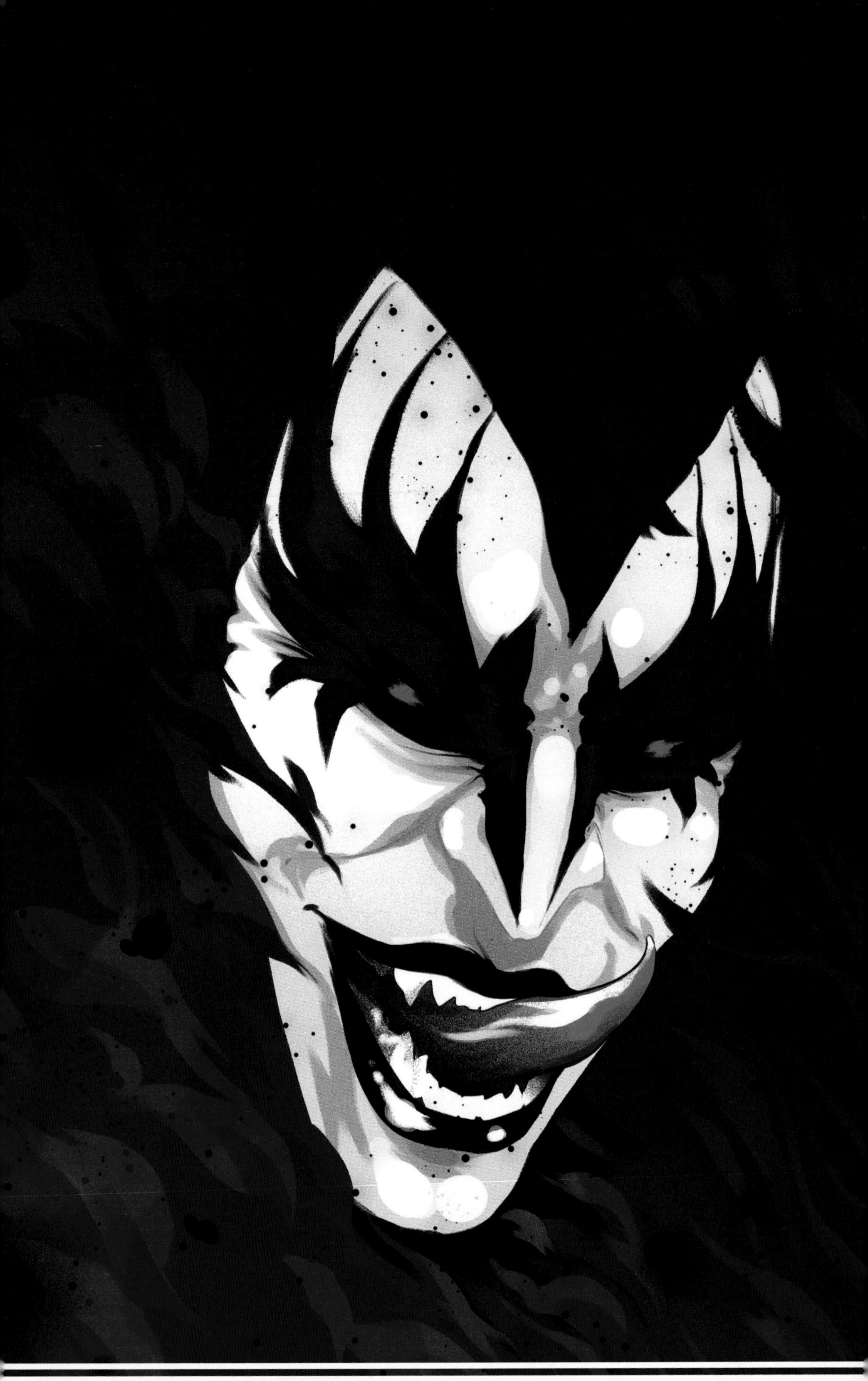

ISSUE 1, MAIN COVER: "Demon" Art by Goni Montes

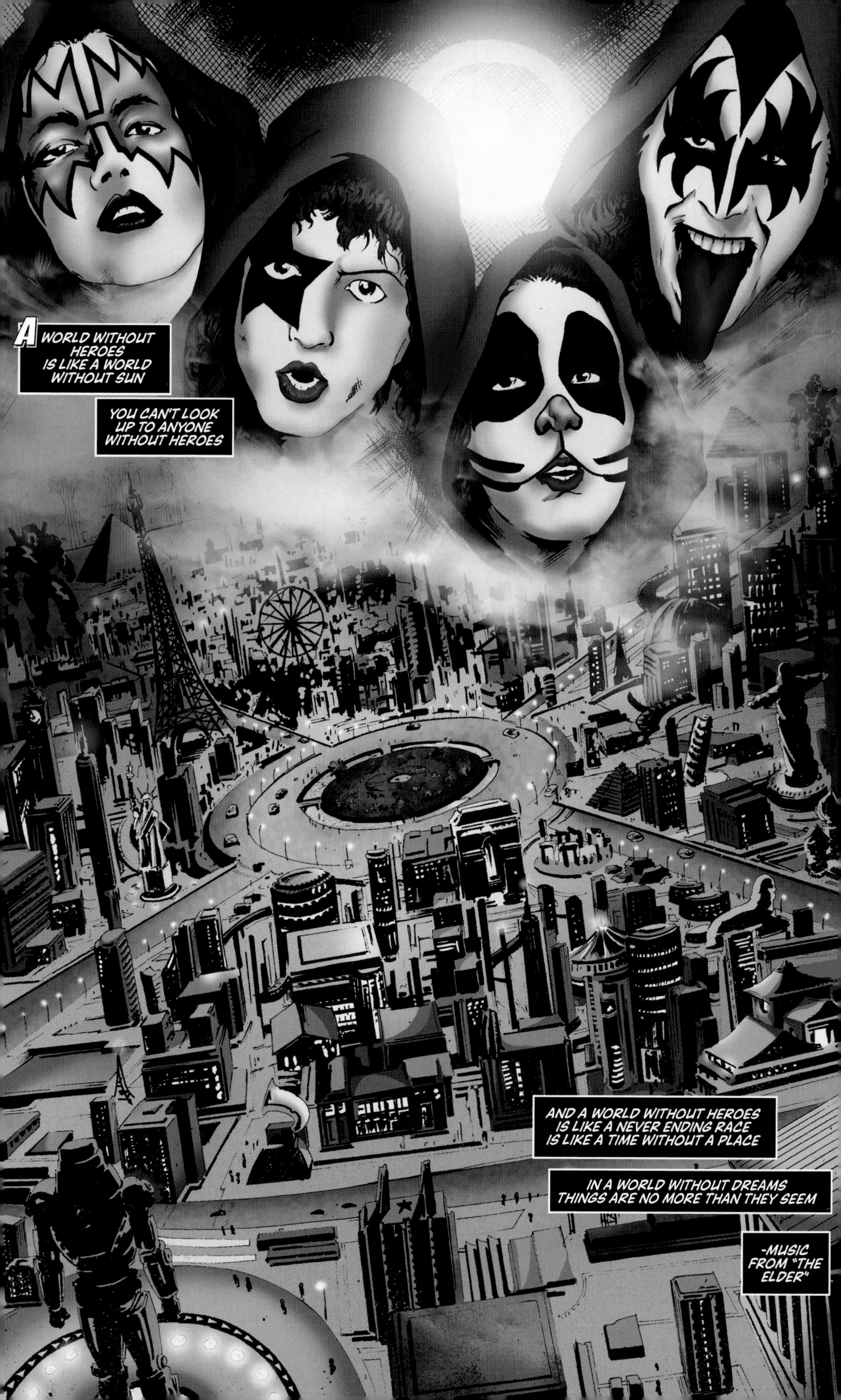
A WORLD WITHOUT HEROES IS LIKE A WORLD WITHOUT SUN
YOU CAN'T LOOK UP TO ANYONE WITHOUT HEROES
AND A WORLD WITHOUT HEROES IS LIKE A NEVER ENDING RACE IS LIKE A TIME WITHOUT A PLACE
IN A WORLD WITHOUT DREAMS THINGS ARE NO MORE THAN THEY SEEM
-MUSIC FROM "THE ELDER"

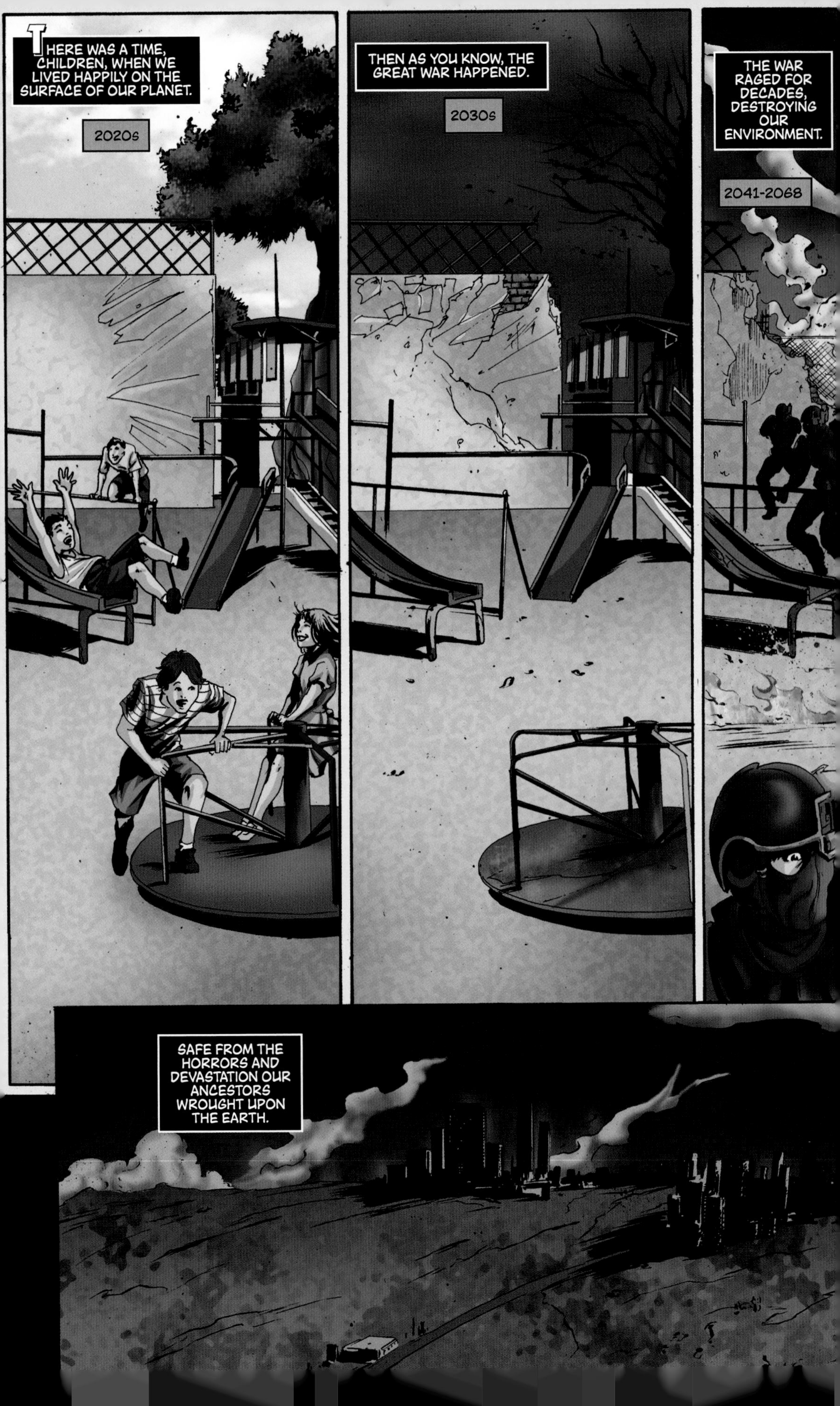
THERE WAS A TIME, CHILDREN, WHEN WE LIVED HAPPILY ON THE SURFACE OF OUR PLANET.
2020s
THEN AS YOU KNOW, THE GREAT WAR HAPPENED.
2030s
THE WAR RAGED FOR DECADES, DESTROYING OUR ENVIRONMENT.
2041-2068
SAFE FROM THE HORRORS AND DEVASTATION OUR ANCESTORS WROUGHT UPON THE EARTH.

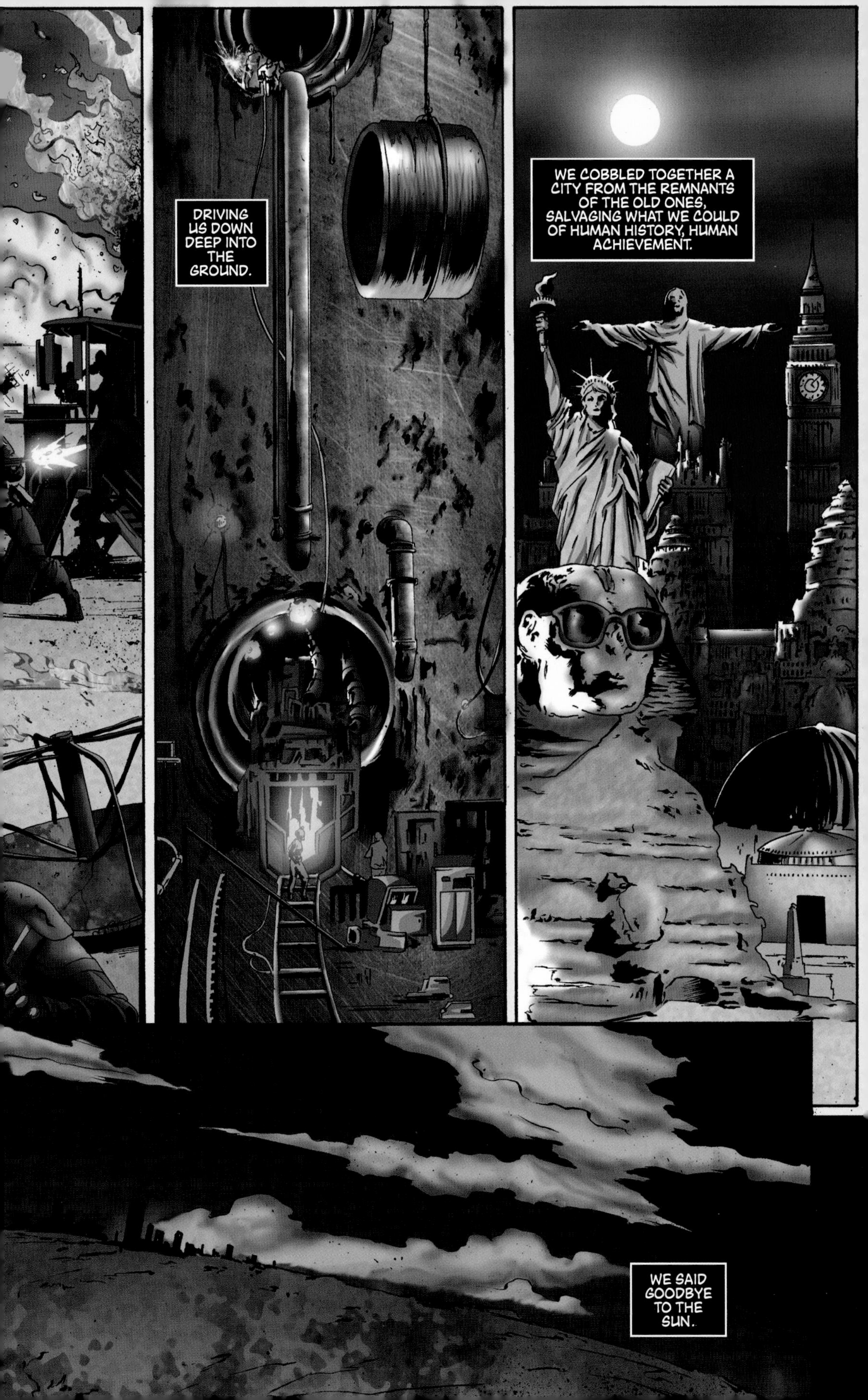
DRIVING US DOWN DEEP INTO THE GROUND.
WE COBBLED TOGETHER A CITY FROM THE REMNANTS OF THE OLD ONES, SALVAGING WHAT WE COULD OF HUMAN HISTORY, HUMAN ACHIEVEMENT.
WE SAID GOODBYE TO THE SUN.

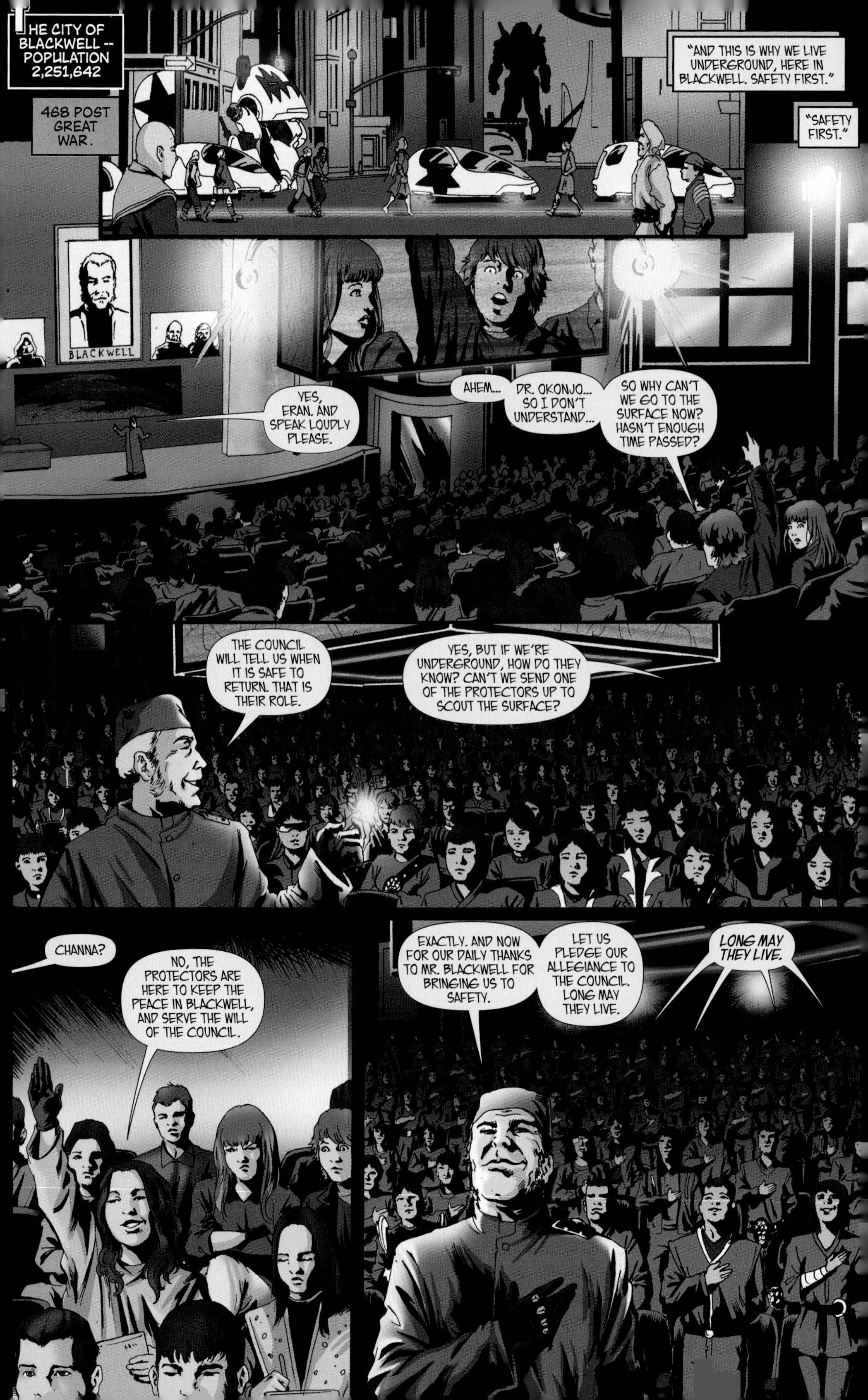
THE CITY OF BLACKWELL -- POPULATION 2,251,642
468 POST GREAT WAR.
"AND THIS IS WHY WE LIVE UNDERGROUND, HERE IN BLACKWELL. SAFETY FIRST."
"SAFETY FIRST."
BLACKWELL
AHEM...
DR. OKONJO... SO I DON'T UNDERSTAND...
SO WHY CAN'T WE GO TO THE SURFACE NOW? HASN'T ENOUGH TIME PASSED?
YES, ERAN. AND SPEAK LOUDLY PLEASE.
THE COUNCIL WILL TELL US WHEN IT IS SAFE TO RETURN. THAT IS THEIR ROLE.
YES, BUT IF WE'RE UNDERGROUND, HOW DO THEY KNOW? CAN'T WE SEND ONE OF THE PROTECTORS UP TO SCOUT THE SURFACE?
CHANNA?
NO, THE PROTECTORS ARE HERE TO KEEP THE PEACE IN BLACKWELL, AND SERVE THE WILL OF THE COUNCIL.
EXACTLY. AND NOW FOR OUR DAILY THANKS TO MR. BLACKWELL FOR BRINGING US TO SAFETY.
LET US PLEDGE OUR ALLEGIANCE TO THE COUNCIL. LONG MAY THEY LIVE.
LONG MAY THEY LIVE.

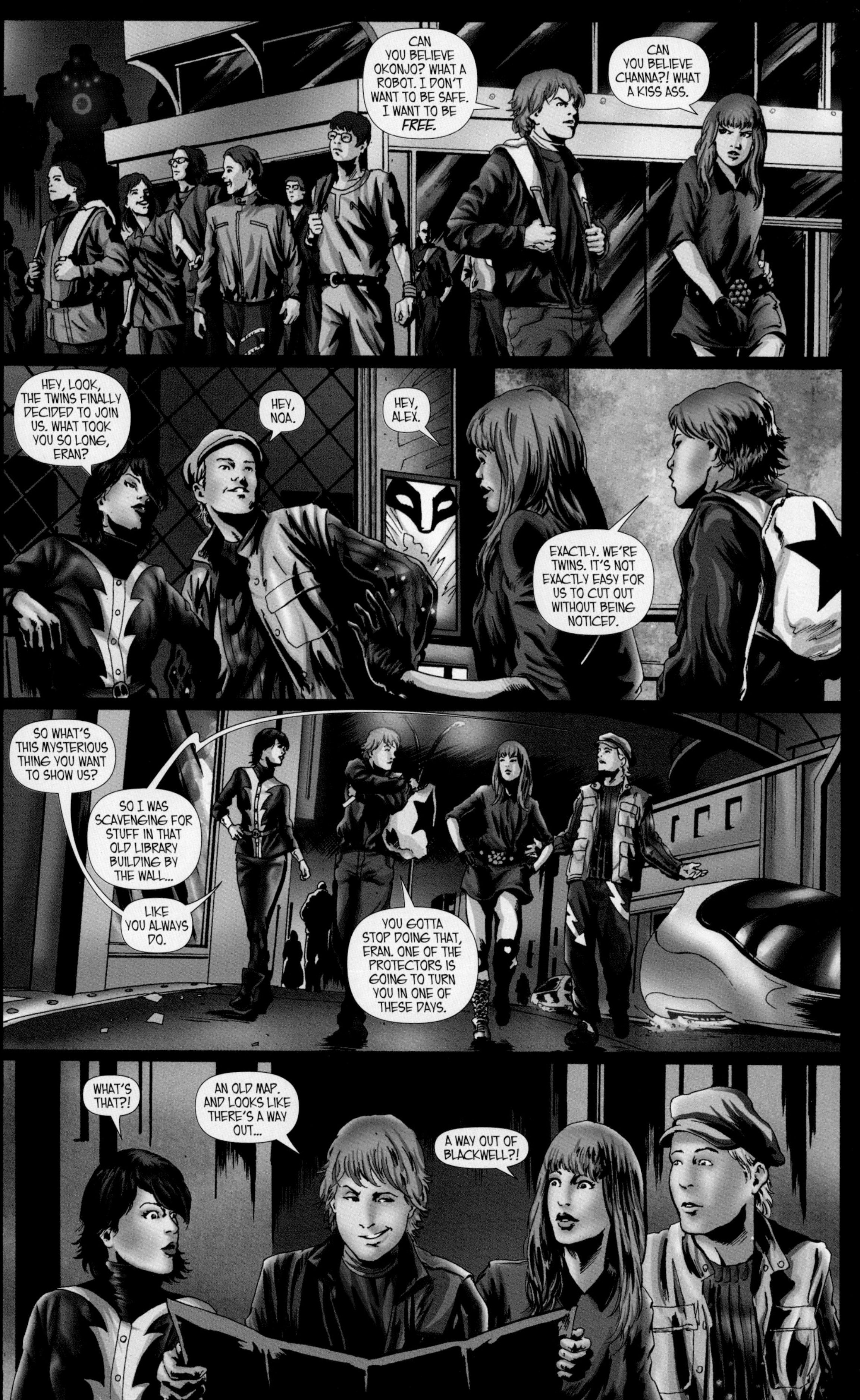
CAN YOU BELIEVE OKONJO? WHAT A ROBOT. I DON'T WANT TO BE SAFE. I WANT TO BE *FREE.*
CAN YOU BELIEVE CHANNA?! WHAT A KISS ASS.
HEY, LOOK, THE TWINS FINALLY DECIDED TO JOIN US. WHAT TOOK YOU SO LONG, ERAN?
HEY, NOA.
HEY, ALEX.
EXACTLY. WE'RE TWINS. IT'S NOT EXACTLY EASY FOR US TO CUT OUT WITHOUT BEING NOTICED.
SO WHAT'S THIS MYSTERIOUS THING YOU WANT TO SHOW US?
SO I WAS SCAVENGING FOR STUFF IN THAT OLD LIBRARY BUILDING BY THE WALL...
LIKE YOU ALWAYS DO.
YOU GOTTA STOP DOING THAT, ERAN. ONE OF THE PROTECTORS IS GOING TO TURN YOU IN ONE OF THESE DAYS.
WHAT'S THAT?!
AN OLD MAP. AND LOOKS LIKE THERE'S A WAY OUT...
A WAY OUT OF BLACKWELL?!

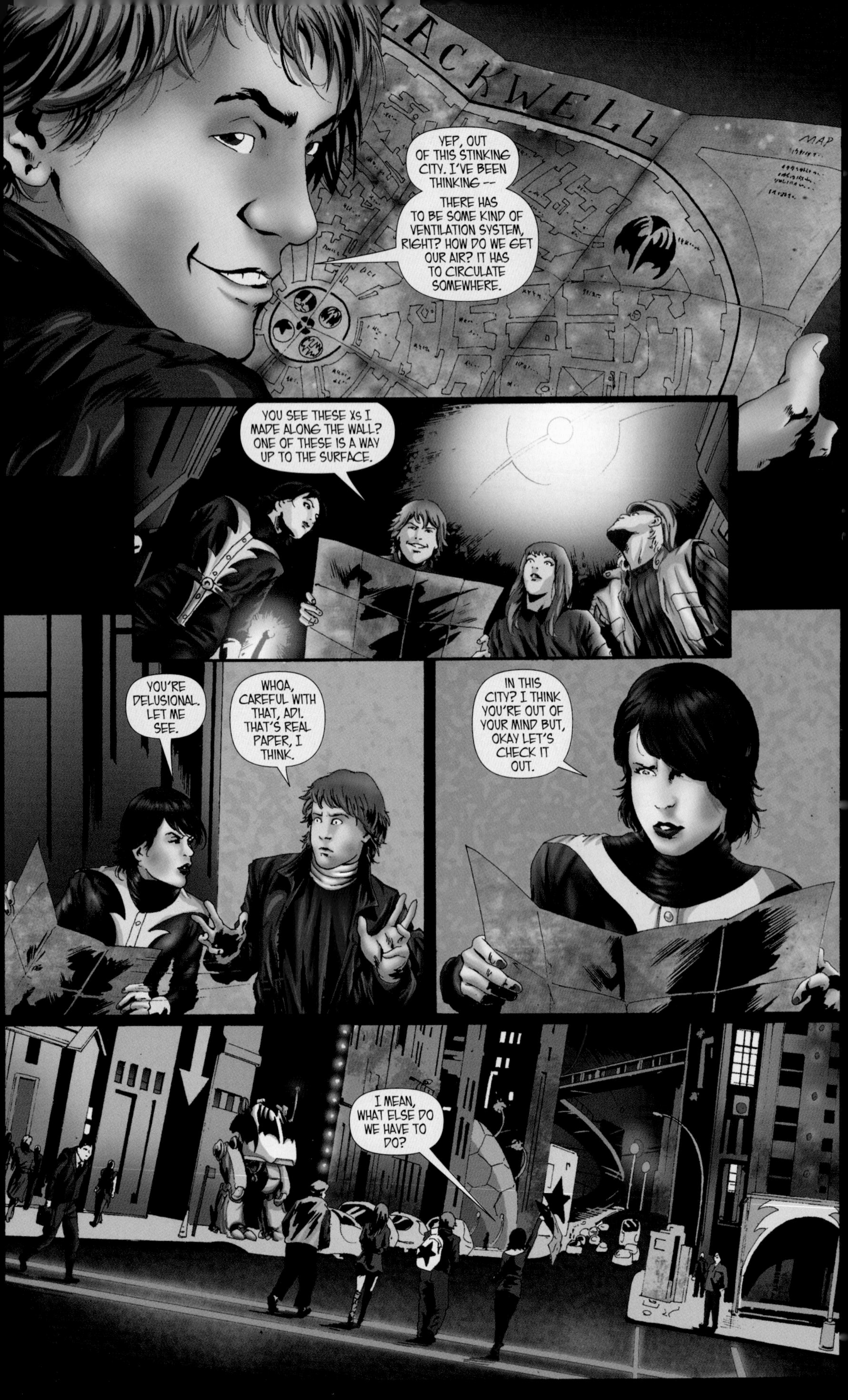

BLACKWELL
MAP
YEP, OUT OF THIS STINKING CITY. I'VE BEEN THINKING --
THERE HAS TO BE SOME KIND OF VENTILATION SYSTEM, RIGHT? HOW DO WE GET OUR AIR? IT HAS TO CIRCULATE SOMEWHERE.
YOU SEE THESE XS I MADE ALONG THE WALL? ONE OF THESE IS A WAY UP TO THE SURFACE.
YOU'RE DELUSIONAL. LET ME SEE.
WHOA, CAREFUL WITH THAT, ADI. THAT'S REAL PAPER, I THINK.
IN THIS CITY? I THINK YOU'RE OUT OF YOUR MIND BUT, OKAY LET'S CHECK IT OUT.
I MEAN, WHAT ELSE DO WE HAVE TO DO?

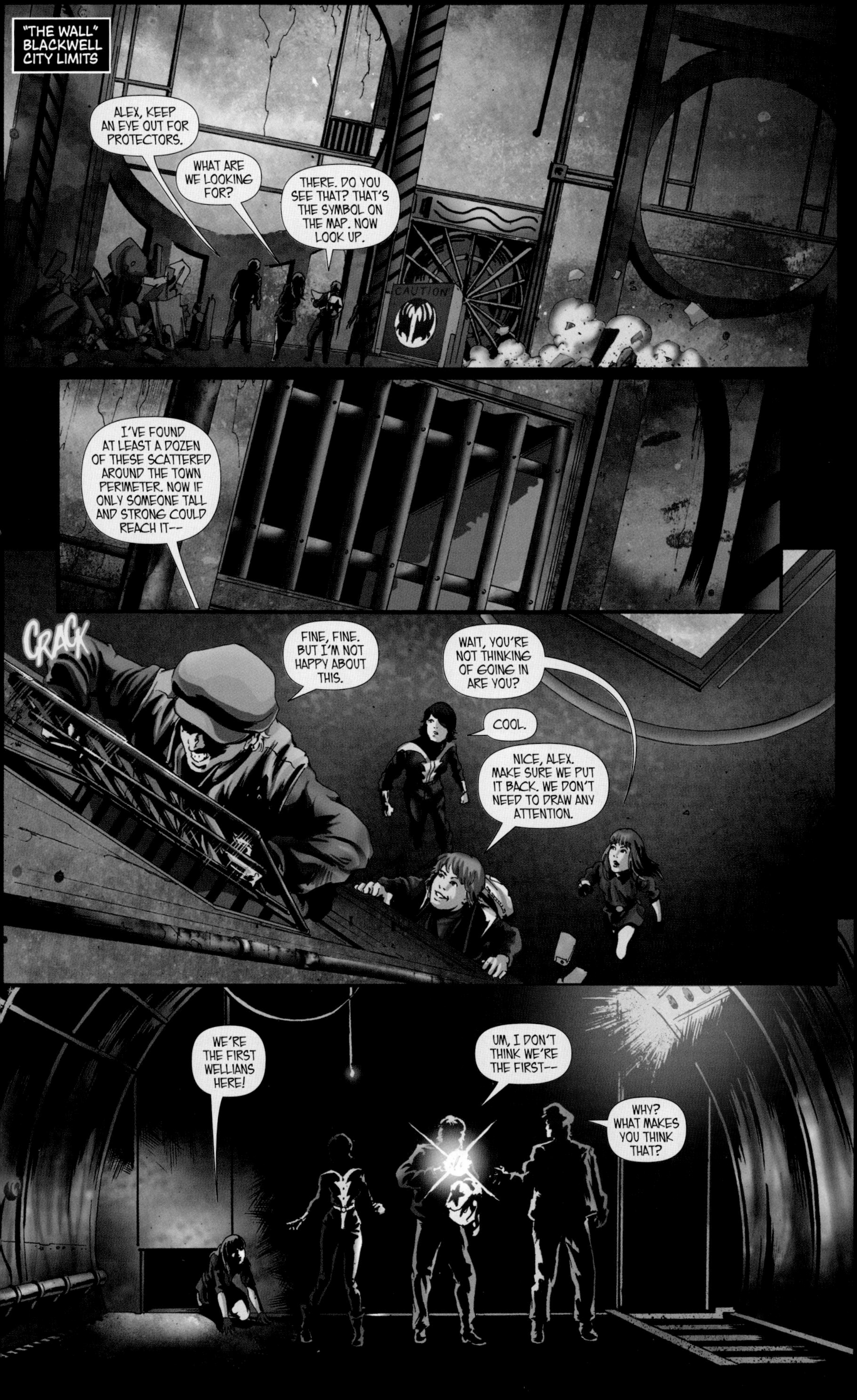
"THE WALL" BLACKWELL CITY LIMITS
ALEX, KEEP AN EYE OUT FOR PROTECTORS.
WHAT ARE WE LOOKING FOR?
THERE. DO YOU SEE THAT? THAT'S THE SYMBOL ON THE MAP. NOW LOOK UP.
CAUTION
I'VE FOUND AT LEAST A DOZEN OF THESE SCATTERED AROUND THE TOWN PERIMETER. NOW IF ONLY SOMEONE TALL AND STRONG COULD REACH IT--
CRACK
FINE, FINE. BUT I'M NOT HAPPY ABOUT THIS.
WAIT, YOU'RE NOT THINKING OF GOING IN ARE YOU?
COOL.
NICE, ALEX. MAKE SURE WE PUT IT BACK. WE DON'T NEED TO DRAW ANY ATTENTION.
WE'RE THE FIRST WELLIANS HERE!
UM, I DON'T THINK WE'RE THE FIRST--
WHY? WHAT MAKES YOU THINK THAT?

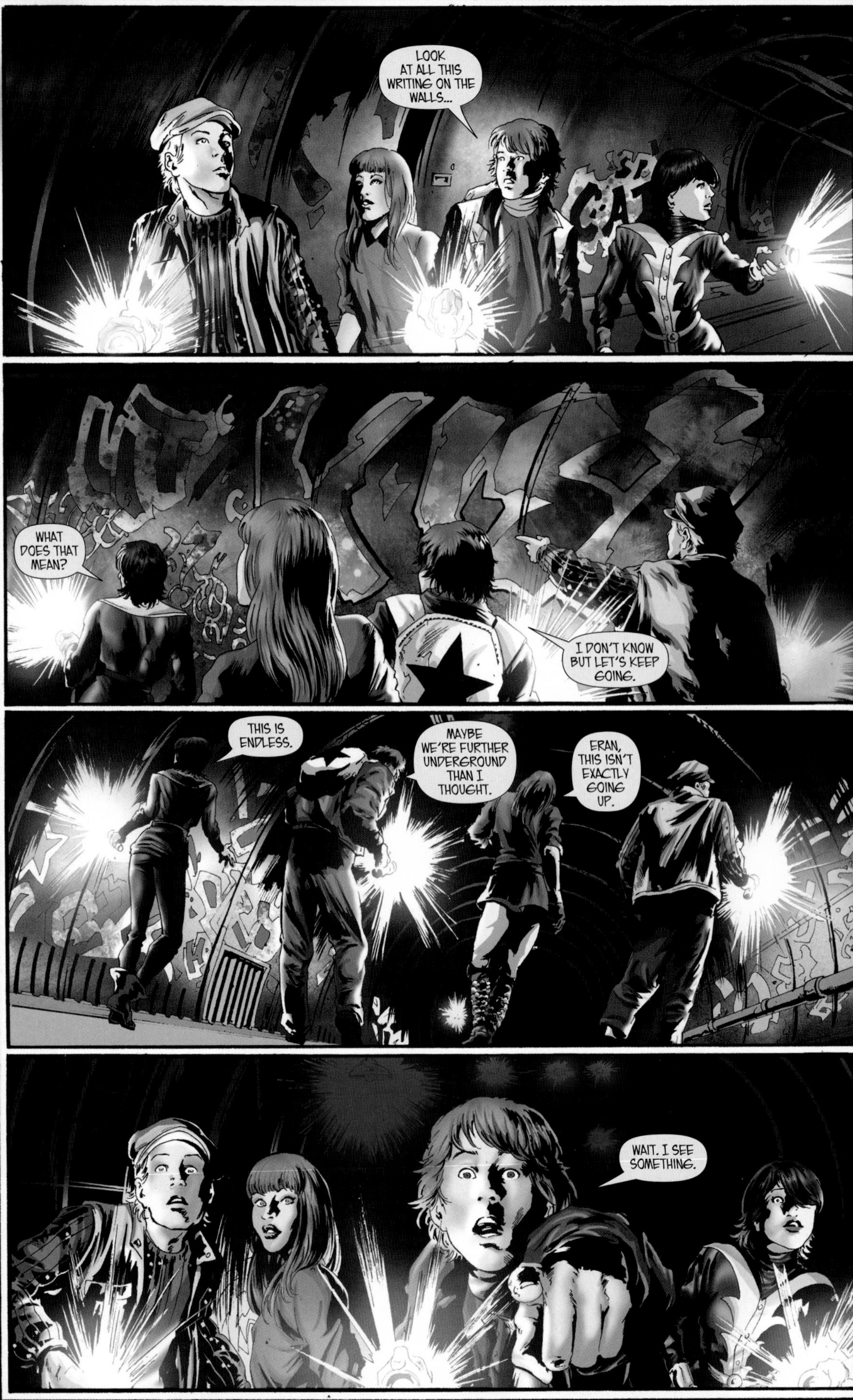

LOOK AT ALL THIS WRITING ON THE WALLS...
WHAT DOES THAT MEAN?
I DON'T KNOW BUT LET'S KEEP GOING.
THIS IS ENDLESS.
MAYBE WE'RE FURTHER UNDERGROUND THAN I THOUGHT.
ERAN, THIS ISN'T EXACTLY GOING UP.
WAIT. I SEE SOMETHING.

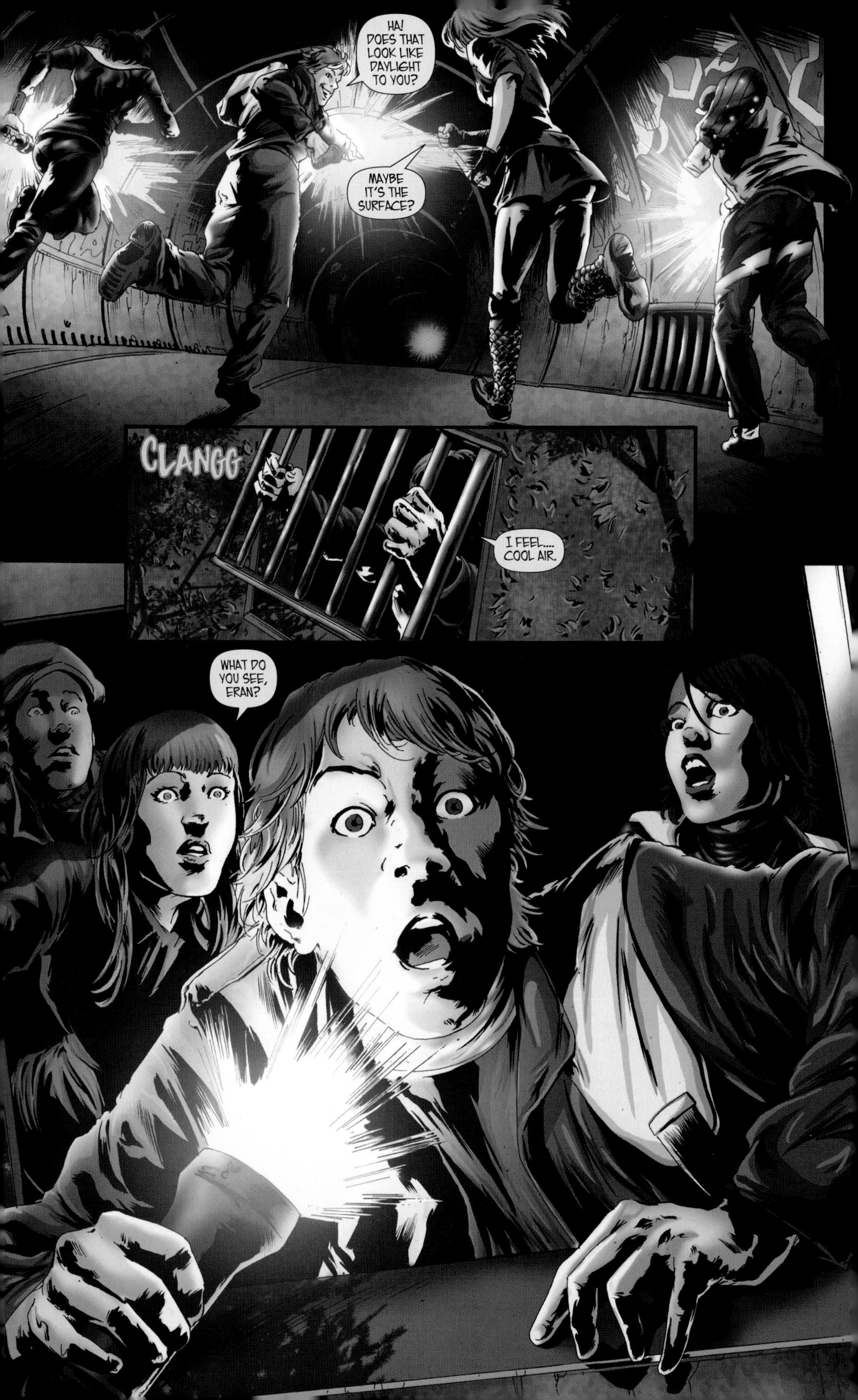
HA! DOES THAT LOOK LIKE DAYLIGHT TO YOU?
MAYBE IT'S THE SURFACE?
CLANGG
I FEEL.... COOL AIR.
WHAT DO YOU SEE, ERAN?

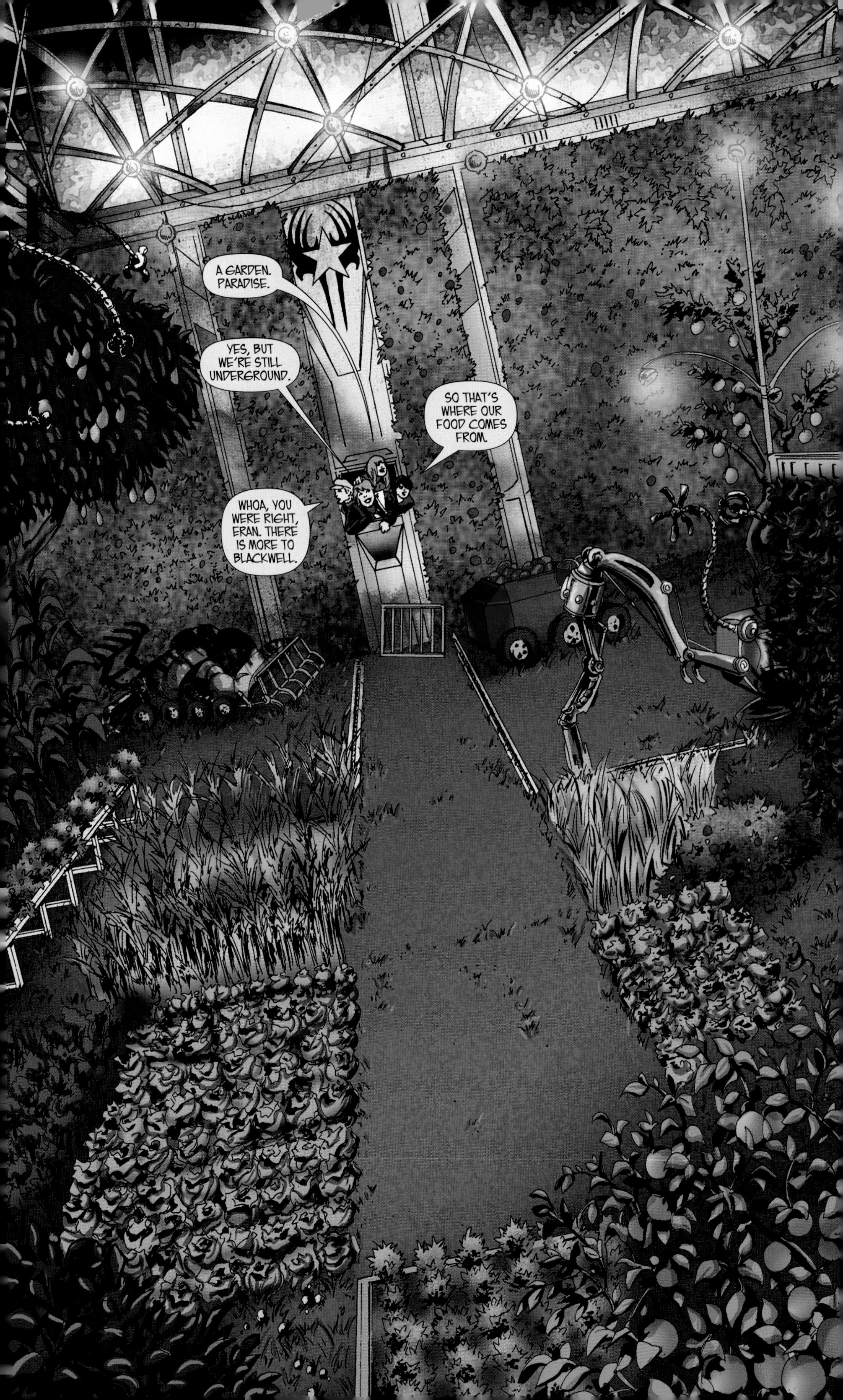
A GARDEN. PARADISE.
YES, BUT WE'RE STILL UNDERGROUND.
SO THAT'S WHERE OUR FOOD COMES FROM.
WHOA, YOU WERE RIGHT, ERAN. THERE IS MORE TO BLACKWELL.

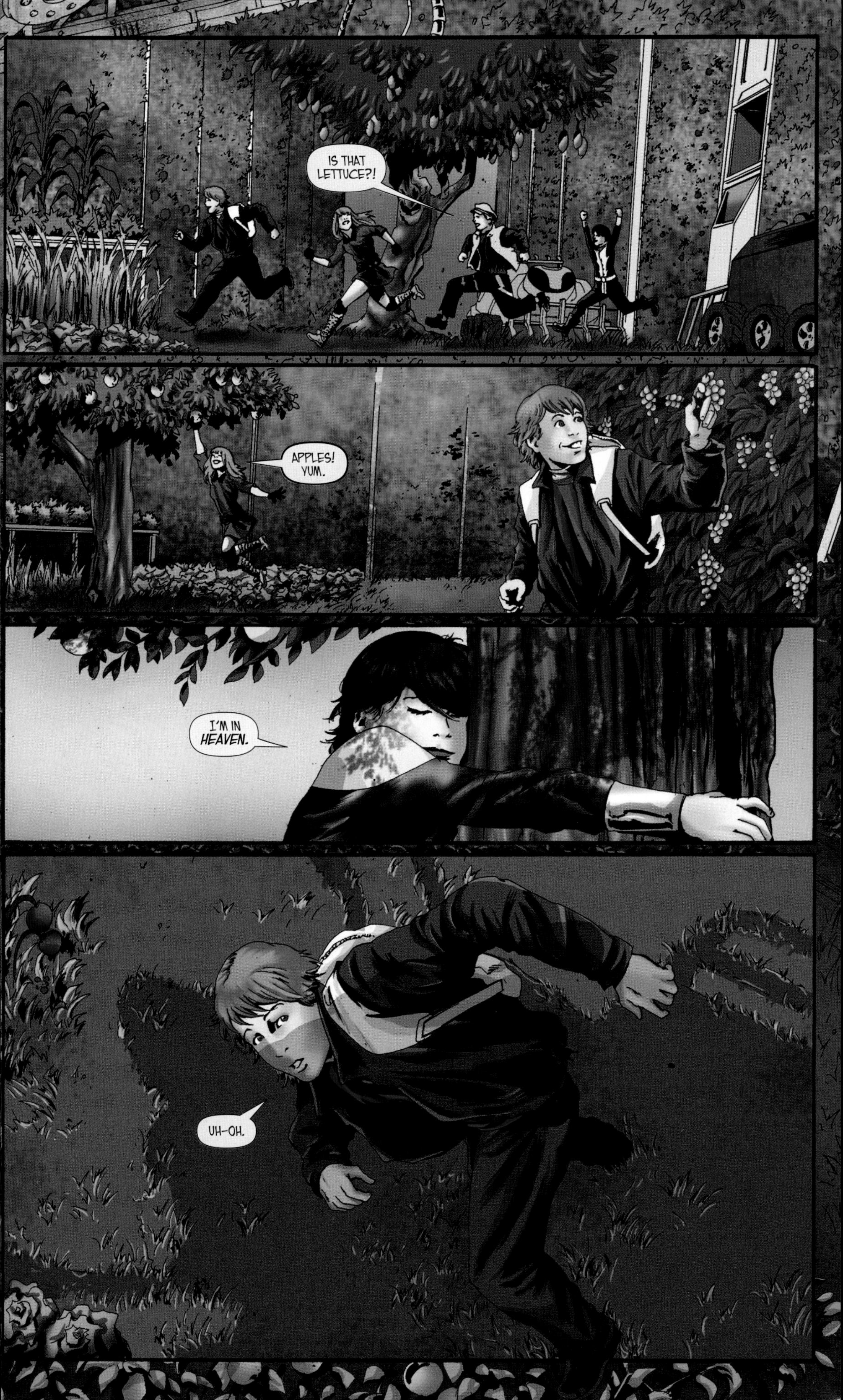
IS THAT LETTUCE?!
APPLES! YUM.
I'M IN HEAVEN.
UH-OH.

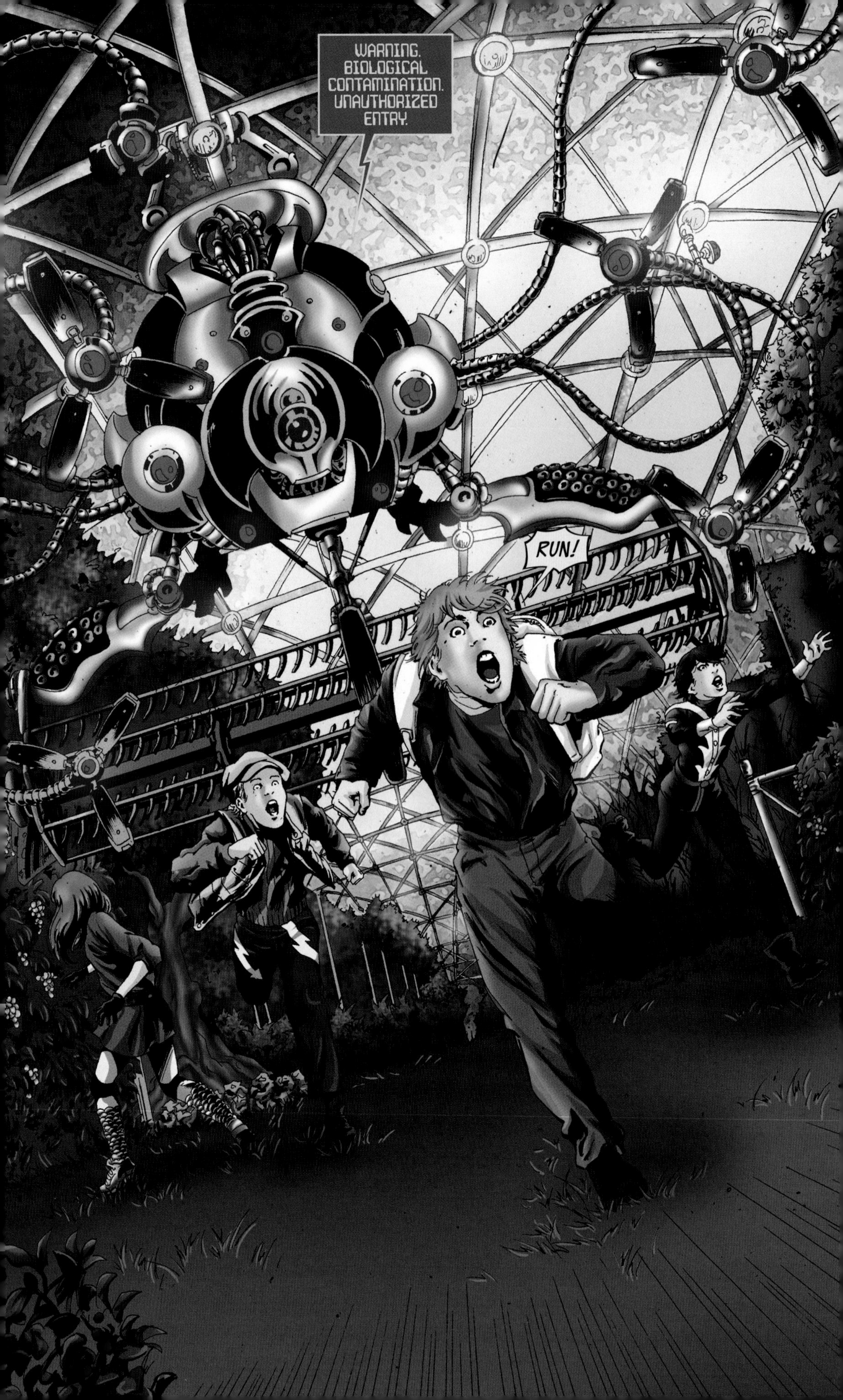
WARNING. BIOLOGICAL CONTAMINATION. UNAUTHORIZED ENTRY.
RUN!

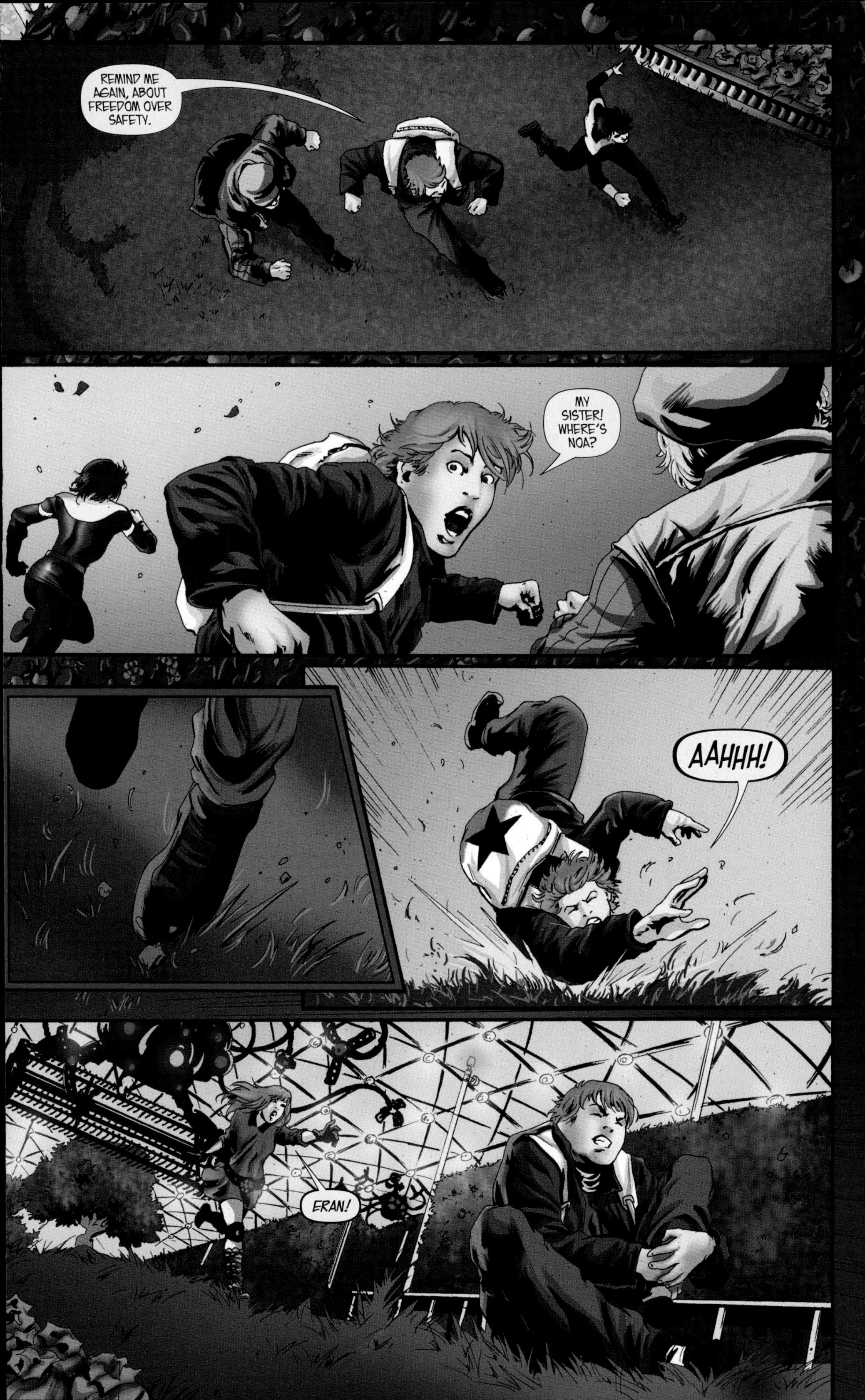
REMIND ME AGAIN, ABOUT FREEDOM OVER SAFETY.
MY SISTER! WHERE'S NOA?
AAHHH!
ERAN!

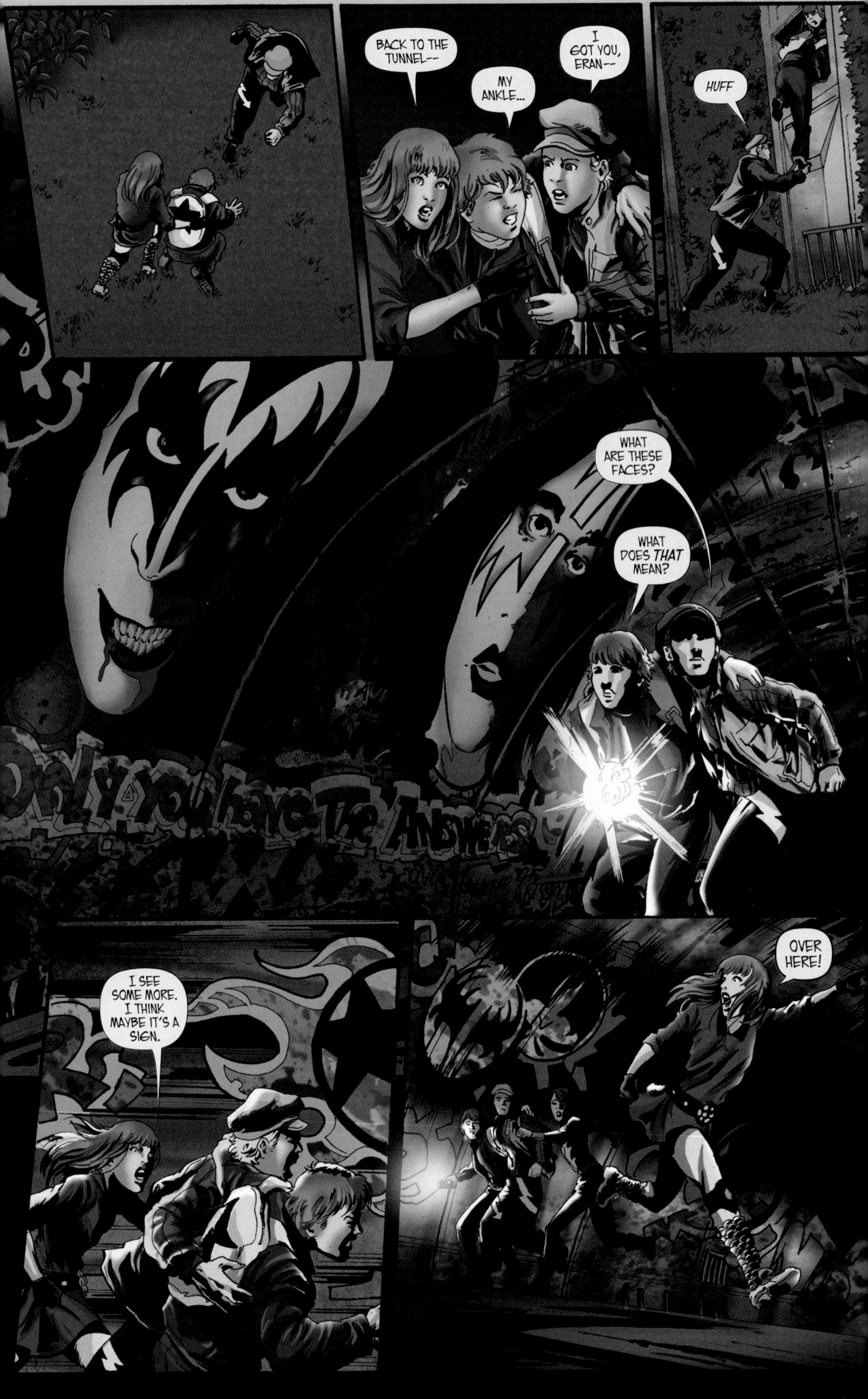

BACK TO THE TUNNEL--
MY ANKLE...
I GOT YOU, ERAN--
HUFF
WHAT ARE THESE FACES?
WHAT DOES *THAT* MEAN?
ONLY YOU HAVE THE ANSWERS
I SEE SOME MORE. I THINK MAYBE IT'S A SIGN.
OVER HERE!

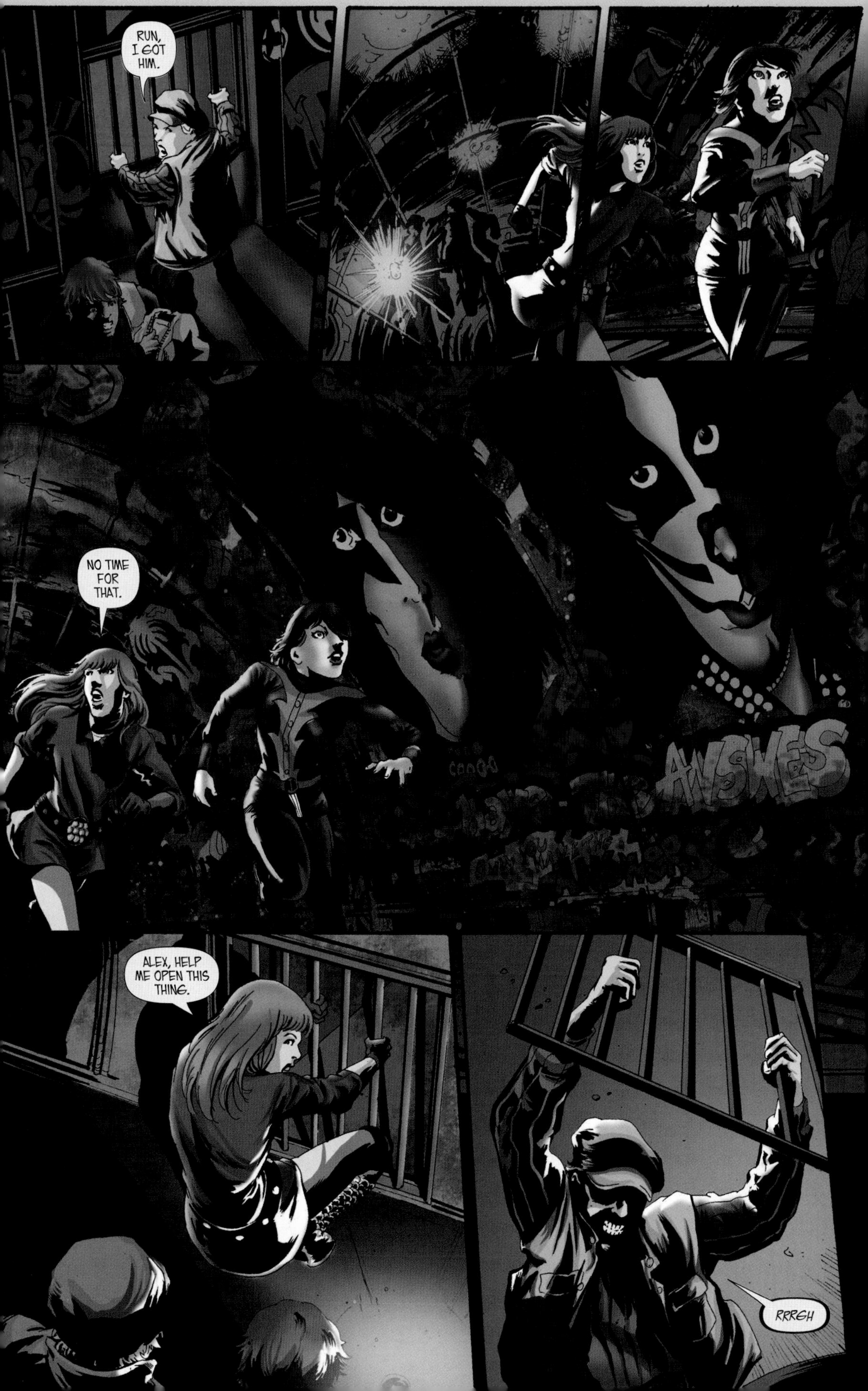
RUN, I GOT HIM.
NO TIME FOR THAT.
ALEX, HELP ME OPEN THIS THING.
RRRGH

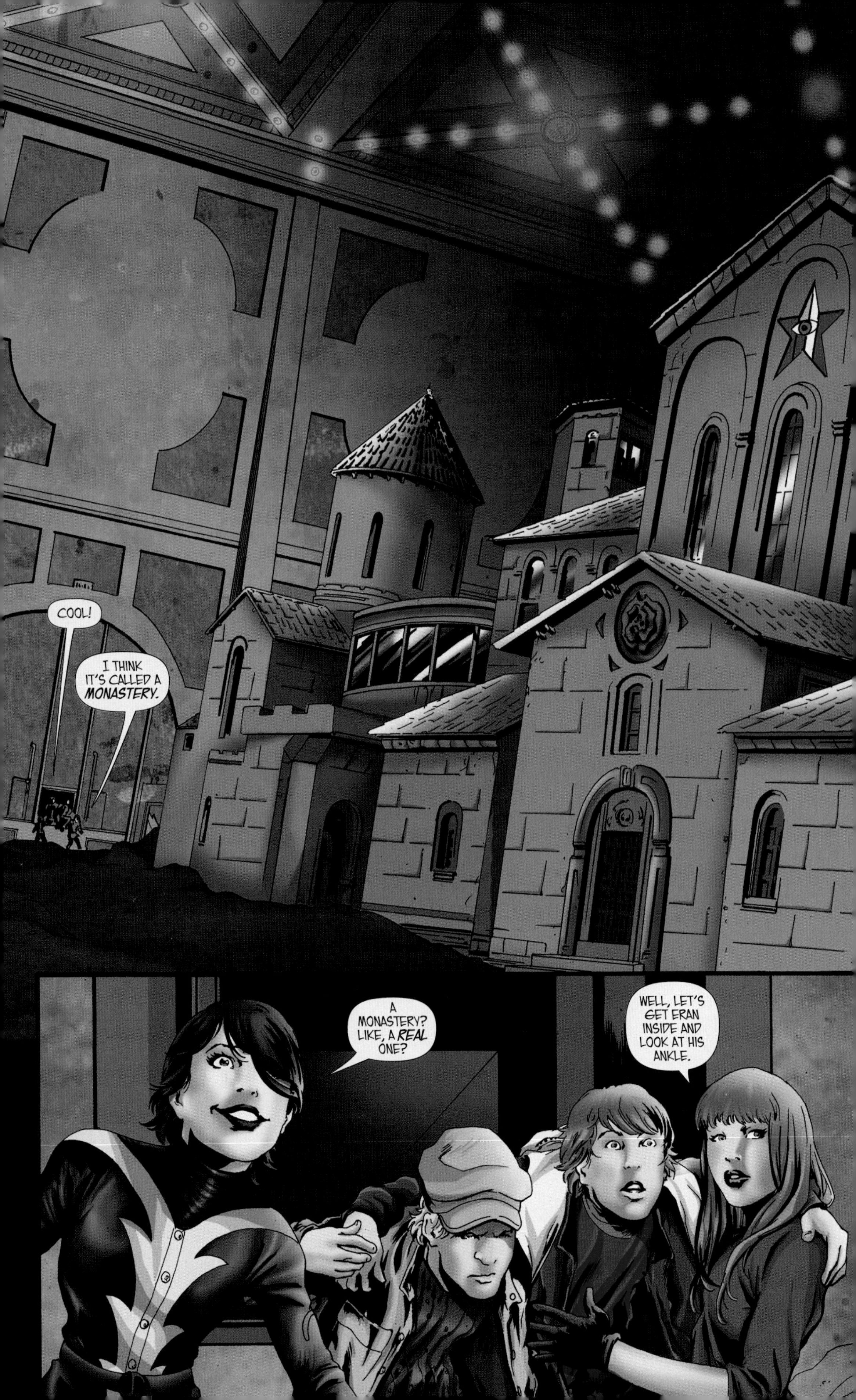
COOL!
I THINK IT'S CALLED A *MONASTERY*.
A MONASTERY? LIKE, A *REAL* ONE?
WELL, LET'S GET ERAN INSIDE AND LOOK AT HIS ANKLE.

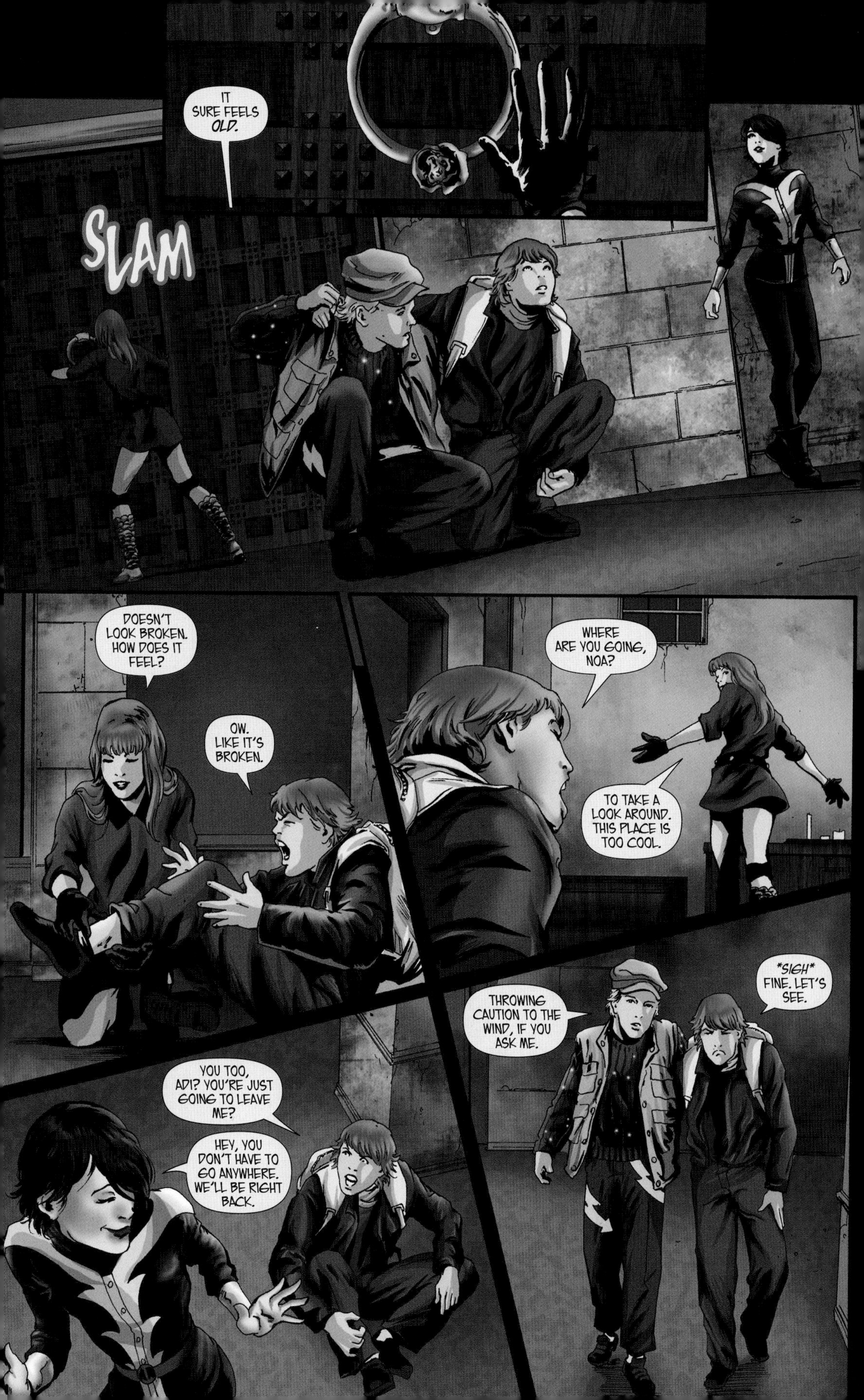
IT SURE FEELS OLD.
SLAM
DOESN'T LOOK BROKEN. HOW DOES IT FEEL?
OW. LIKE IT'S BROKEN.
WHERE ARE YOU GOING, NOA?
TO TAKE A LOOK AROUND. THIS PLACE IS TOO COOL.
YOU TOO, ADI? YOU'RE JUST GOING TO LEAVE ME?
HEY, YOU DON'T HAVE TO GO ANYWHERE. WE'LL BE RIGHT BACK.
THROWING CAUTION TO THE WIND, IF YOU ASK ME.
SIGH FINE. LET'S SEE.

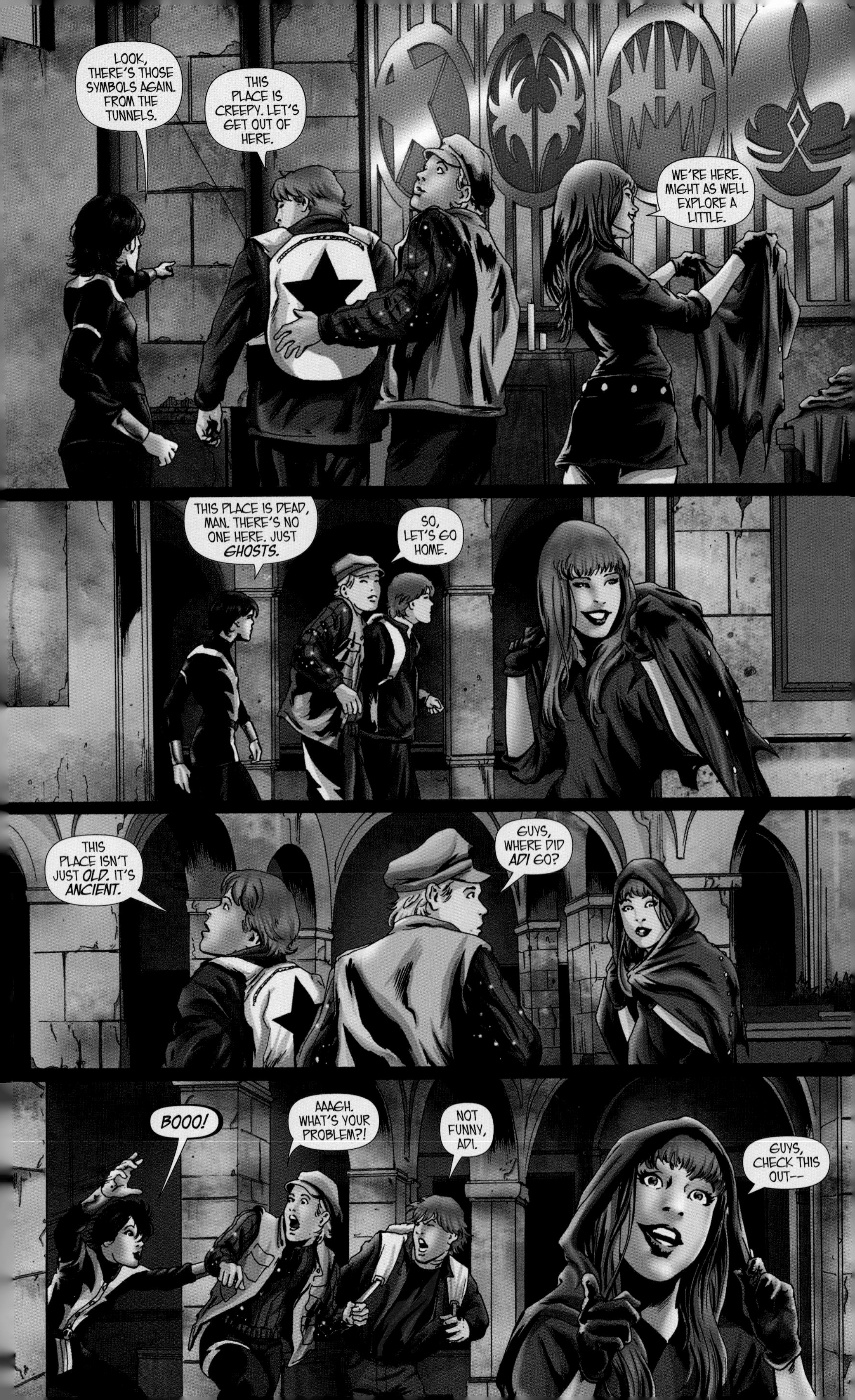
LOOK, THERE'S THOSE SYMBOLS AGAIN. FROM THE TUNNELS.
THIS PLACE IS CREEPY. LET'S GET OUT OF HERE.
WE'RE HERE. MIGHT AS WELL EXPLORE A LITTLE.
THIS PLACE IS DEAD, MAN. THERE'S NO ONE HERE. JUST GHOSTS.
SO, LET'S GO HOME.
THIS PLACE ISN'T JUST OLD. IT'S ANCIENT.
GUYS, WHERE DID ADI GO?
BOOO!
AAAGH. WHAT'S YOUR PROBLEM?!
NOT FUNNY, ADI.
GUYS, CHECK THIS OUT--

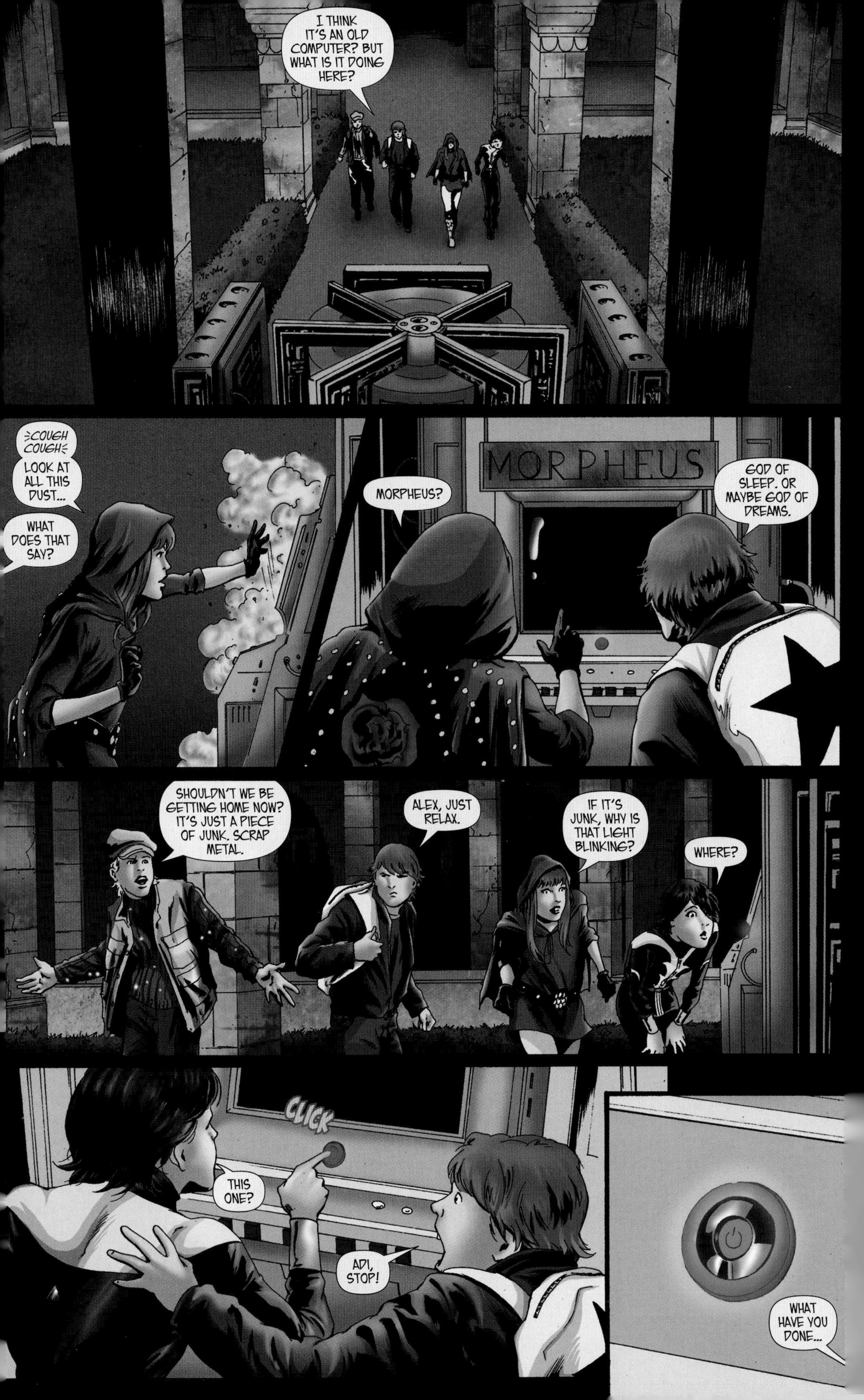
I THINK IT'S AN OLD COMPUTER? BUT WHAT IS IT DOING HERE?
≥COUGH COUGH≤ LOOK AT ALL THIS DUST...
WHAT DOES THAT SAY?
MORPHEUS
MORPHEUS?
GOD OF SLEEP. OR MAYBE GOD OF DREAMS.
SHOULDN'T WE BE GETTING HOME NOW? IT'S JUST A PIECE OF JUNK. SCRAP METAL.
ALEX, JUST RELAX.
IF IT'S JUNK, WHY IS THAT LIGHT BLINKING?
WHERE?
CLICK
THIS ONE?
ADI, STOP!
WHAT HAVE YOU DONE...

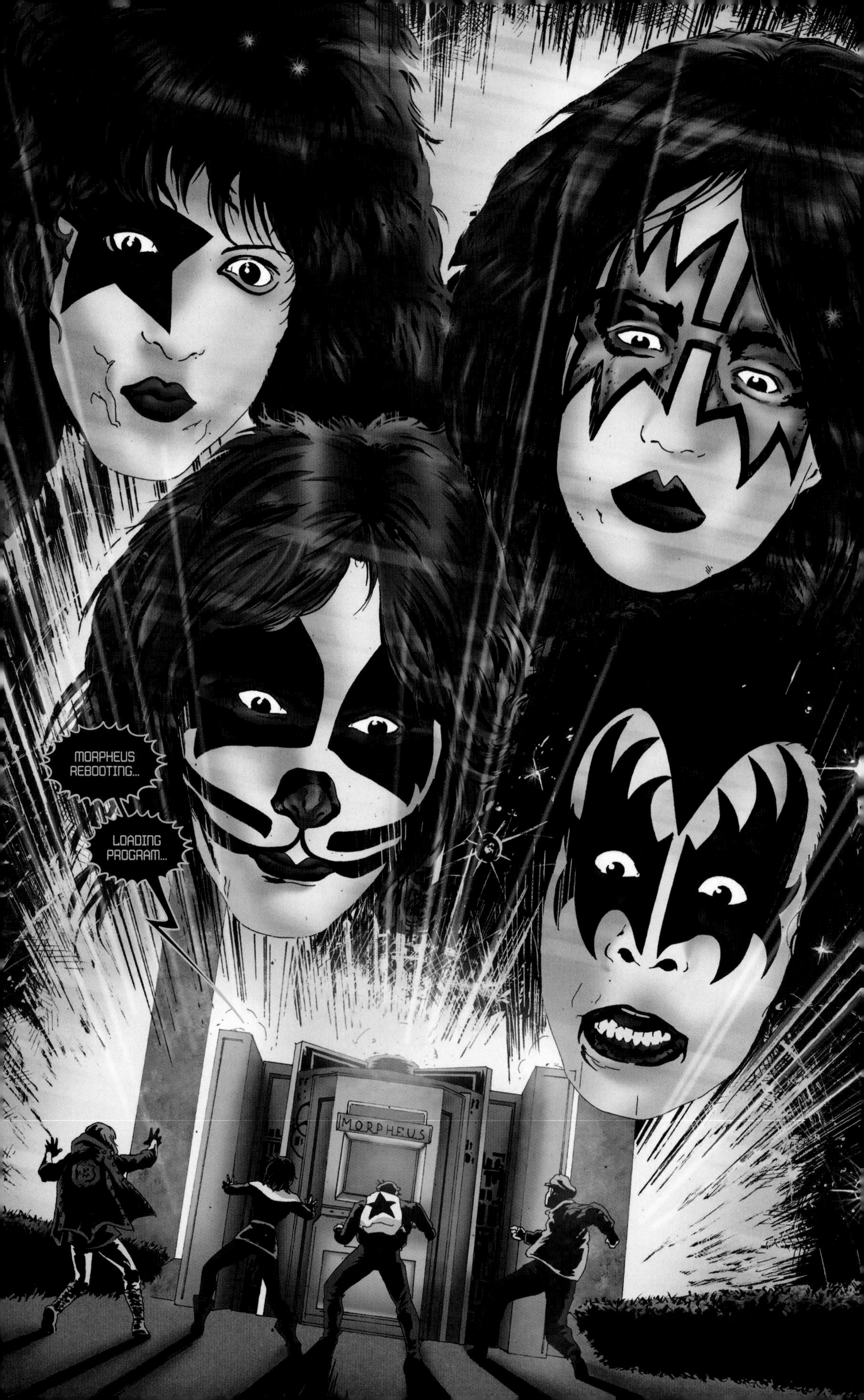
MORPHEUS REBOOTING...
LOADING PROGRAM...
MORPHEUS

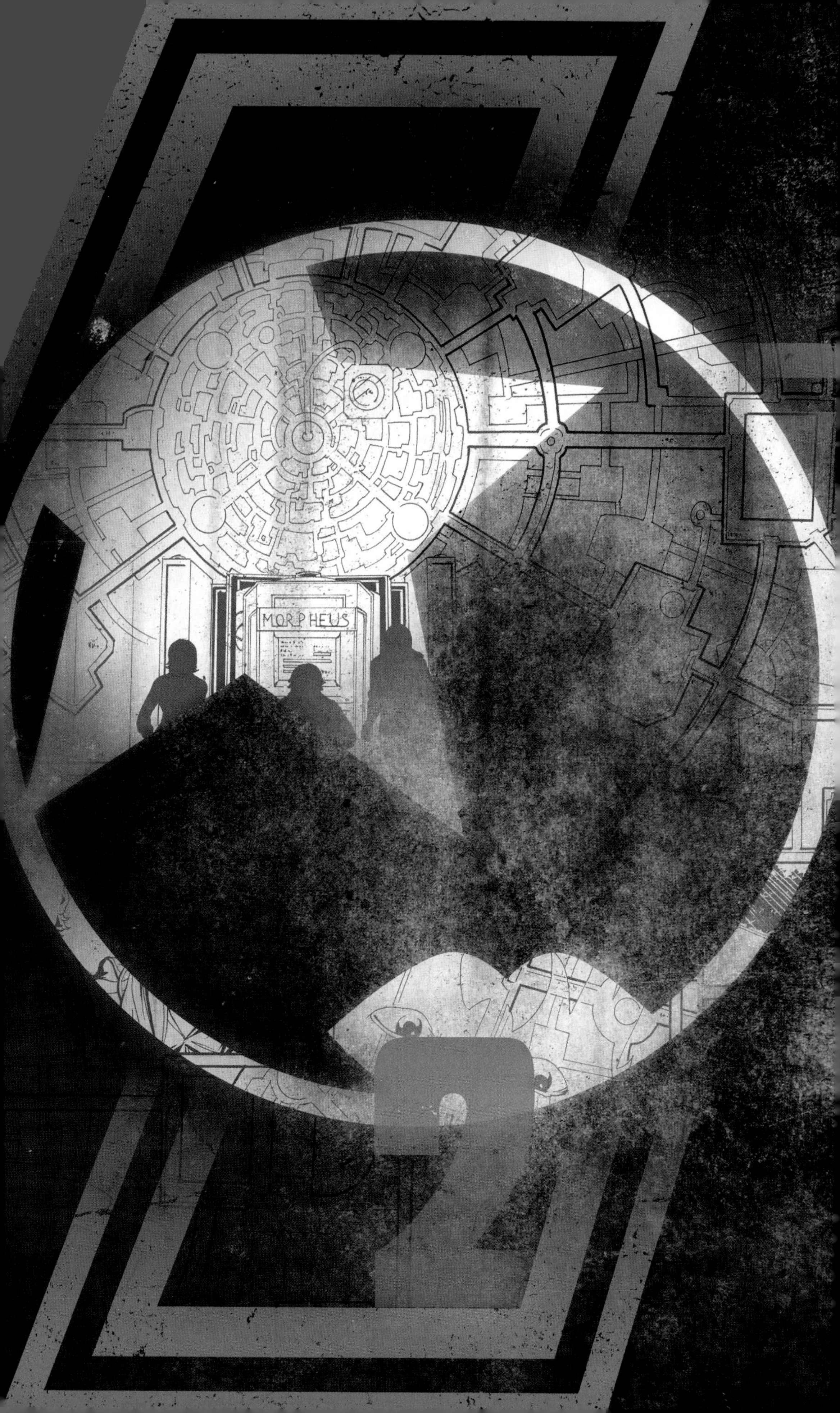
MORPHEUS
2

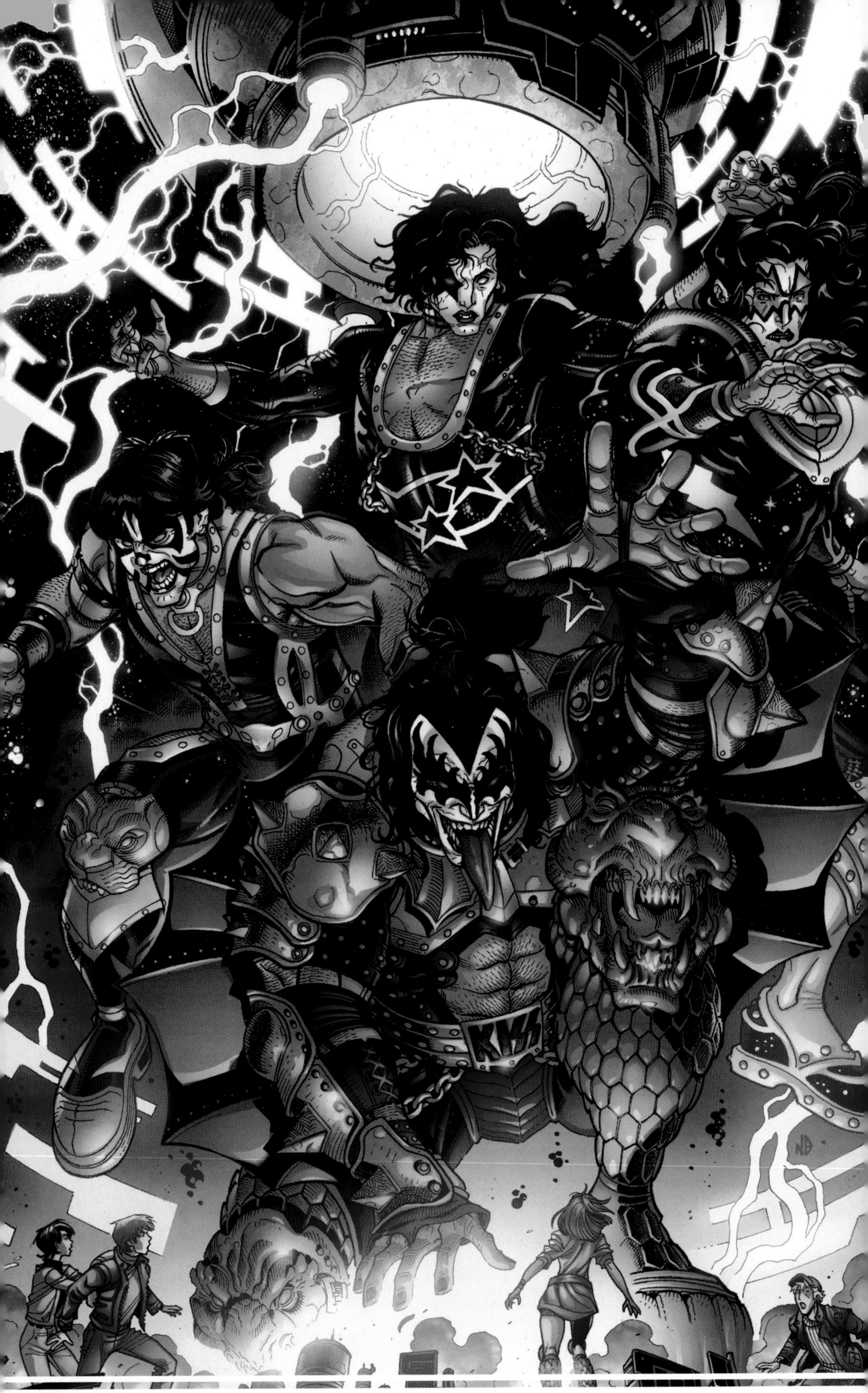

ISSUE 2, MAIN COVER: Art by Nick Bradshaw & Pete Pantazis

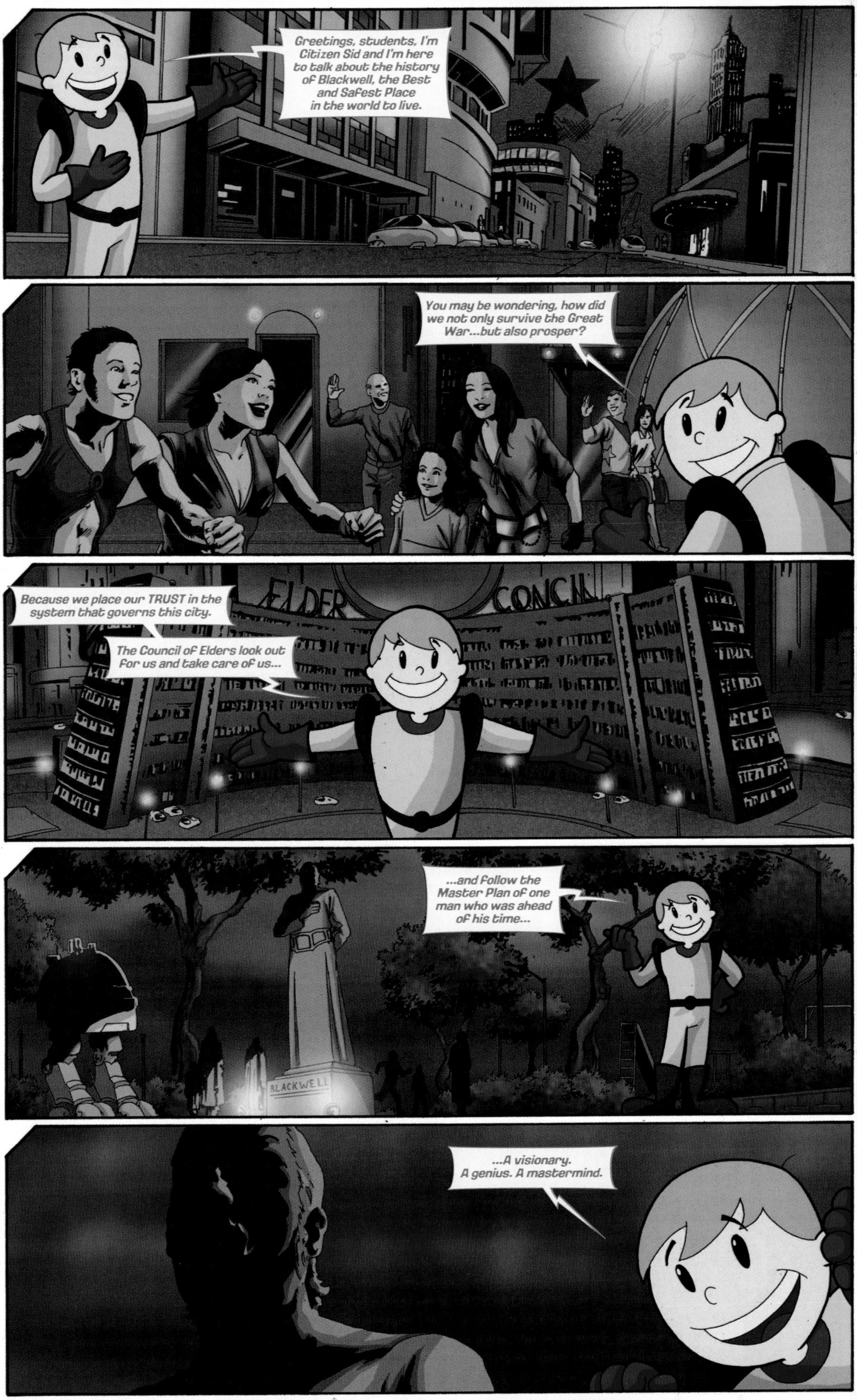
Greetings, students, I'm Citizen Sid and I'm here to talk about the history of Blackwell, the Best and Safest Place in the world to live.
You may be wondering, how did we not only survive the Great War...but also prosper?
ELDER CONCIL
Because we place our TRUST in the system that governs this city.
The Council of Elders look out for us and take care of us...
...and follow the Master Plan of one man who was ahead of his time...
BLACKWELL
...A visionary. A genius. A mastermind.

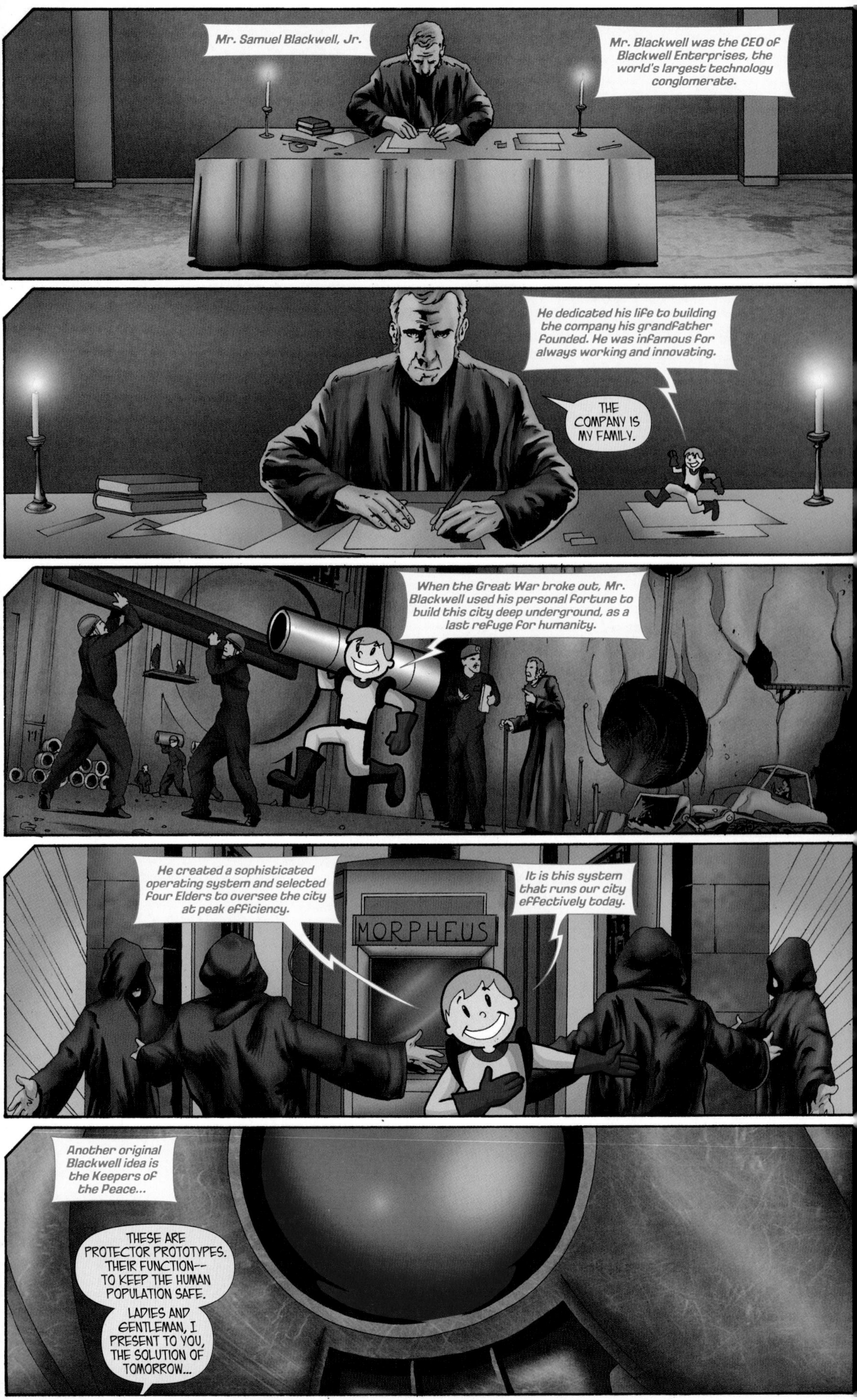

Mr. Samuel Blackwell, Jr.
Mr. Blackwell was the CEO of Blackwell Enterprises, the world's largest technology conglomerate.
He dedicated his life to building the company his grandfather founded. He was infamous for always working and innovating.
THE COMPANY IS MY FAMILY.
When the Great War broke out, Mr. Blackwell used his personal fortune to build this city deep underground, as a last refuge for humanity.
He created a sophisticated operating system and selected Four Elders to oversee the city at peak efficiency.
It is this system that runs our city effectively today.
MORPHEUS
Another original Blackwell idea is the Keepers of the Peace...
THESE ARE PROTECTOR PROTOTYPES. THEIR FUNCTION-- TO KEEP THE HUMAN POPULATION SAFE.
LADIES AND GENTLEMAN, I PRESENT TO YOU, THE SOLUTION OF TOMORROW...

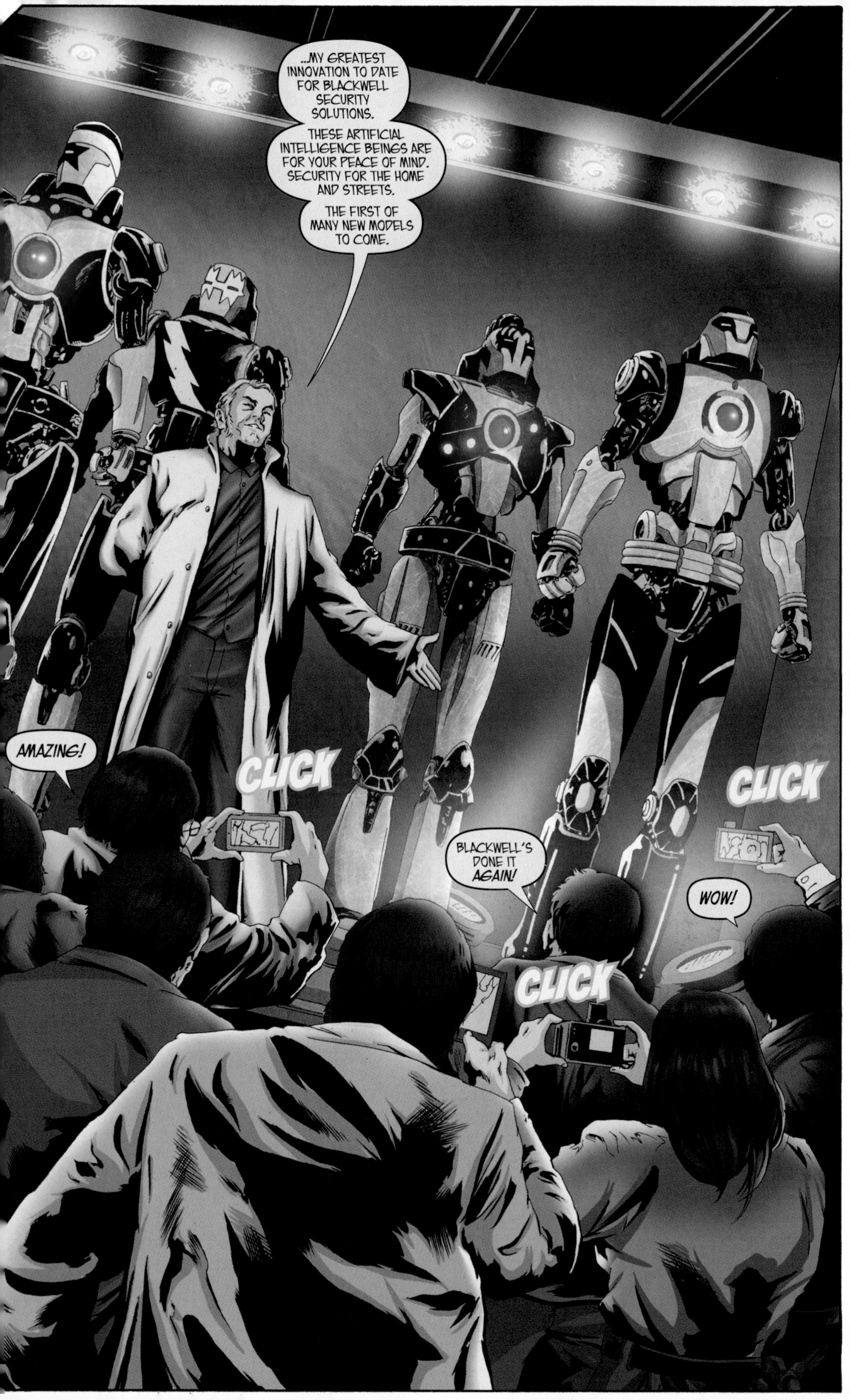
...MY GREATEST INNOVATION TO DATE FOR BLACKWELL SECURITY SOLUTIONS.
THESE ARTIFICIAL INTELLIGENCE BEINGS ARE FOR YOUR PEACE OF MIND. SECURITY FOR THE HOME AND STREETS.
THE FIRST OF MANY NEW MODELS TO COME.
AMAZING!
CLICK
CLICK
BLACKWELL'S DONE IT AGAIN!
WOW!
CLICK

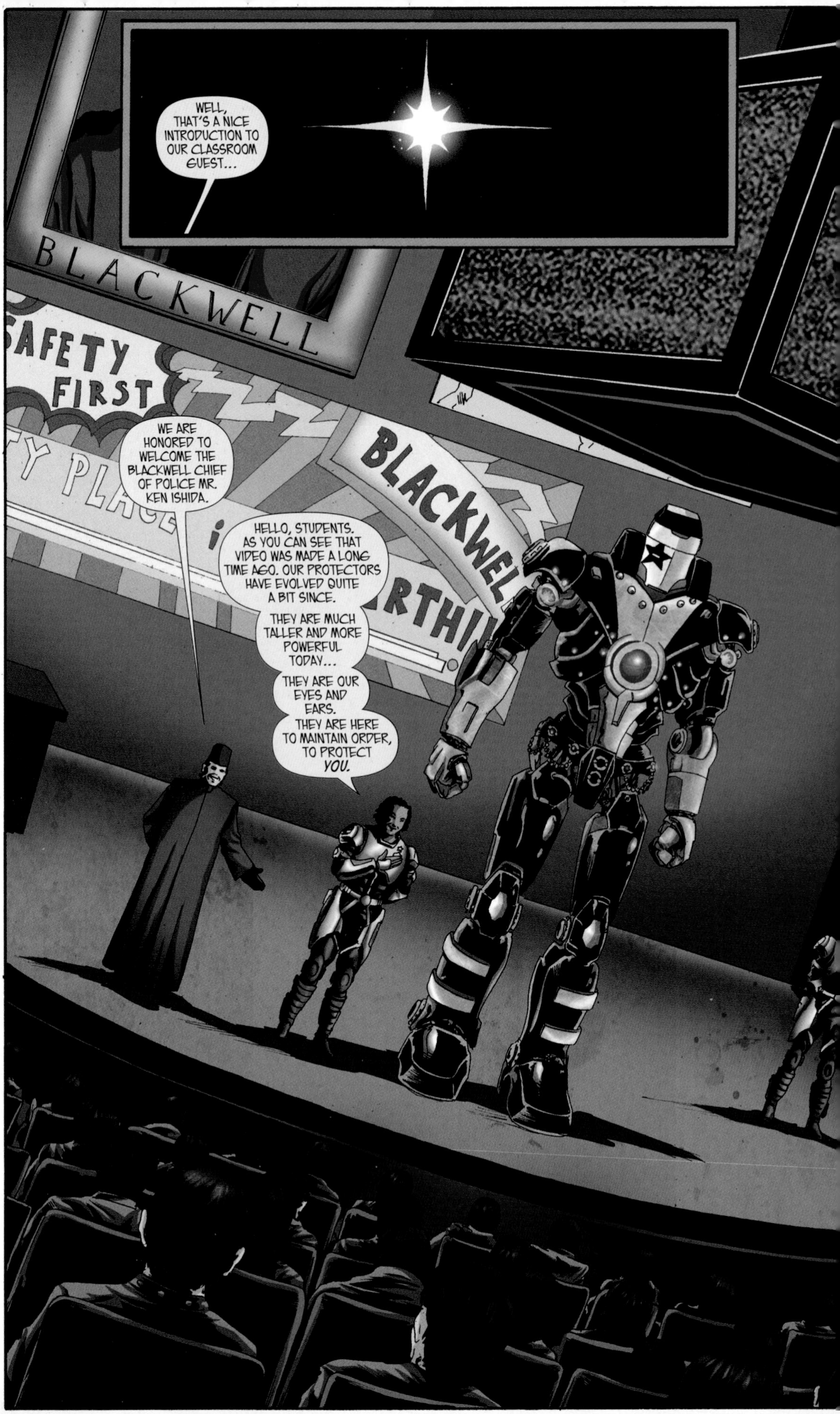
WELL, THAT'S A NICE INTRODUCTION TO OUR CLASSROOM GUEST...
BLACKWELL
SAFETY FIRST
WE ARE HONORED TO WELCOME THE BLACKWELL CHIEF OF POLICE MR. KEN ISHIDA.
HELLO, STUDENTS. AS YOU CAN SEE THAT VIDEO WAS MADE A LONG TIME AGO. OUR PROTECTORS HAVE EVOLVED QUITE A BIT SINCE.
THEY ARE MUCH TALLER AND MORE POWERFUL TODAY...
THEY ARE OUR EYES AND EARS.
THEY ARE HERE TO MAINTAIN ORDER, TO PROTECT *YOU.*

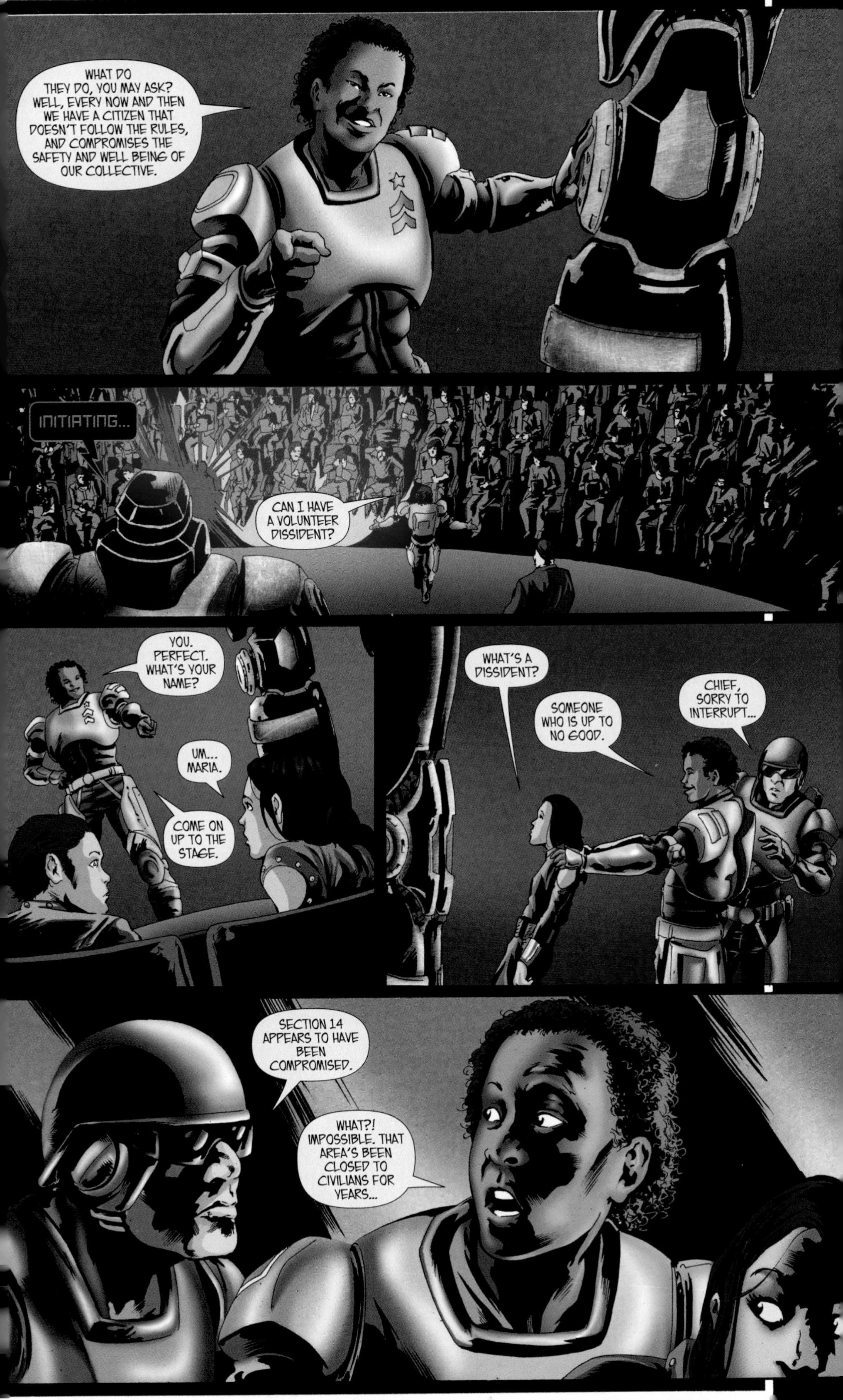
WHAT DO THEY DO, YOU MAY ASK? WELL, EVERY NOW AND THEN WE HAVE A CITIZEN THAT DOESN'T FOLLOW THE RULES, AND COMPROMISES THE SAFETY AND WELL BEING OF OUR COLLECTIVE.
INITIATING...
CAN I HAVE A VOLUNTEER DISSIDENT?
YOU. PERFECT. WHAT'S YOUR NAME?
UM... MARIA.
COME ON UP TO THE STAGE.
WHAT'S A DISSIDENT?
SOMEONE WHO IS UP TO NO GOOD.
CHIEF, SORRY TO INTERRUPT...
SECTION 14 APPEARS TO HAVE BEEN COMPROMISED.
WHAT?! IMPOSSIBLE. THAT AREA'S BEEN CLOSED TO CIVILIANS FOR YEARS...

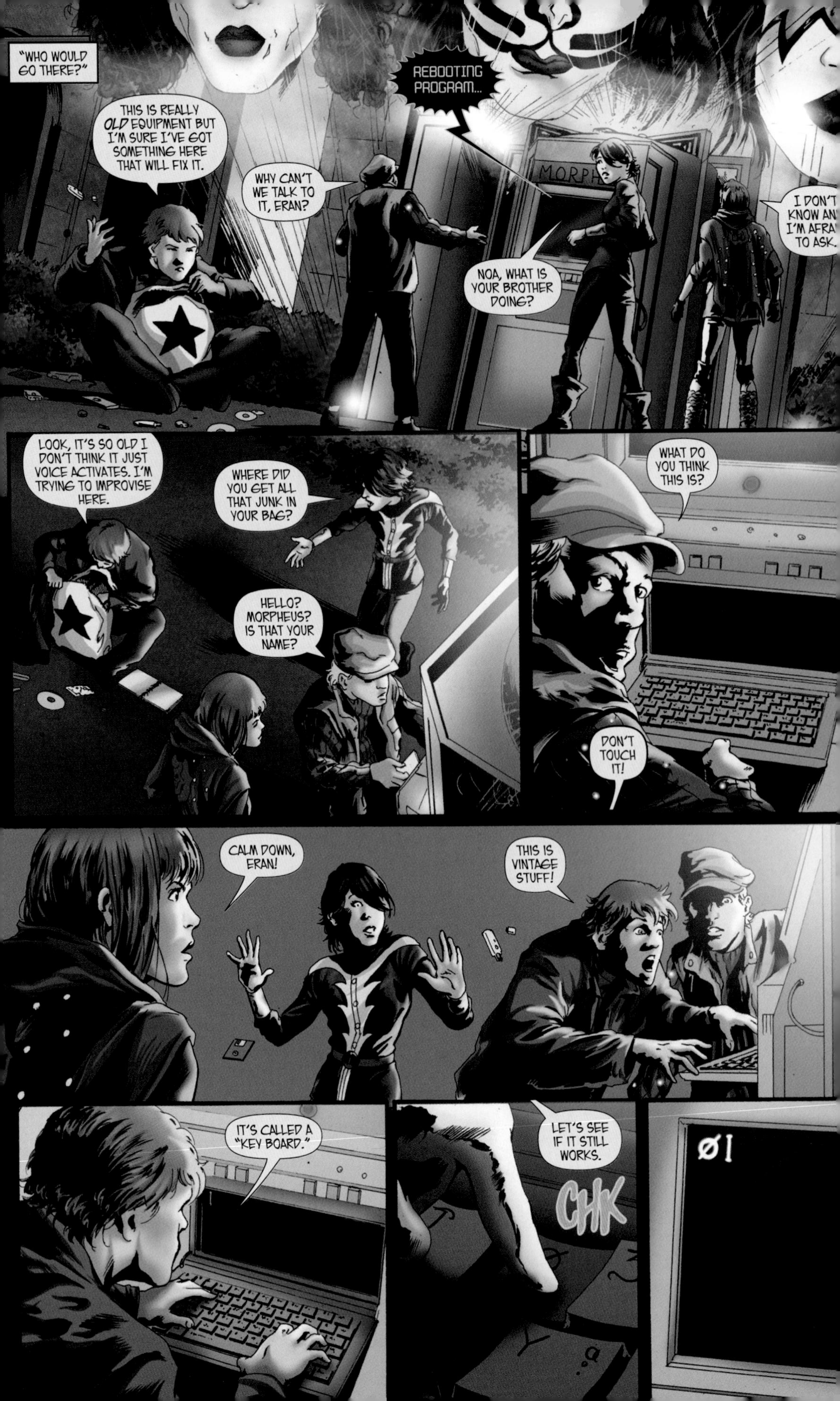
"WHO WOULD GO THERE?"
REBOOTING PROGRAM...
THIS IS REALLY OLD EQUIPMENT BUT I'M SURE I'VE GOT SOMETHING HERE THAT WILL FIX IT.
WHY CAN'T WE TALK TO IT, ERAN?
MORPH
NOA, WHAT IS YOUR BROTHER DOING?
I DON'T KNOW AN I'M AFRA TO ASK.
LOOK, IT'S SO OLD I DON'T THINK IT JUST VOICE ACTIVATES. I'M TRYING TO IMPROVISE HERE.
WHERE DID YOU GET ALL THAT JUNK IN YOUR BAG?
HELLO? MORPHEUS? IS THAT YOUR NAME?
WHAT DO YOU THINK THIS IS?
DON'T TOUCH IT!
CALM DOWN, ERAN!
THIS IS VINTAGE STUFF!
IT'S CALLED A "KEY BOARD."
LET'S SEE IF IT STILL WORKS.
CHK
Ø1

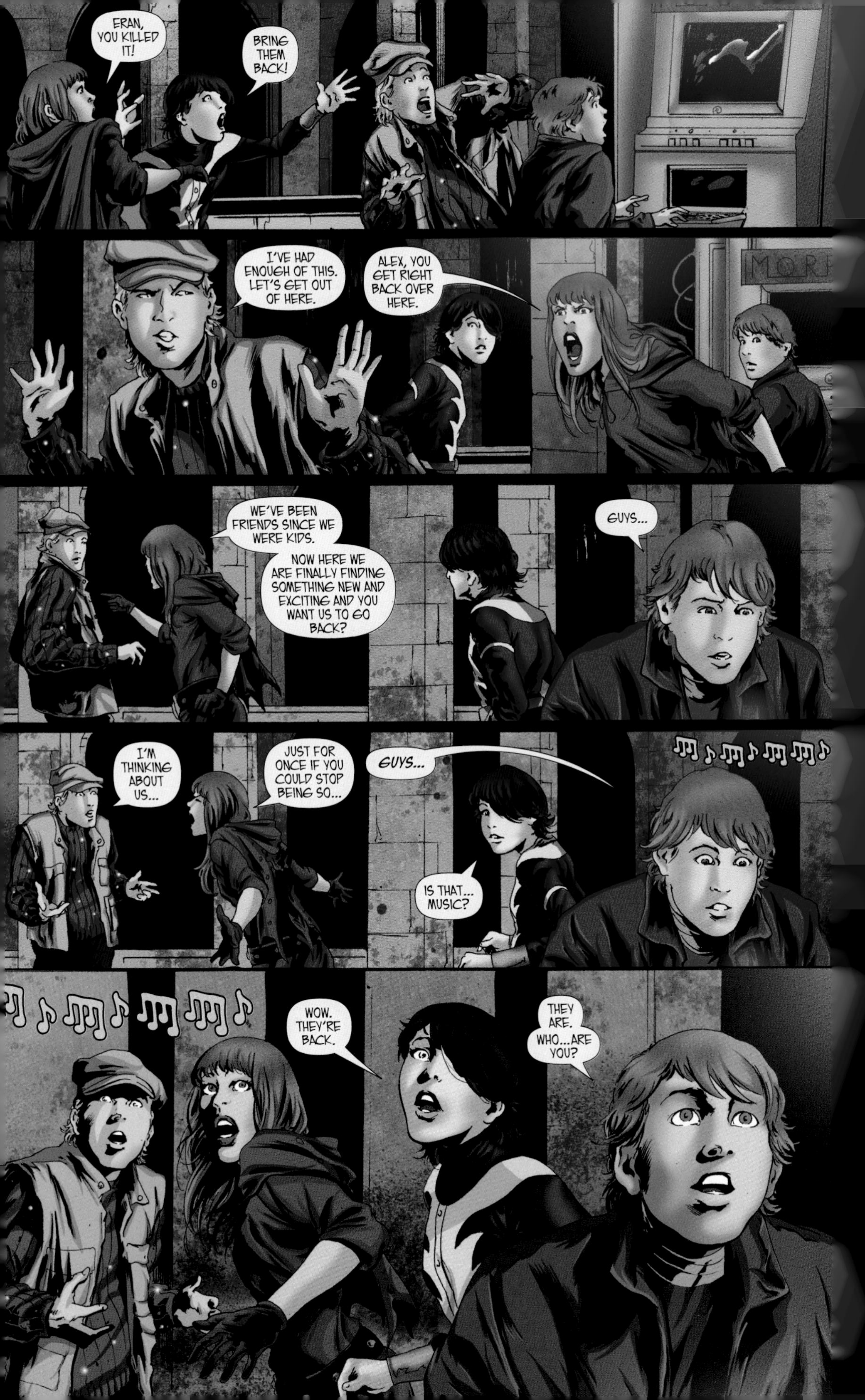
ERAN, YOU KILLED IT!
BRING THEM BACK!
I'VE HAD ENOUGH OF THIS. LET'S GET OUT OF HERE.
ALEX, YOU GET RIGHT BACK OVER HERE.
WE'VE BEEN FRIENDS SINCE WE WERE KIDS.
NOW HERE WE ARE FINALLY FINDING SOMETHING NEW AND EXCITING AND YOU WANT US TO GO BACK?
GUYS...
I'M THINKING ABOUT US...
JUST FOR ONCE IF YOU COULD STOP BEING SO...
GUYS...
IS THAT... MUSIC?
WOW. THEY'RE BACK.
THEY ARE. WHO...ARE YOU?

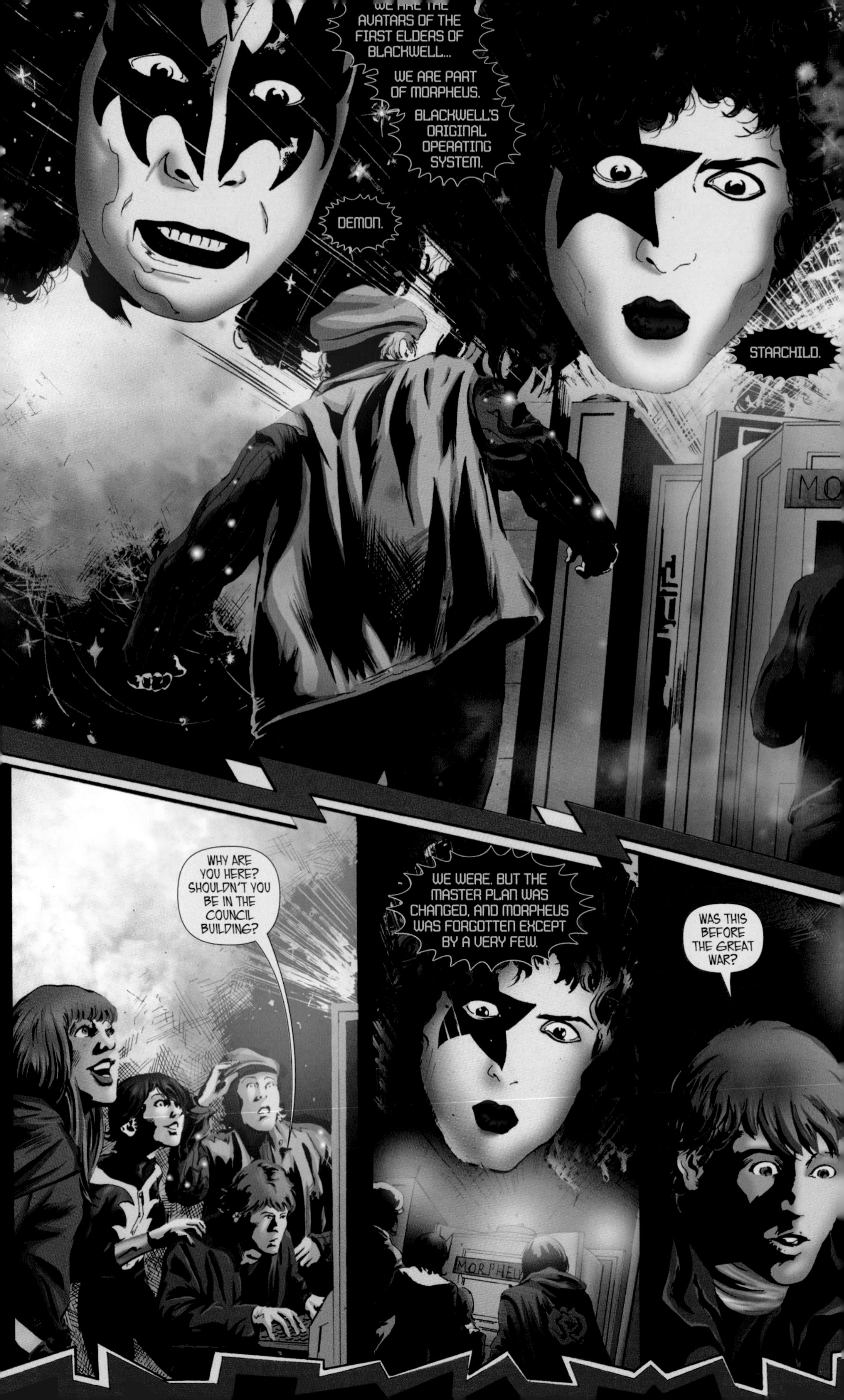
WE ARE THE AVATARS OF THE FIRST ELDERS OF BLACKWELL...
WE ARE PART OF MORPHEUS.
BLACKWELL'S ORIGINAL OPERATING SYSTEM.
DEMON.
STARCHILD.
WHY ARE YOU HERE? SHOULDN'T YOU BE IN THE COUNCIL BUILDING?
WE WERE. BUT THE MASTER PLAN WAS CHANGED, AND MORPHEUS WAS FORGOTTEN EXCEPT BY A VERY FEW.
WAS THIS BEFORE THE GREAT WAR?

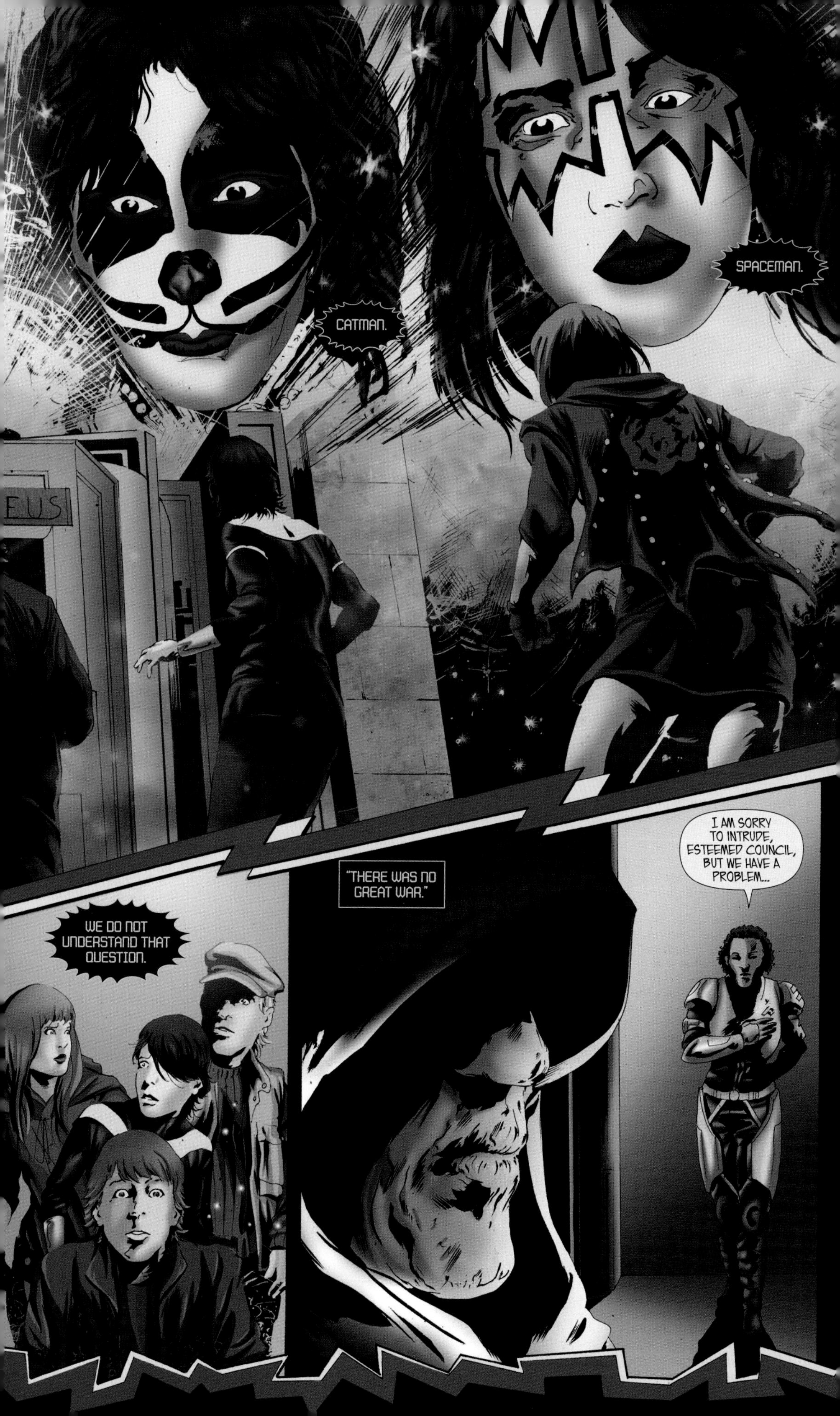
CATMAN.
SPACEMAN.
EUS
WE DO NOT UNDERSTAND THAT QUESTION.
"THERE WAS NO GREAT WAR."
I AM SORRY TO INTRUDE, ESTEEMED COUNCIL, BUT WE HAVE A PROBLEM...

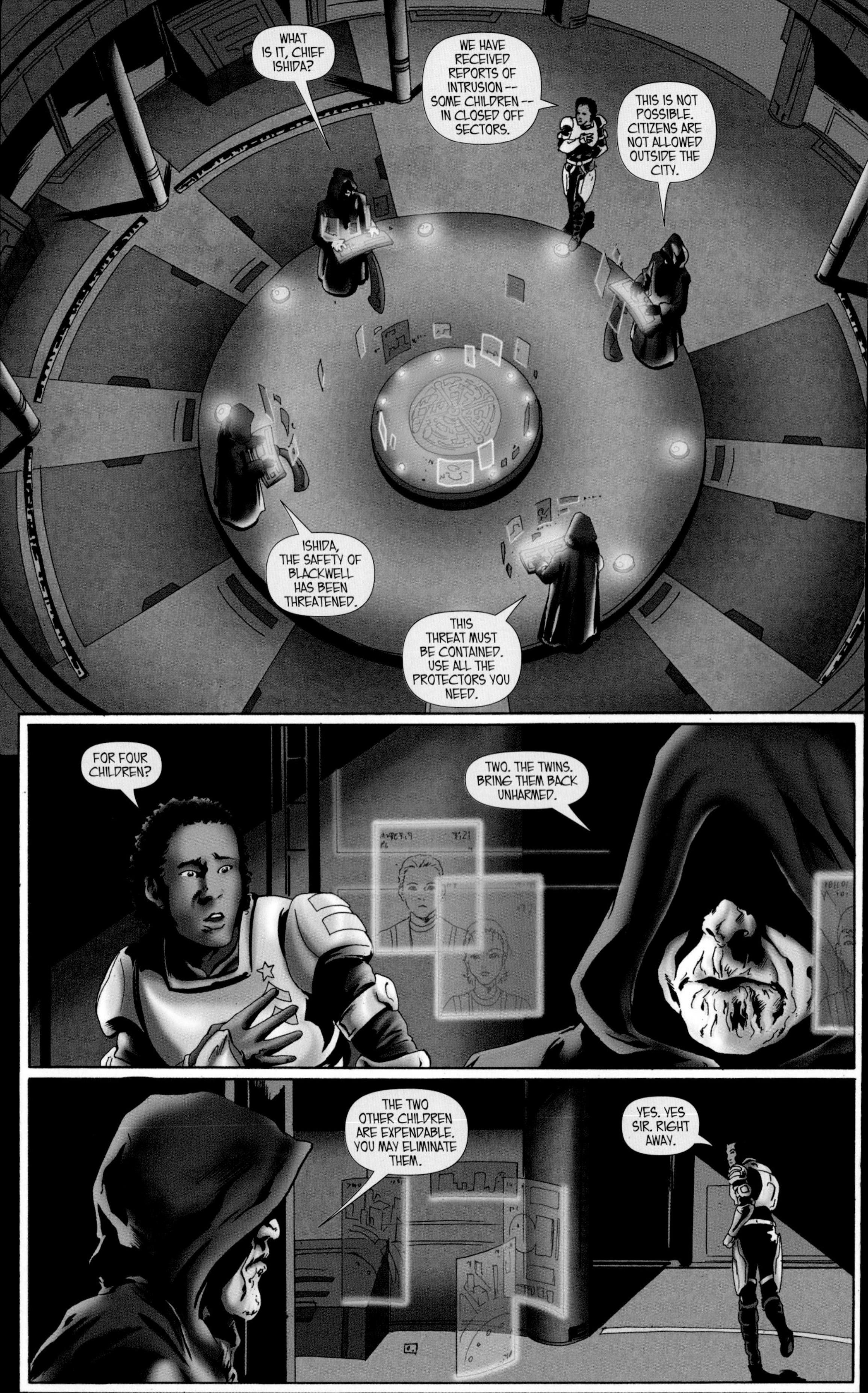
WHAT IS IT, CHIEF ISHIDA?
WE HAVE RECEIVED REPORTS OF INTRUSION -- SOME CHILDREN -- IN CLOSED OFF SECTORS.
THIS IS NOT POSSIBLE. CITIZENS ARE NOT ALLOWED OUTSIDE THE CITY.
ISHIDA, THE SAFETY OF BLACKWELL HAS BEEN THREATENED.
THIS THREAT MUST BE CONTAINED. USE ALL THE PROTECTORS YOU NEED.
FOR FOUR CHILDREN?
TWO. THE TWINS. BRING THEM BACK UNHARMED.
THE TWO OTHER CHILDREN ARE EXPENDABLE. YOU MAY ELIMINATE THEM.
YES. YES SIR. RIGHT AWAY.

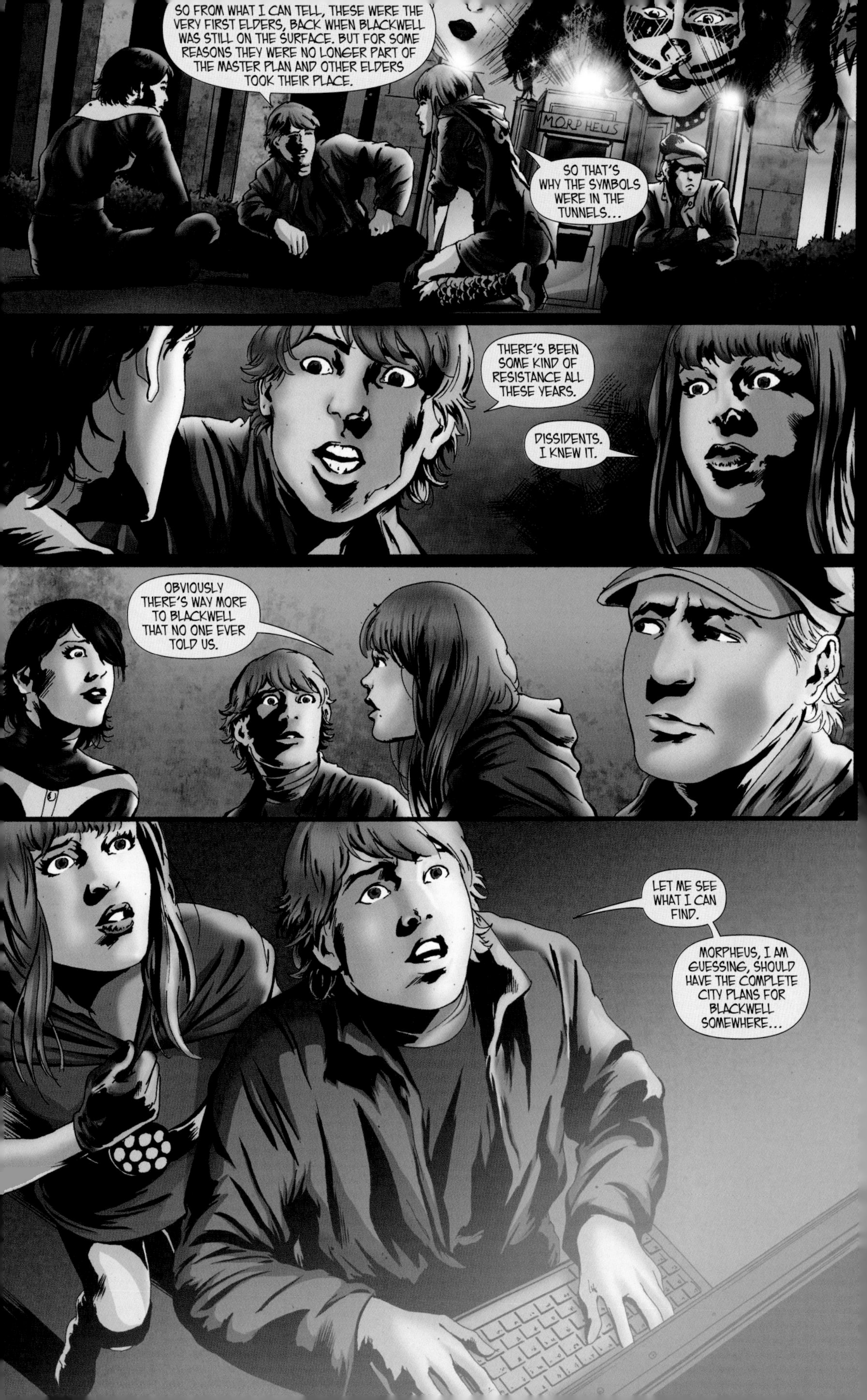
SO FROM WHAT I CAN TELL, THESE WERE THE VERY FIRST ELDERS, BACK WHEN BLACKWELL WAS STILL ON THE SURFACE. BUT FOR SOME REASONS THEY WERE NO LONGER PART OF THE MASTER PLAN AND OTHER ELDERS TOOK THEIR PLACE.
MORPHEUS
SO THAT'S WHY THE SYMBOLS WERE IN THE TUNNELS...
THERE'S BEEN SOME KIND OF RESISTANCE ALL THESE YEARS.
DISSIDENTS. I KNEW IT.
OBVIOUSLY THERE'S WAY MORE TO BLACKWELL THAT NO ONE EVER TOLD US.
LET ME SEE WHAT I CAN FIND.
MORPHEUS, I AM GUESSING, SHOULD HAVE THE COMPLETE CITY PLANS FOR BLACKWELL SOMEWHERE...

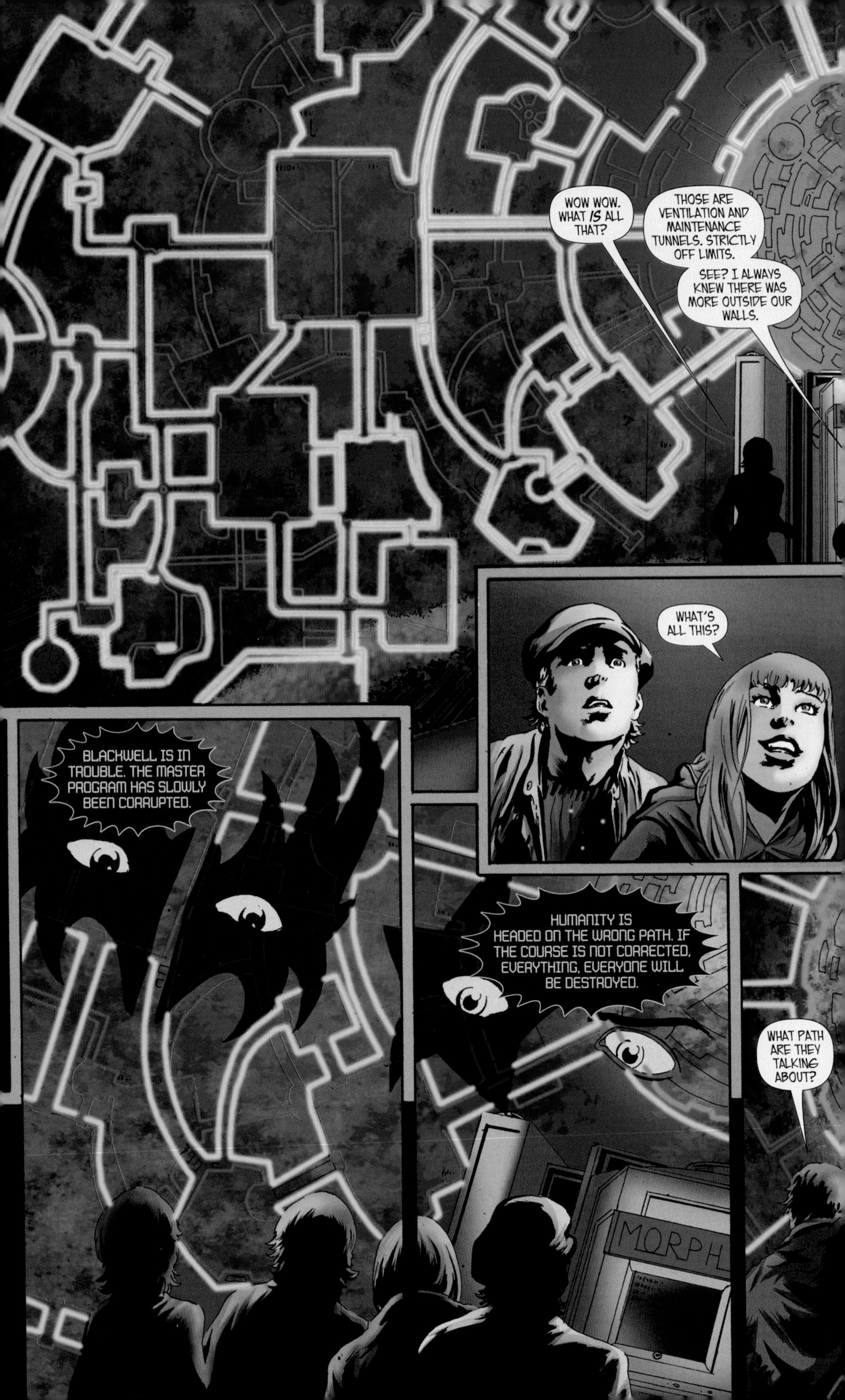
WOW WOW. WHAT IS ALL THAT?
THOSE ARE VENTILATION AND MAINTENANCE TUNNELS. STRICTLY OFF LIMITS.
SEE? I ALWAYS KNEW THERE WAS MORE OUTSIDE OUR WALLS.
WHAT'S ALL THIS?
BLACKWELL IS IN TROUBLE. THE MASTER PROGRAM HAS SLOWLY BEEN CORRUPTED.
HUMANITY IS HEADED ON THE WRONG PATH. IF THE COURSE IS NOT CORRECTED, EVERYTHING, EVERYONE WILL BE DESTROYED.
WHAT PATH ARE THEY TALKING ABOUT?
MORPH

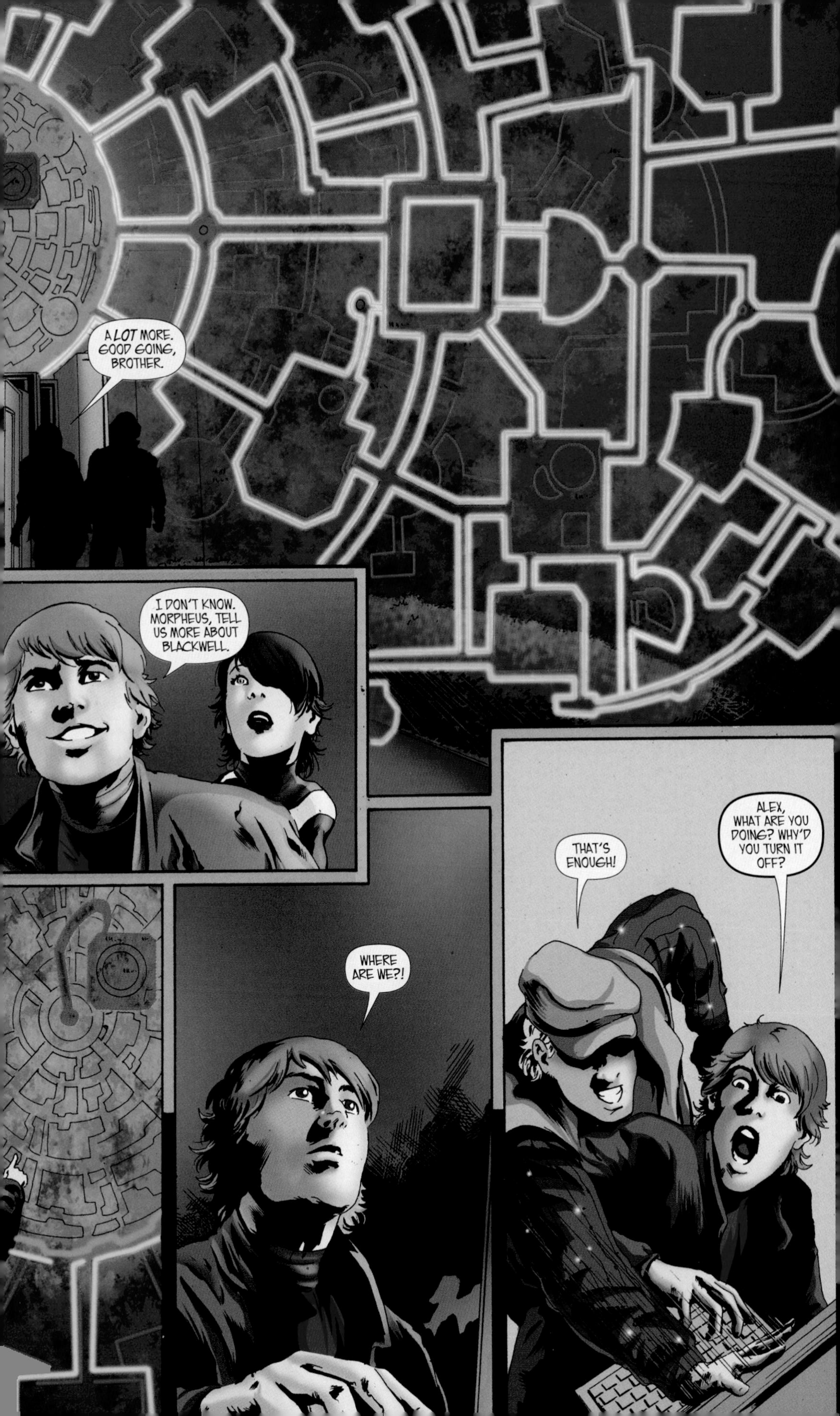
A LOT MORE. GOOD GOING, BROTHER.
I DON'T KNOW. MORPHEUS, TELL US MORE ABOUT BLACKWELL.
WHERE ARE WE?!
THAT'S ENOUGH!
ALEX, WHAT ARE YOU DOING? WHY'D YOU TURN IT OFF?

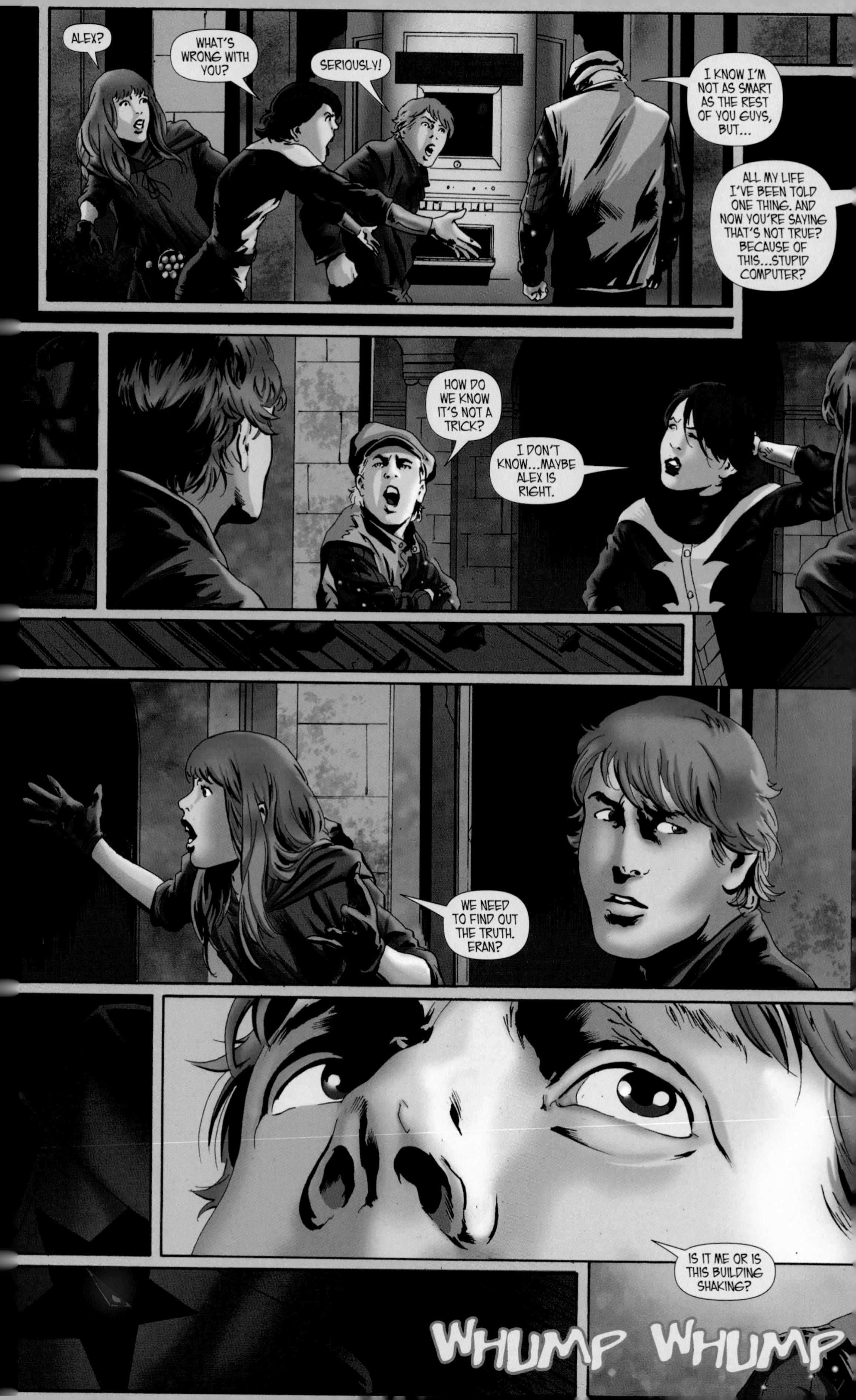

ALEX?
WHAT'S WRONG WITH YOU?
SERIOUSLY!
I KNOW I'M NOT AS SMART AS THE REST OF YOU GUYS, BUT...
ALL MY LIFE I'VE BEEN TOLD ONE THING. AND NOW YOU'RE SAYING THAT'S NOT TRUE? BECAUSE OF THIS...STUPID COMPUTER?
HOW DO WE KNOW IT'S NOT A TRICK?
I DON'T KNOW...MAYBE ALEX IS RIGHT.
WE NEED TO FIND OUT THE TRUTH. ERAN?
IS IT ME OR IS THIS BUILDING SHAKING?
WHUMP WHUMP

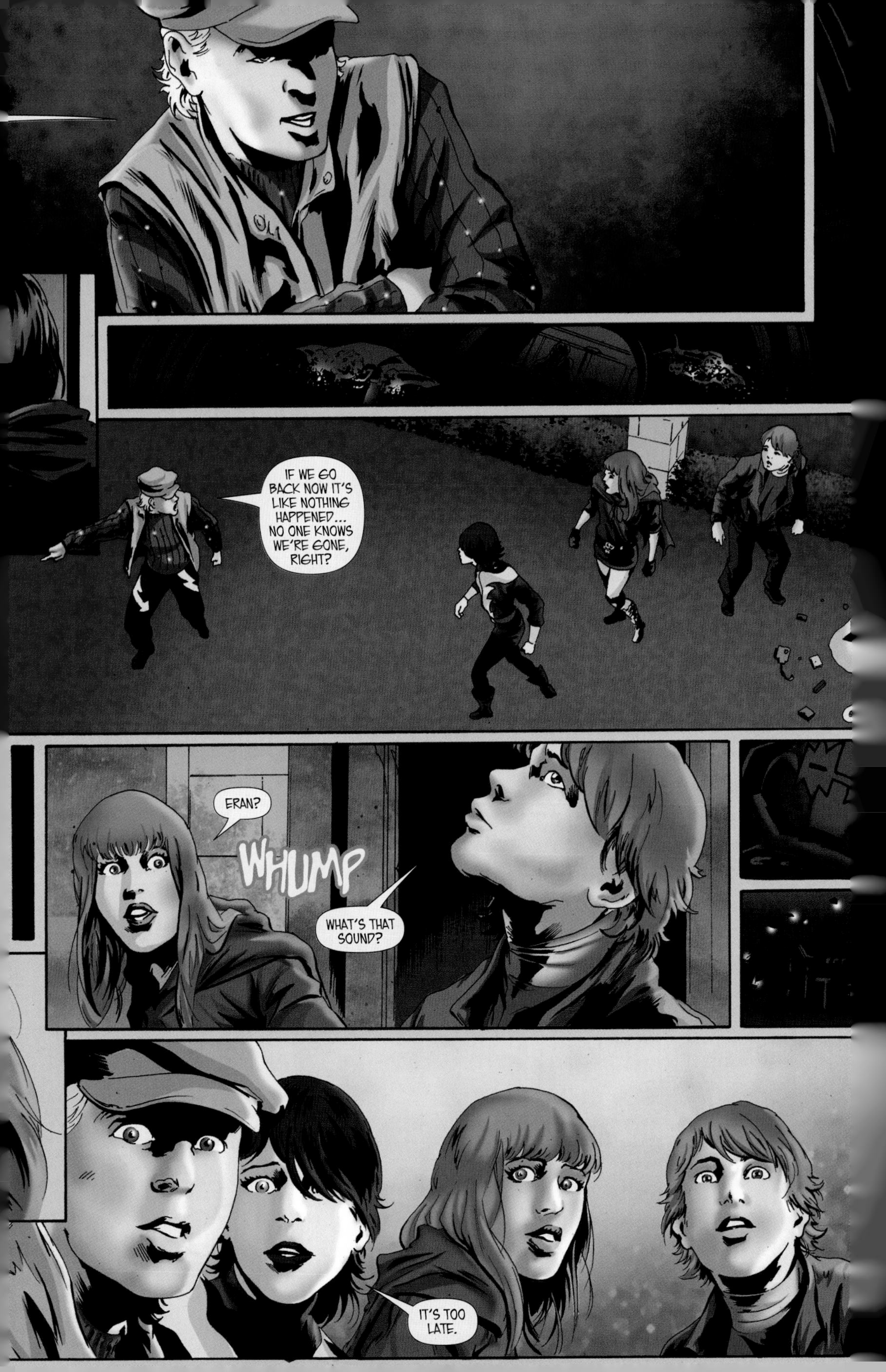
IF WE GO BACK NOW IT'S LIKE NOTHING HAPPENED... NO ONE KNOWS WE'RE GONE, RIGHT?
ERAN?
WHUMP
WHAT'S THAT SOUND?
IT'S TOO LATE.

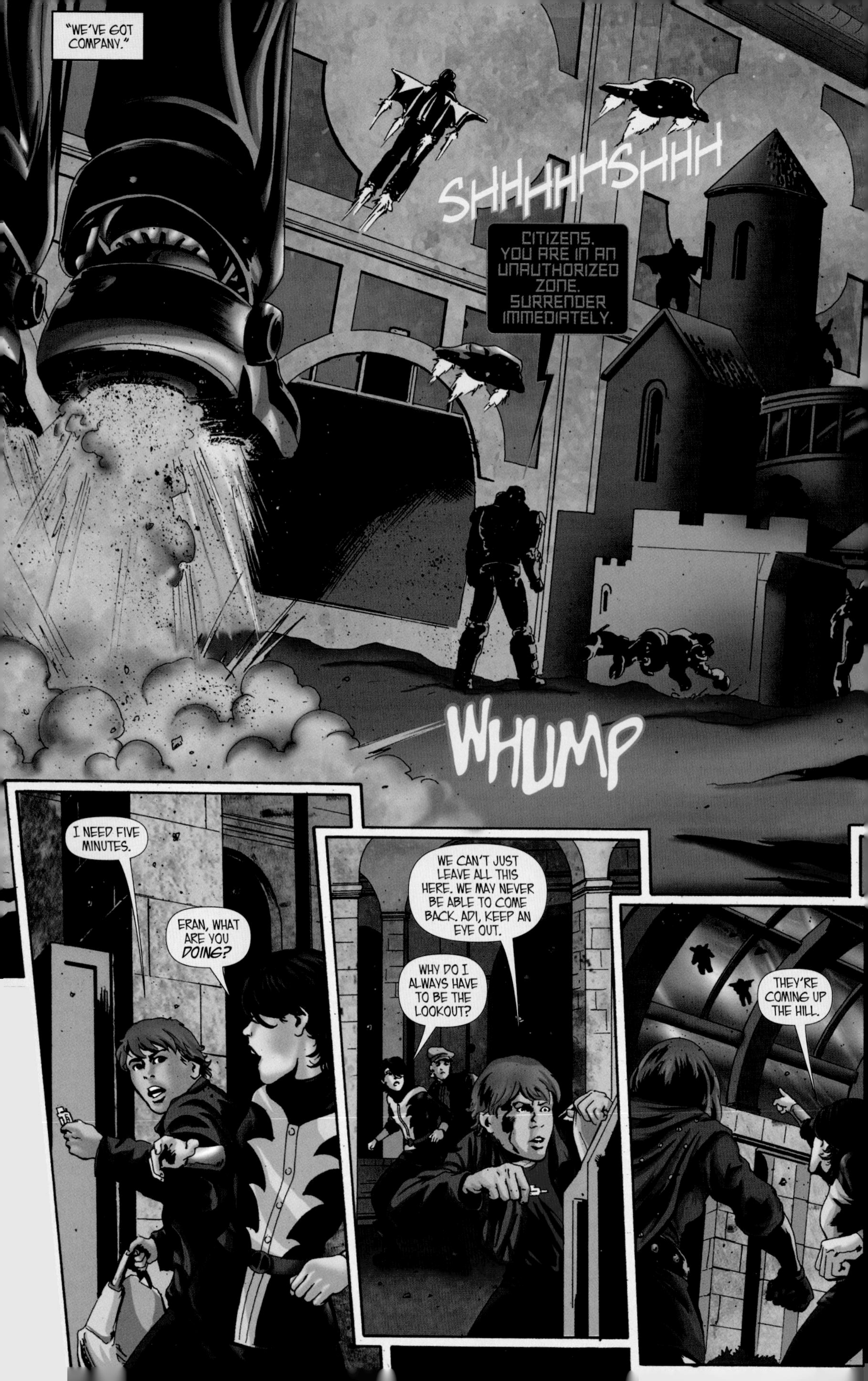
"WE'VE GOT COMPANY."
SHHHHHSHHH
CITIZENS. YOU ARE IN AN UNAUTHORIZED ZONE. SURRENDER IMMEDIATELY.
WHUMP
I NEED FIVE MINUTES.
ERAN, WHAT ARE YOU DOING?
WE CAN'T JUST LEAVE ALL THIS HERE. WE MAY NEVER BE ABLE TO COME BACK. ADI, KEEP AN EYE OUT.
WHY DO I ALWAYS HAVE TO BE THE LOOKOUT?
THEY'RE COMING UP THE HILL.

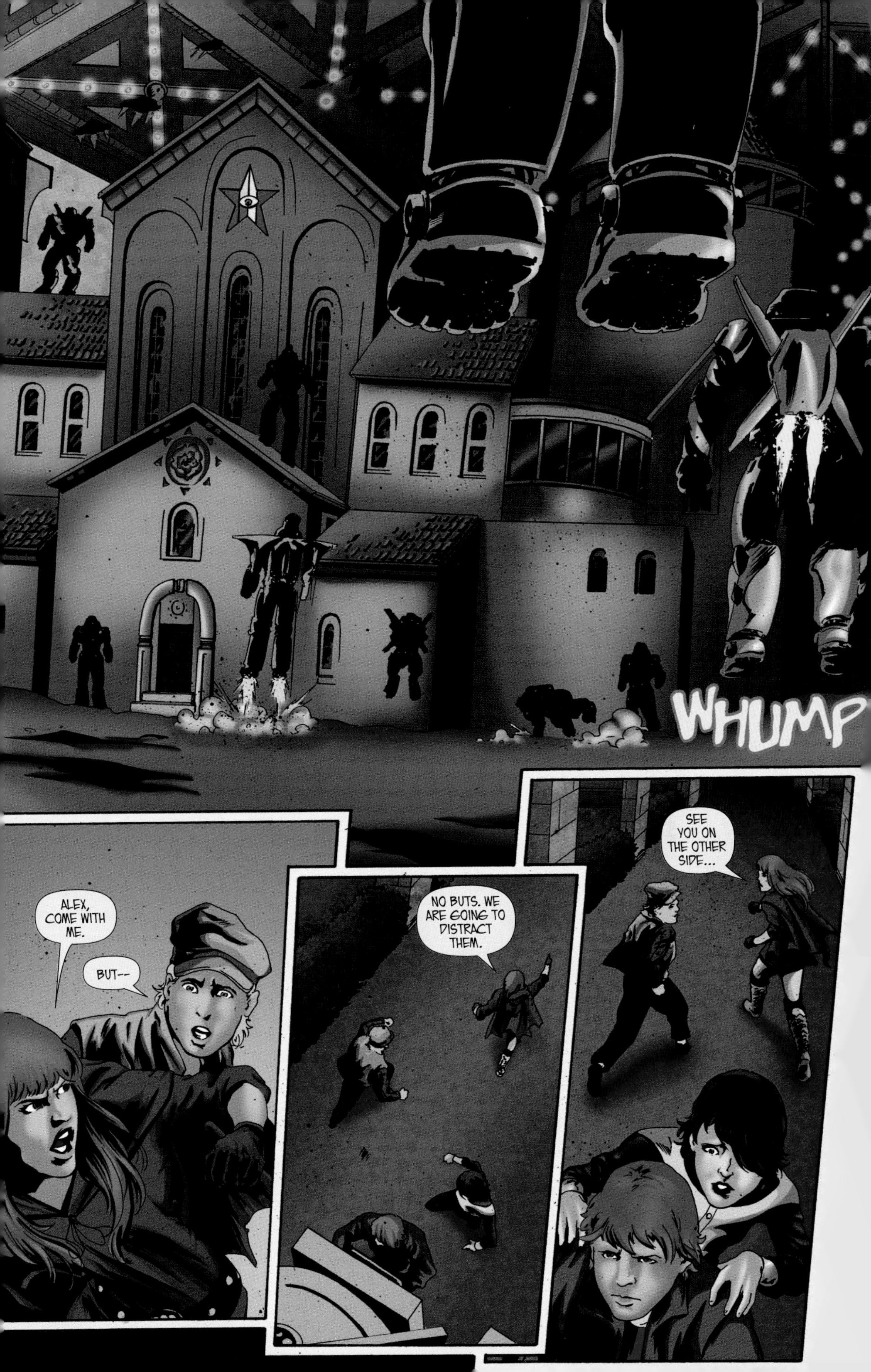
WHUMP
ALEX, COME WITH ME.
BUT--
NO BUTS. WE ARE GOING TO DISTRACT THEM.
SEE YOU ON THE OTHER SIDE...

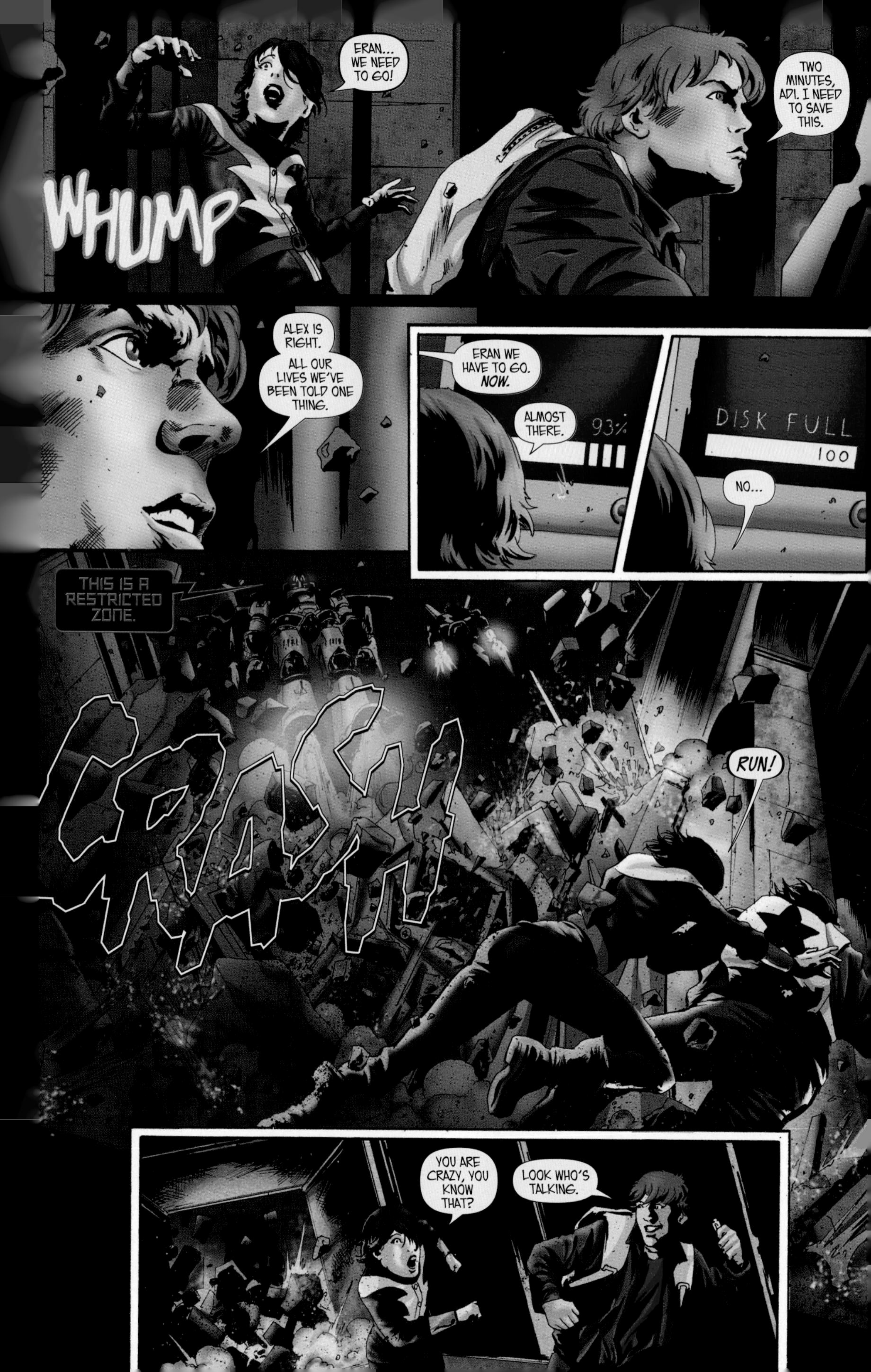
ERAN... WE NEED TO GO!
WHUMP
TWO MINUTES, ADI. I NEED TO SAVE THIS.
ALEX IS RIGHT.
ALL OUR LIVES WE'VE BEEN TOLD ONE THING.
ERAN WE HAVE TO GO. NOW.
ALMOST THERE.
93%
DISK FULL
100
NO...
THIS IS A RESTRICTED ZONE.
CRASH
RUN!
YOU ARE CRAZY, YOU KNOW THAT?
LOOK WHO'S TALKING.

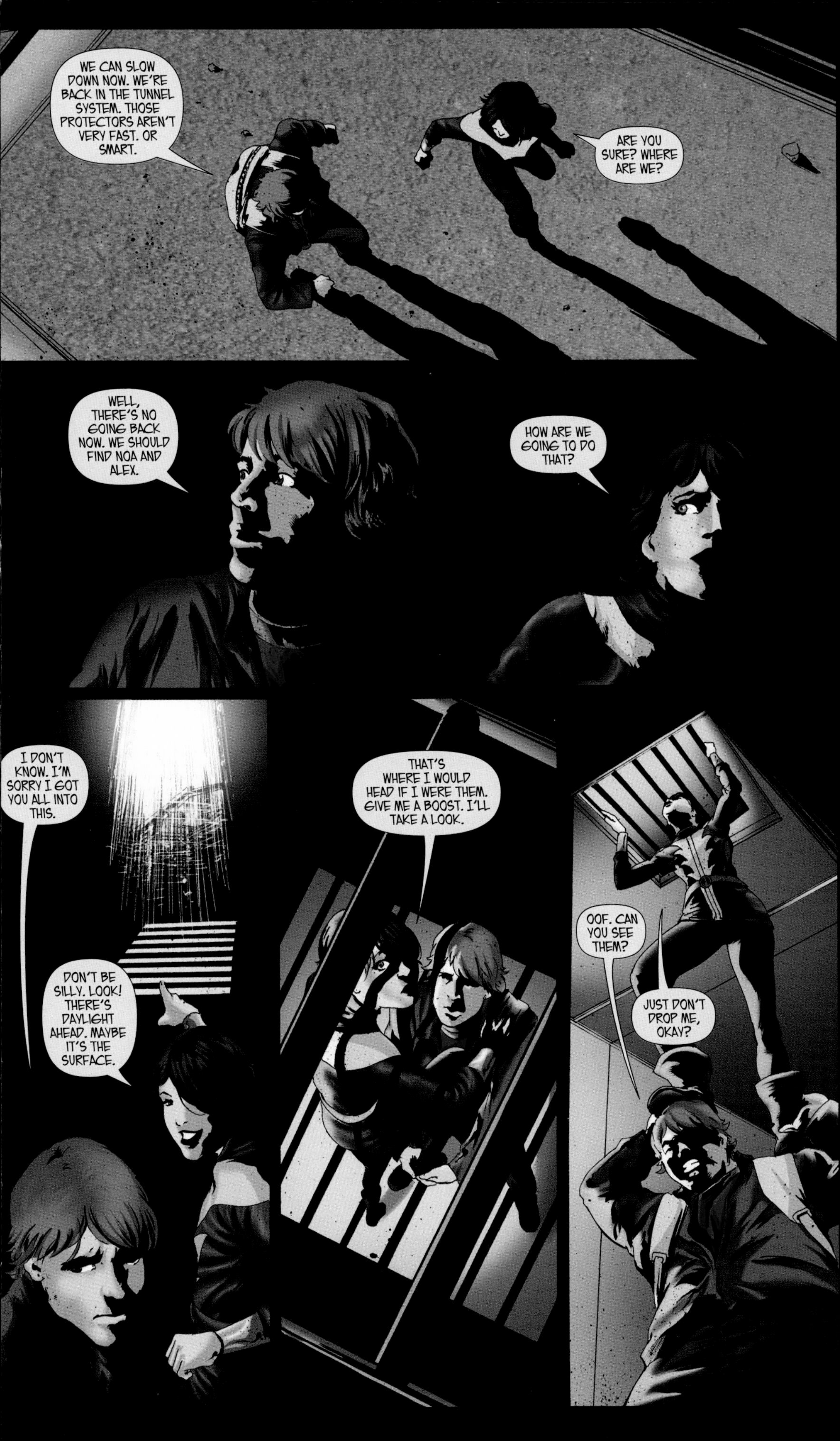
WE CAN SLOW DOWN NOW. WE'RE BACK IN THE TUNNEL SYSTEM. THOSE PROTECTORS AREN'T VERY FAST. OR SMART.
ARE YOU SURE? WHERE ARE WE?
WELL, THERE'S NO GOING BACK NOW. WE SHOULD FIND NOA AND ALEX.
HOW ARE WE GOING TO DO THAT?
I DON'T KNOW. I'M SORRY I GOT YOU ALL INTO THIS.
DON'T BE SILLY. LOOK! THERE'S DAYLIGHT AHEAD. MAYBE IT'S THE SURFACE.
THAT'S WHERE I WOULD HEAD IF I WERE THEM. GIVE ME A BOOST. I'LL TAKE A LOOK.
OOF. CAN YOU SEE THEM?
JUST DON'T DROP ME, OKAY?

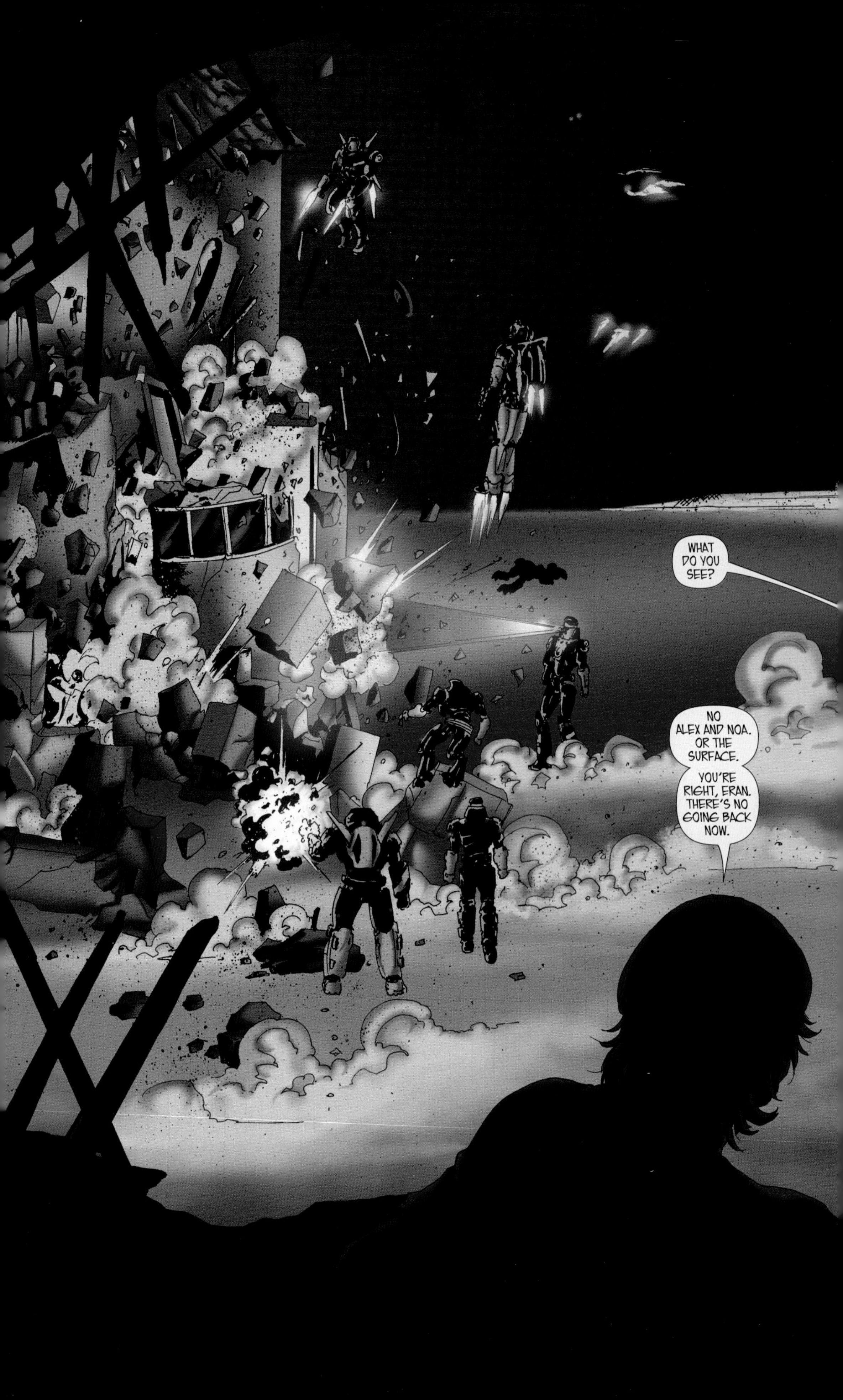
WHAT DO YOU SEE?
NO ALEX AND NOA. OR THE SURFACE.
YOU'RE RIGHT, ERAN. THERE'S NO GOING BACK NOW.

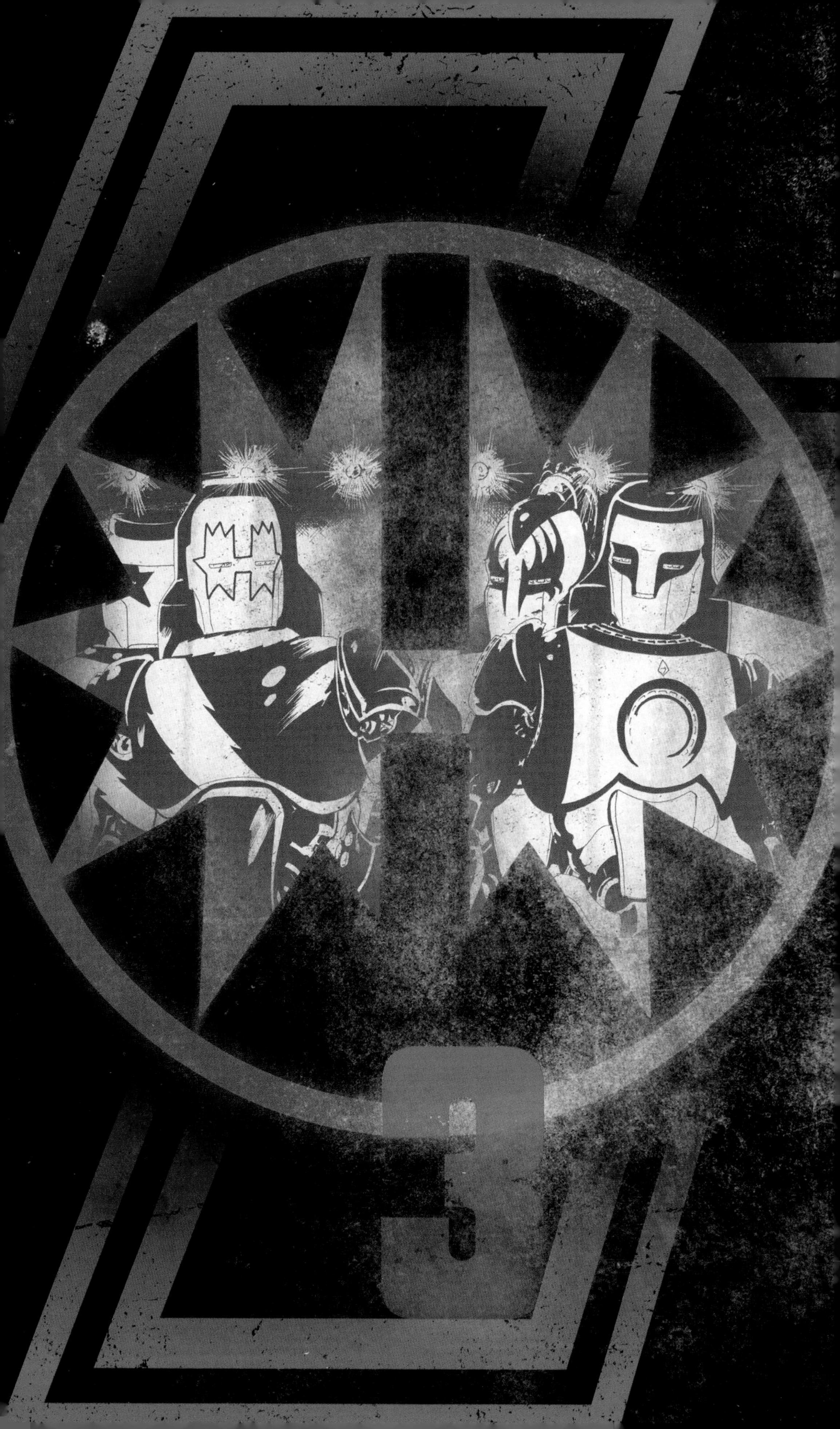
3

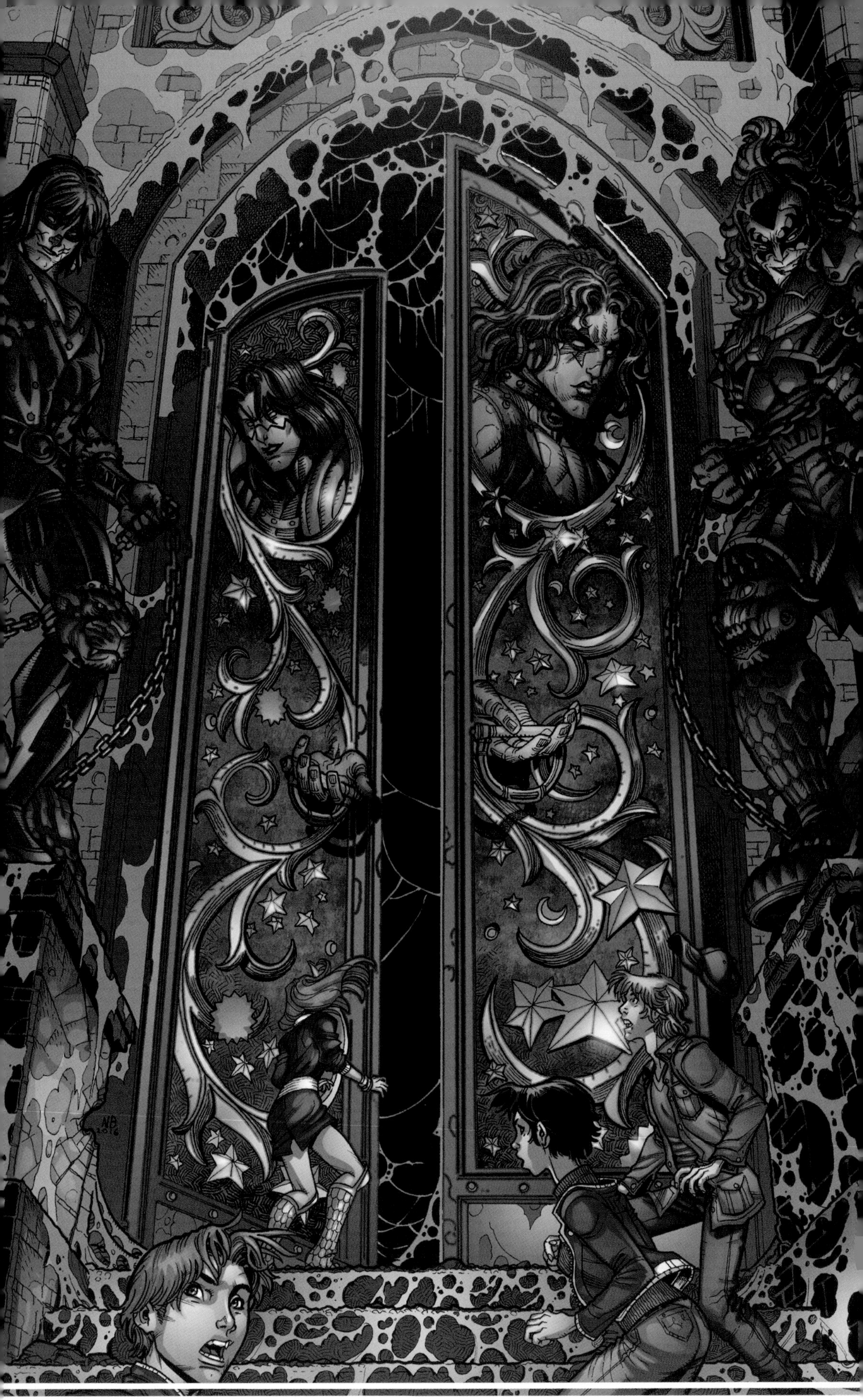

ISSUE 3, MAIN COVER: Art by Nick Bradshaw & Pete Pantazis

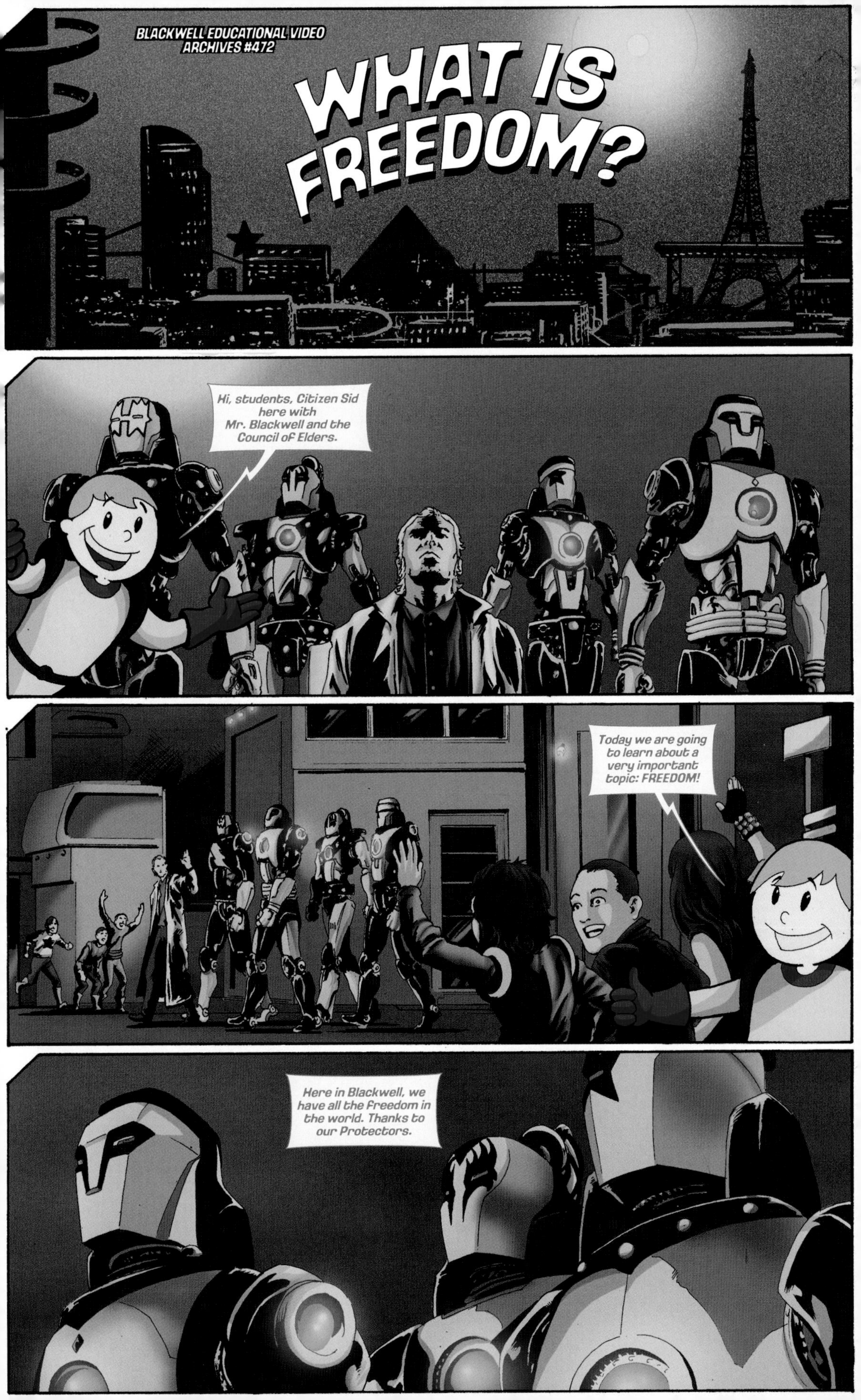
BLACKWELL EDUCATIONAL VIDEO ARCHIVES #472
WHAT IS FREEDOM?
Hi, students, Citizen Sid here with Mr. Blackwell and the Council of Elders.
Today we are going to learn about a very important topic: FREEDOM!
Here in Blackwell, we have all the freedom in the world. Thanks to our Protectors.

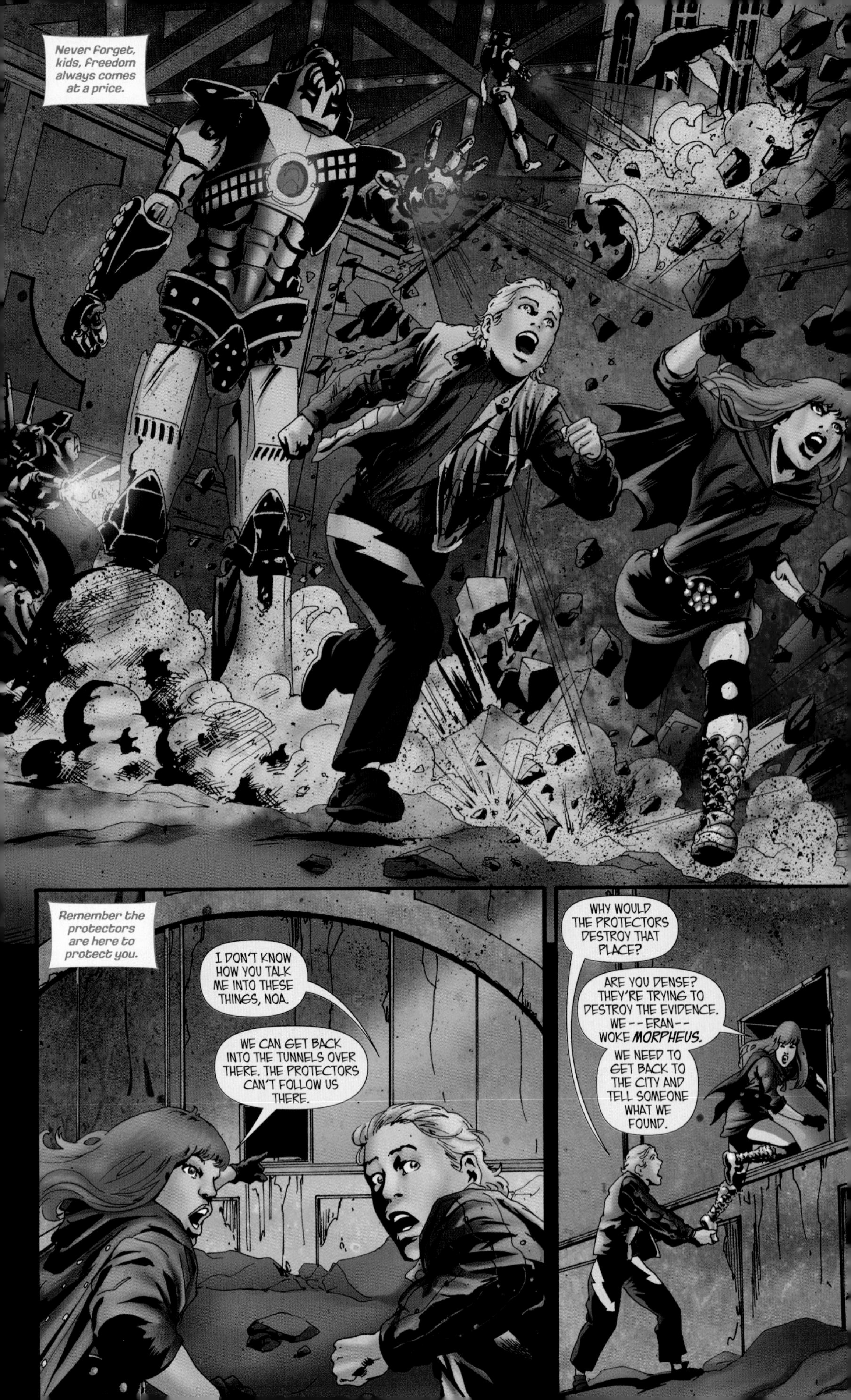
Never forget, kids, freedom always comes at a price.
Remember the protectors are here to protect you.
I DON'T KNOW HOW YOU TALK ME INTO THESE THINGS, NOA.
WE CAN GET BACK INTO THE TUNNELS OVER THERE. THE PROTECTORS CAN'T FOLLOW US THERE.
WHY WOULD THE PROTECTORS DESTROY THAT PLACE?
ARE YOU DENSE? THEY'RE TRYING TO DESTROY THE EVIDENCE. WE--ERAN--WOKE MORPHEUS.
WE NEED TO GET BACK TO THE CITY AND TELL SOMEONE WHAT WE FOUND.

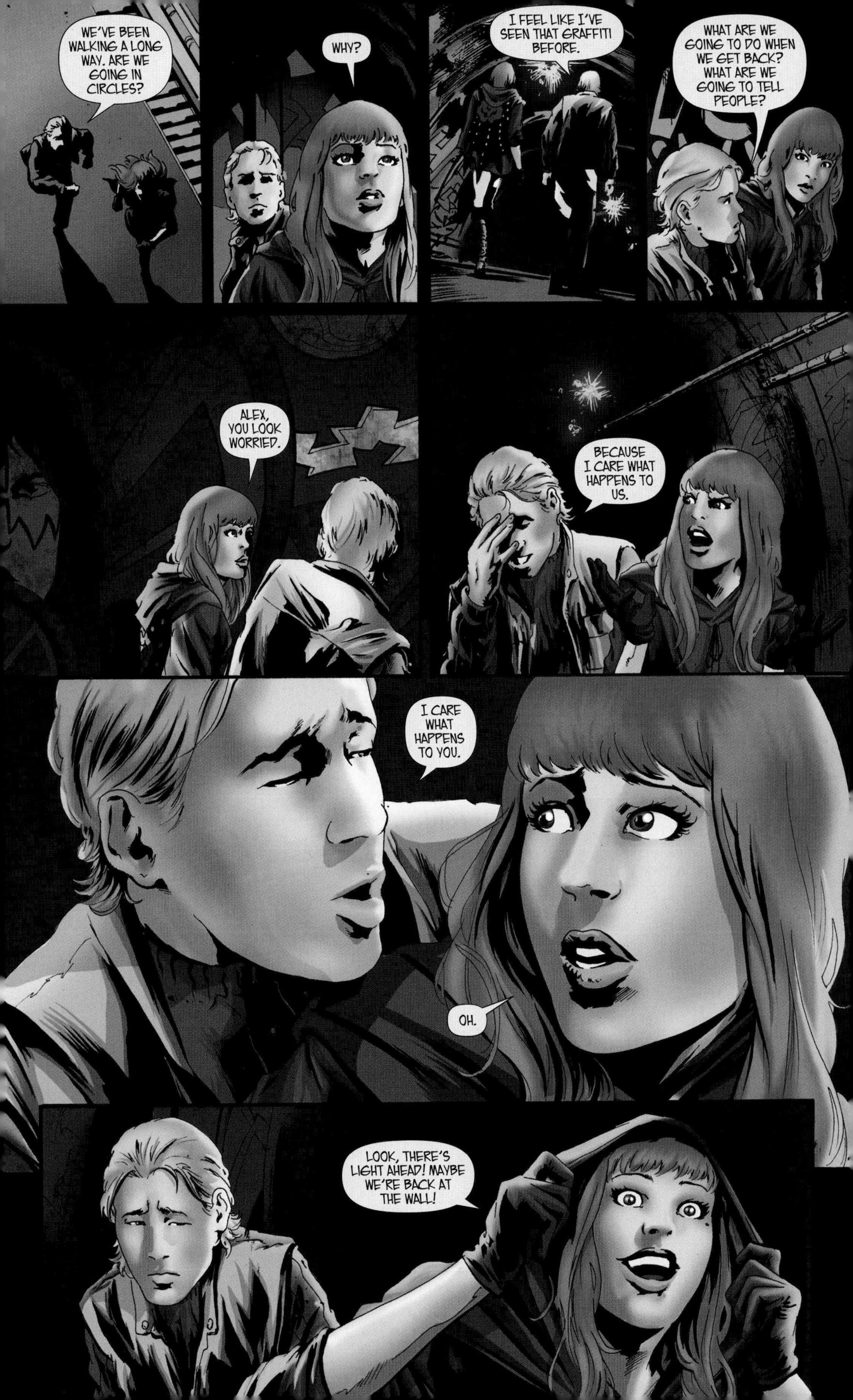
WE'VE BEEN WALKING A LONG WAY. ARE WE GOING IN CIRCLES?
WHY?
I FEEL LIKE I'VE SEEN THAT GRAFFITI BEFORE.
WHAT ARE WE GOING TO DO WHEN WE GET BACK? WHAT ARE WE GOING TO TELL PEOPLE?
ALEX, YOU LOOK WORRIED.
BECAUSE I CARE WHAT HAPPENS TO US.
I CARE WHAT HAPPENS TO YOU.
OH.
LOOK, THERE'S LIGHT AHEAD! MAYBE WE'RE BACK AT THE WALL!

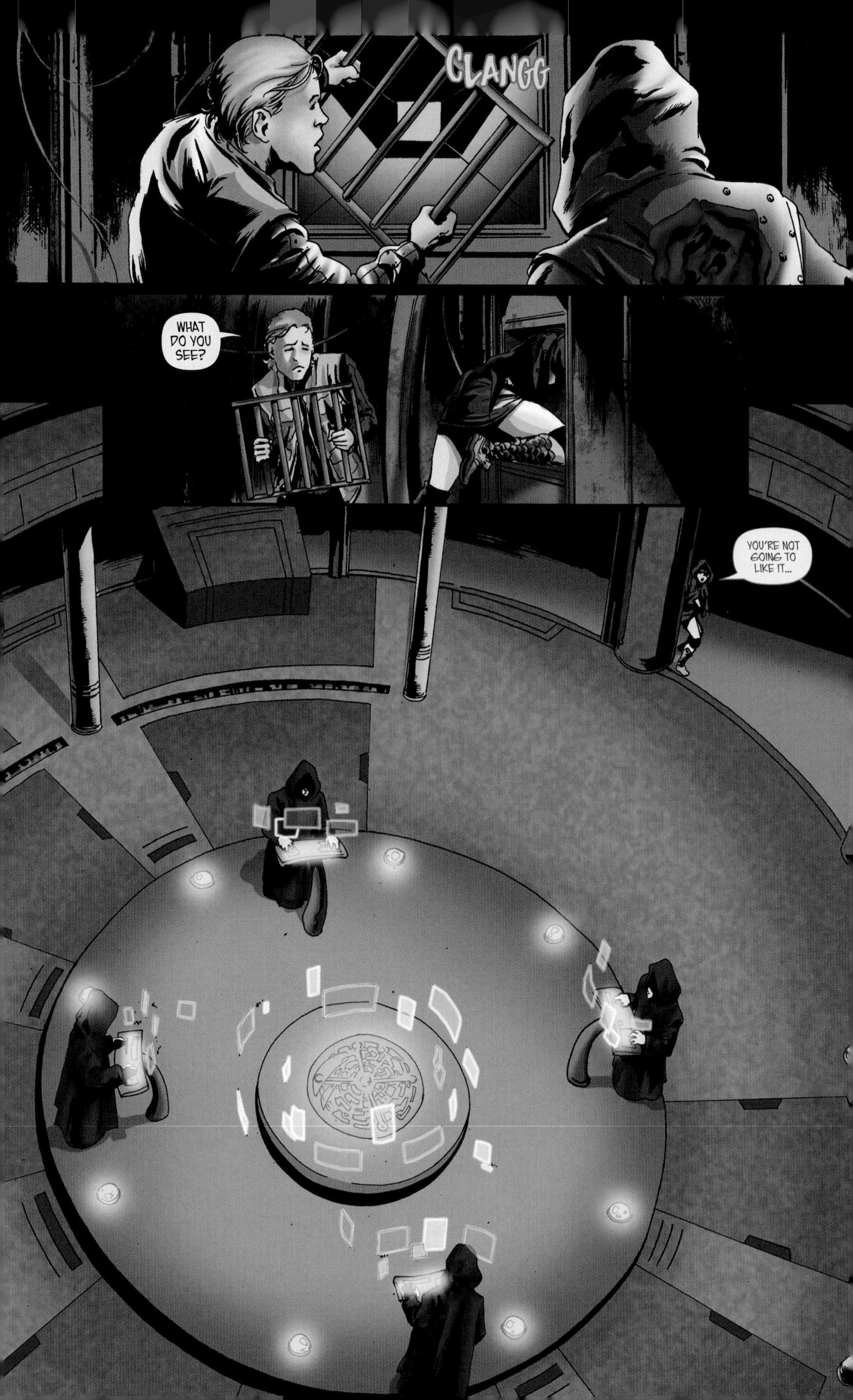
CLANGG
WHAT DO YOU SEE?
YOU'RE NOT GOING TO LIKE IT...

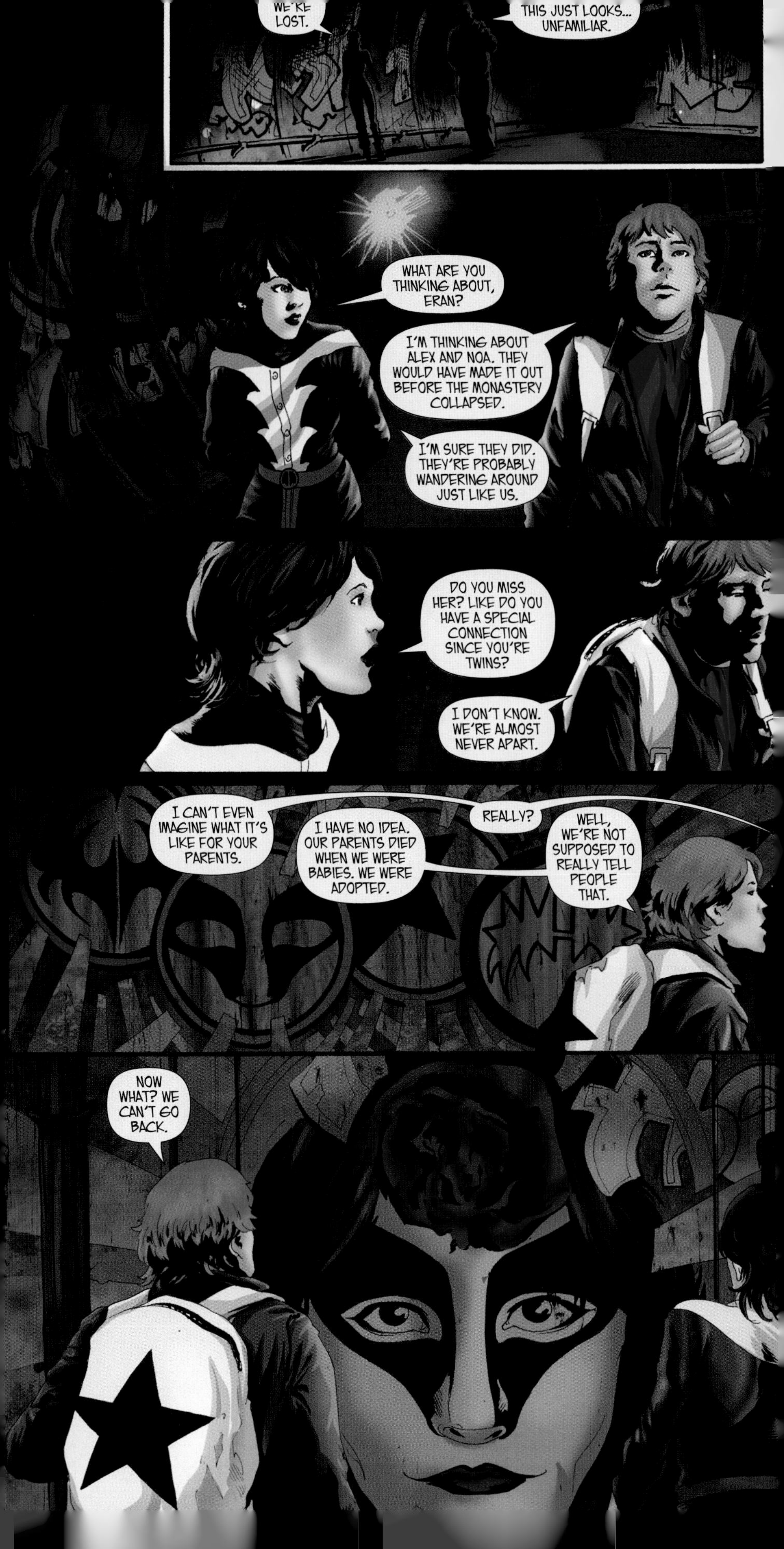
WE'RE LOST.
THIS JUST LOOKS... UNFAMILIAR.
WHAT ARE YOU THINKING ABOUT, ERAN?
I'M THINKING ABOUT ALEX AND NOA. THEY WOULD HAVE MADE IT OUT BEFORE THE MONASTERY COLLAPSED.
I'M SURE THEY DID. THEY'RE PROBABLY WANDERING AROUND JUST LIKE US.
DO YOU MISS HER? LIKE DO YOU HAVE A SPECIAL CONNECTION SINCE YOU'RE TWINS?
I DON'T KNOW. WE'RE ALMOST NEVER APART.
I CAN'T EVEN IMAGINE WHAT IT'S LIKE FOR YOUR PARENTS.
I HAVE NO IDEA. OUR PARENTS DIED WHEN WE WERE BABIES. WE WERE ADOPTED.
REALLY?
WELL, WE'RE NOT SUPPOSED TO REALLY TELL PEOPLE THAT.
NOW WHAT? WE CAN'T GO BACK.

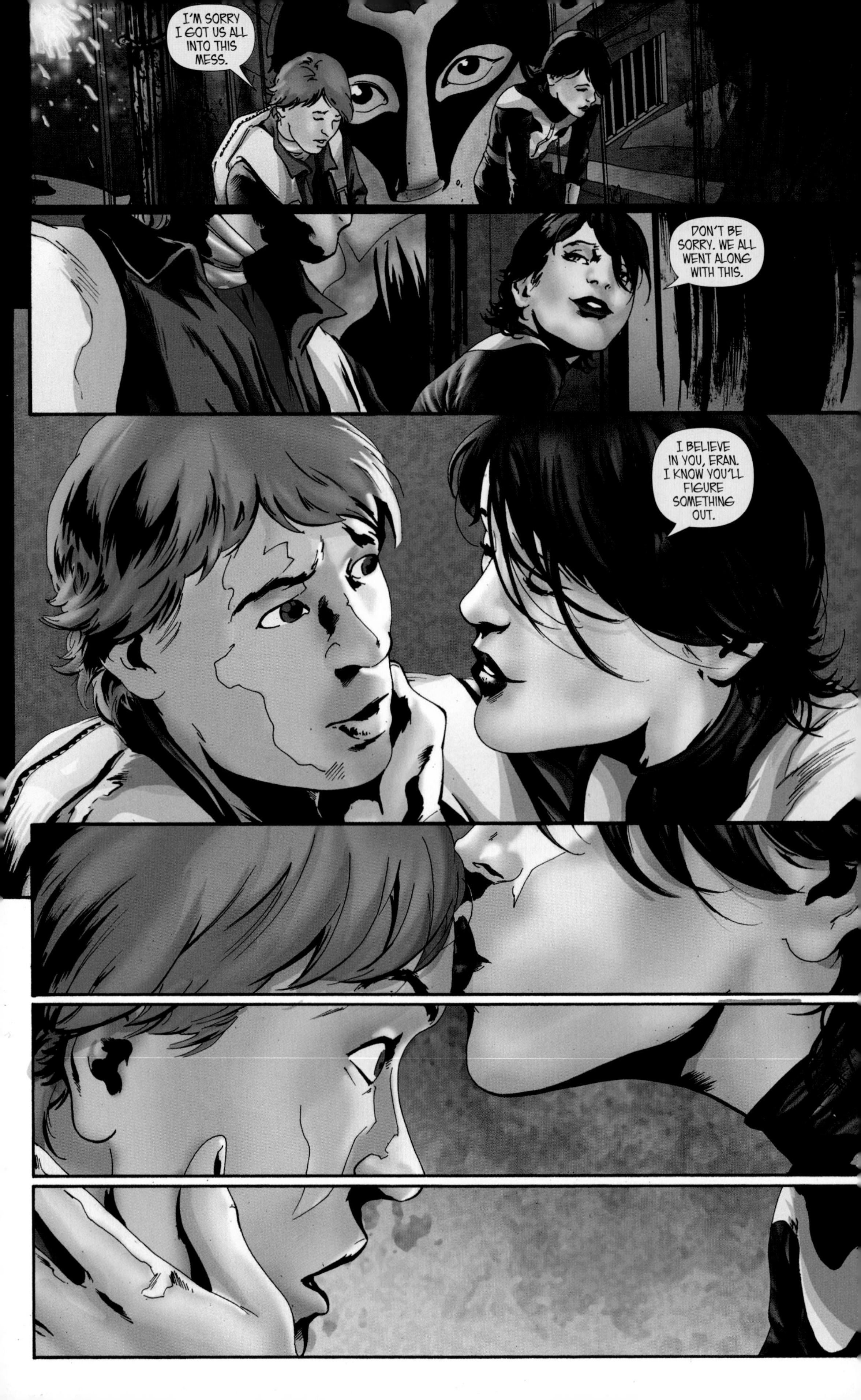
I'M SORRY I GOT US ALL INTO THIS MESS.
DON'T BE SORRY. WE ALL WENT ALONG WITH THIS.
I BELIEVE IN YOU, ERAN. I KNOW YOU'LL FIGURE SOMETHING OUT.

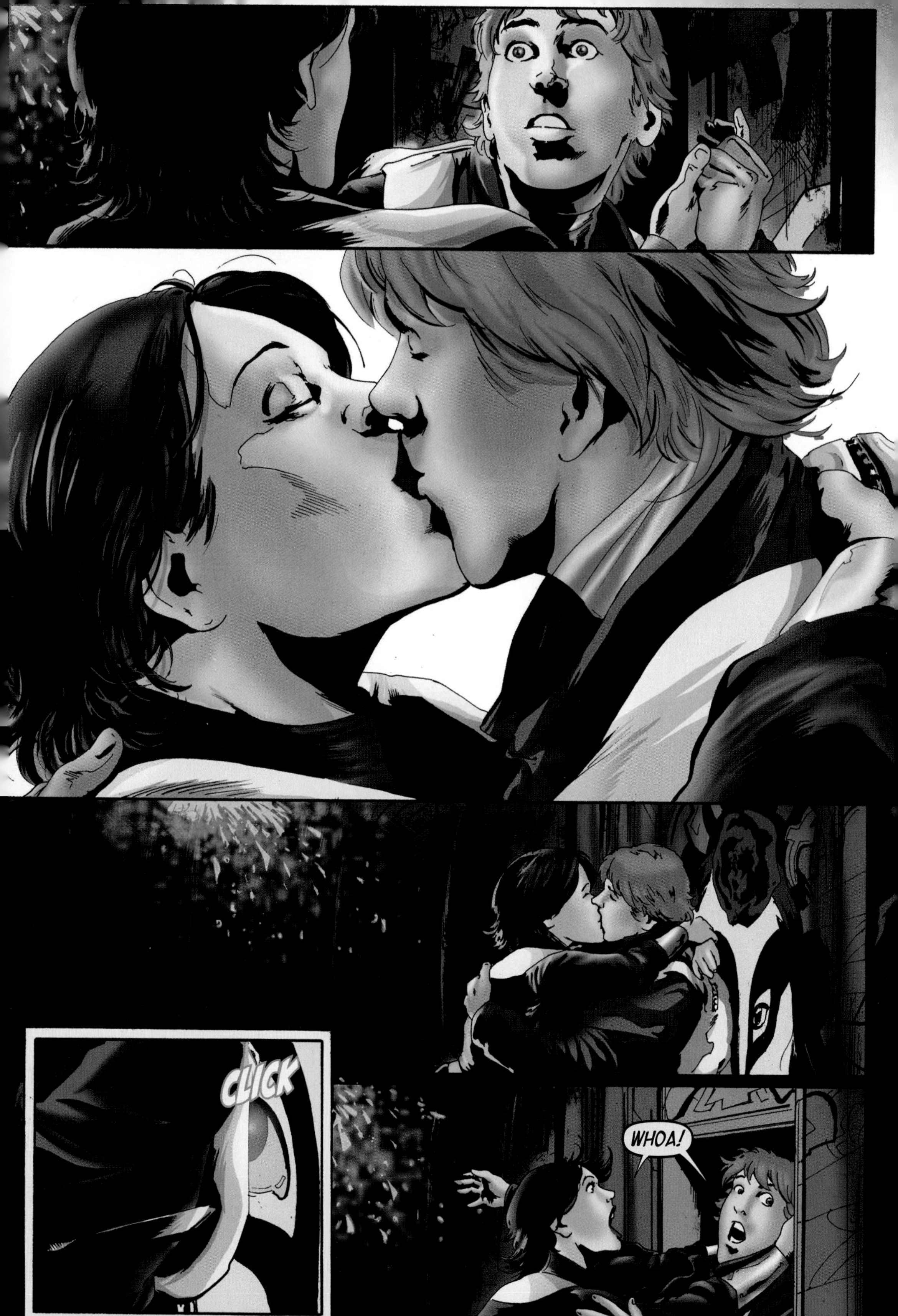
CLICK
WHOA!

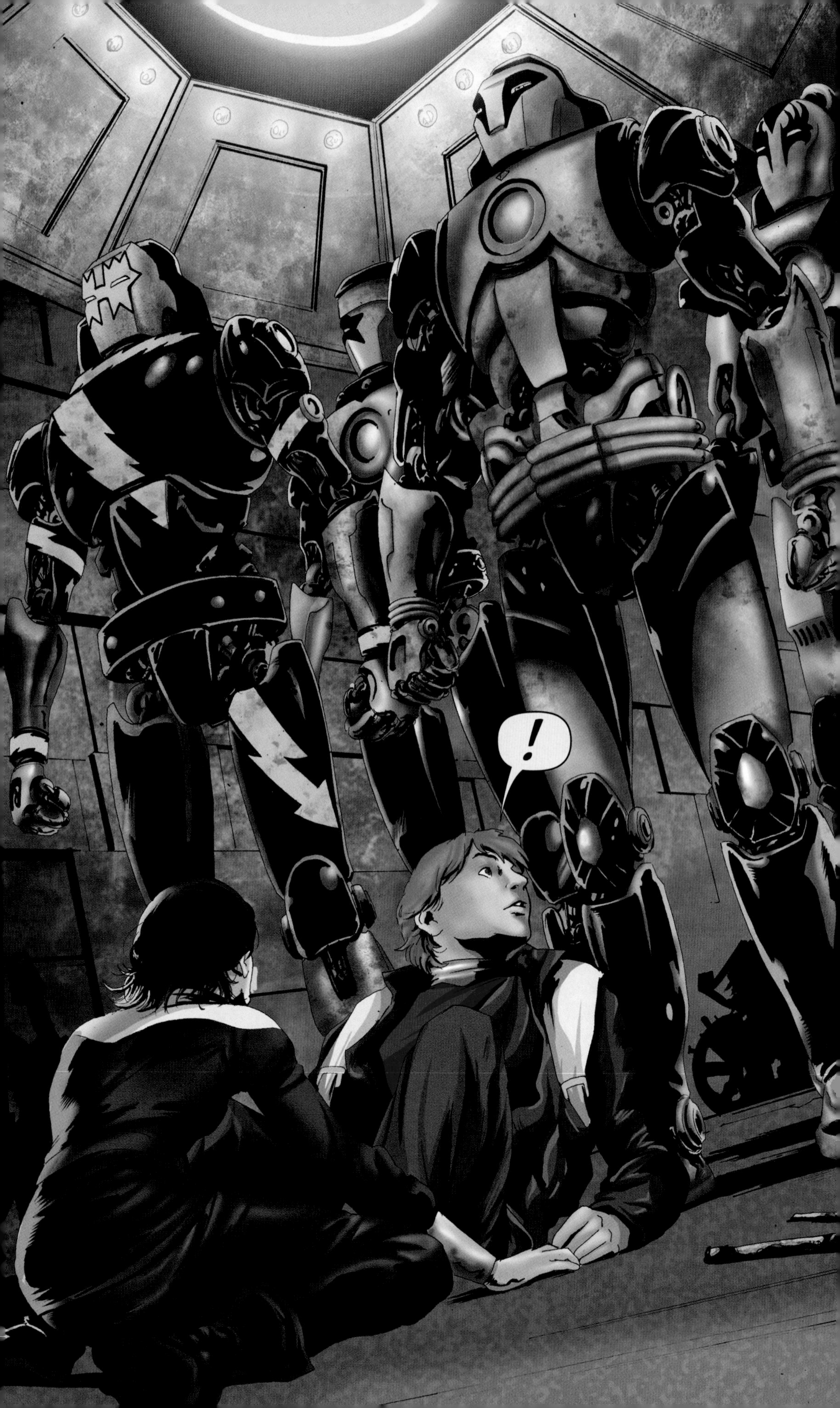
!

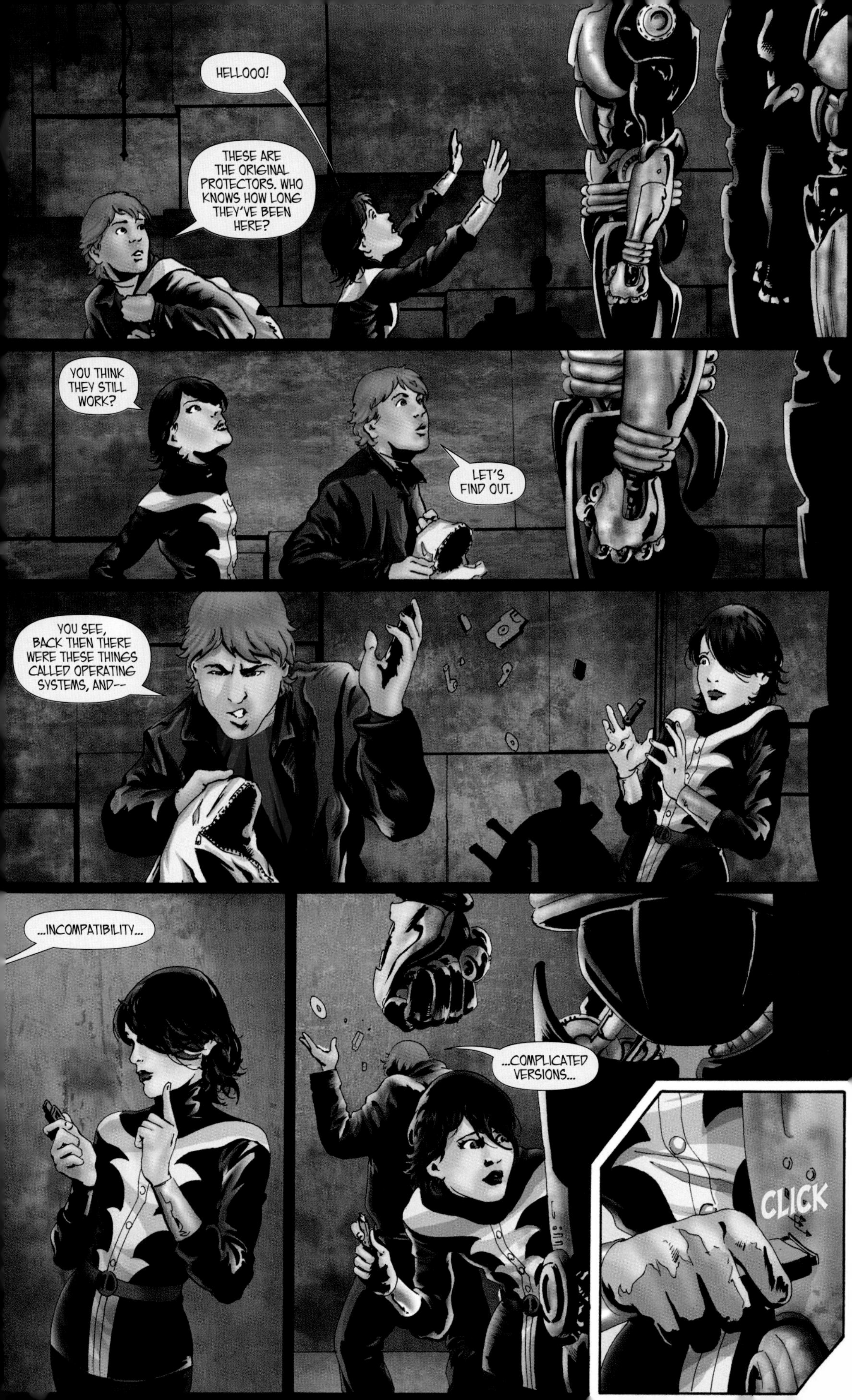
HELLOOO!
THESE ARE THE ORIGINAL PROTECTORS. WHO KNOWS HOW LONG THEY'VE BEEN HERE?
YOU THINK THEY STILL WORK?
LET'S FIND OUT.
YOU SEE, BACK THEN THERE WERE THESE THINGS CALLED OPERATING SYSTEMS, AND--
...INCOMPATIBILITY...
...COMPLICATED VERSIONS...
CLICK

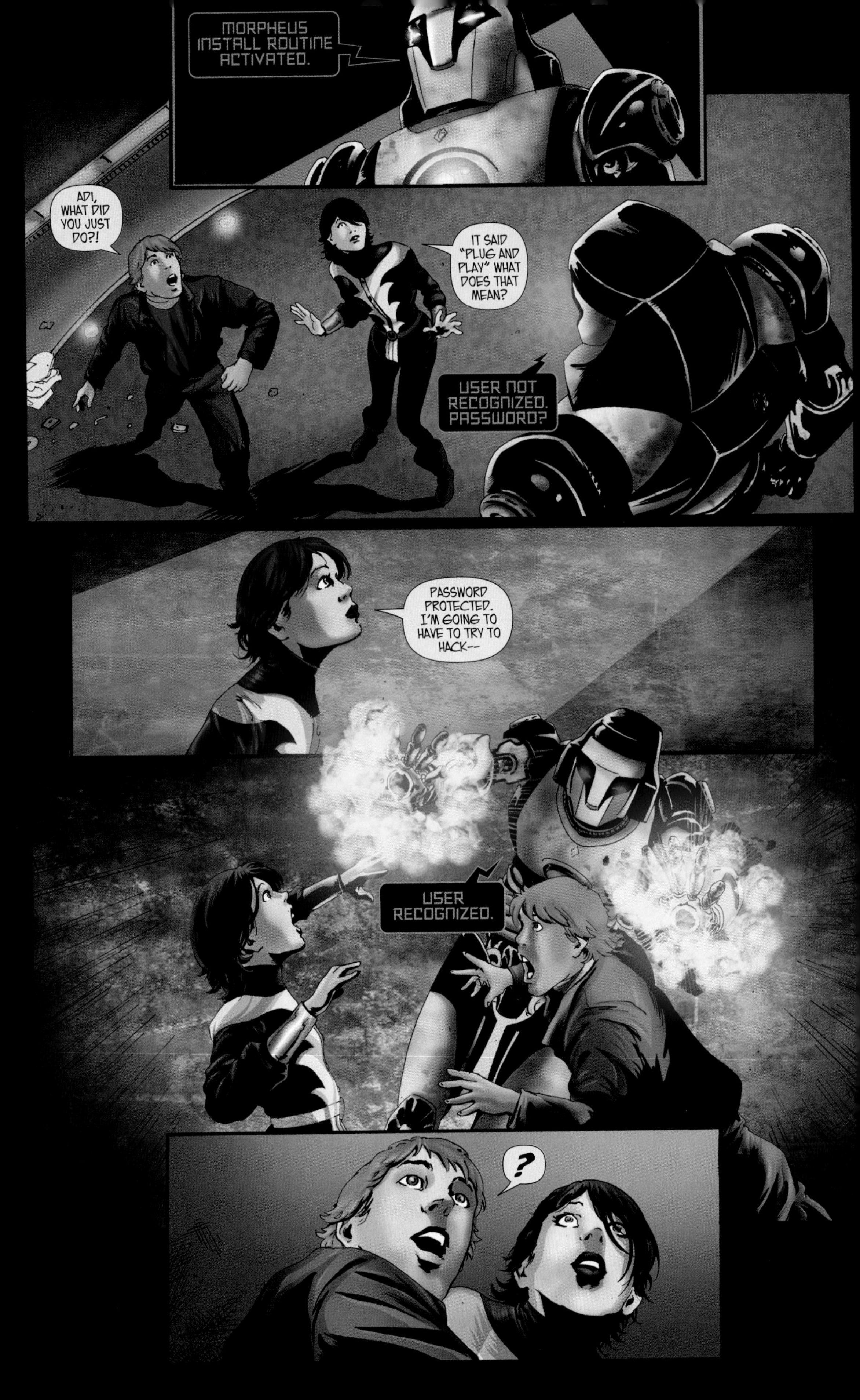
MORPHEUS INSTALL ROUTINE ACTIVATED.
ADI, WHAT DID YOU JUST DO?!
IT SAID "PLUG AND PLAY" WHAT DOES THAT MEAN?
USER NOT RECOGNIZED. PASSWORD?
PASSWORD PROTECTED. I'M GOING TO HAVE TO TRY TO HACK--
USER RECOGNIZED.
?

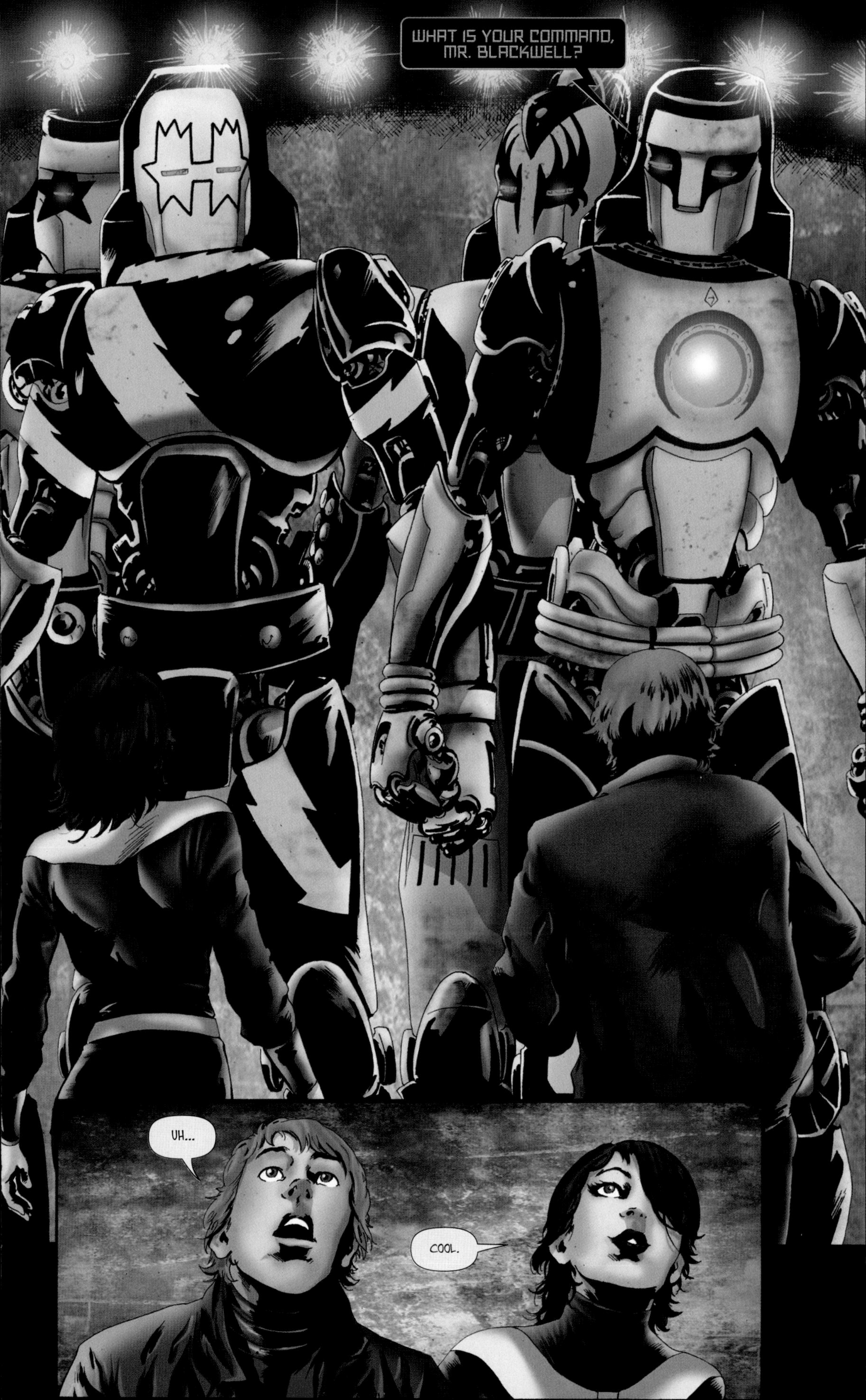
WHAT IS YOUR COMMAND, MR. BLACKWELL?
UH...
COOL.

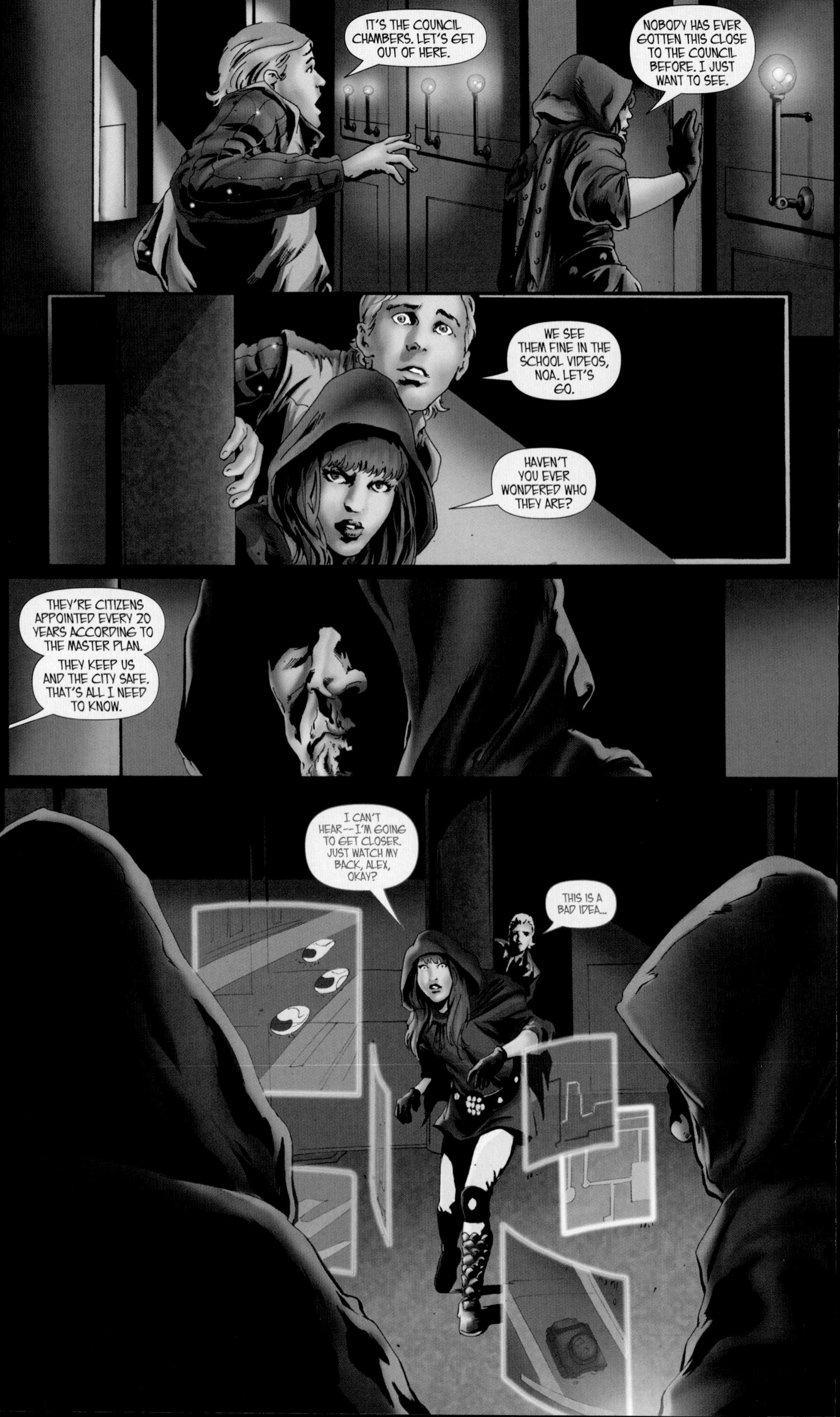
IT'S THE COUNCIL CHAMBERS. LET'S GET OUT OF HERE.
NOBODY HAS EVER GOTTEN THIS CLOSE TO THE COUNCIL BEFORE. I JUST WANT TO SEE.
WE SEE THEM FINE IN THE SCHOOL VIDEOS, NOA. LET'S GO.
HAVEN'T YOU EVER WONDERED WHO THEY ARE?
THEY'RE CITIZENS APPOINTED EVERY 20 YEARS ACCORDING TO THE MASTER PLAN.
THEY KEEP US AND THE CITY SAFE. THAT'S ALL I NEED TO KNOW.
I CAN'T HEAR-- I'M GOING TO GET CLOSER. JUST WATCH MY BACK, ALEX, OKAY?
THIS IS A BAD IDEA...

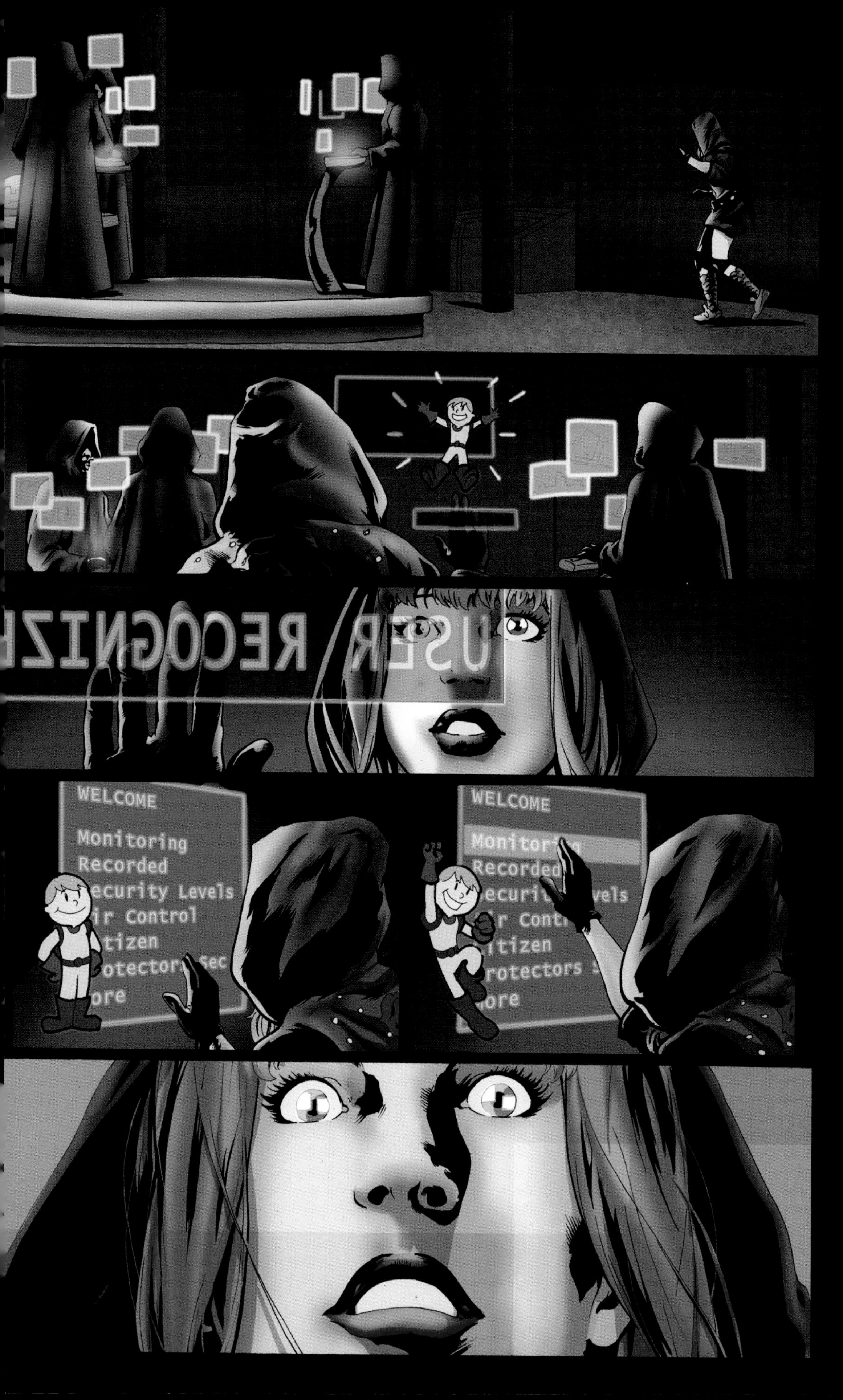

USER RECOGNIZ
WELCOME
Monitoring
Recorded
ecurity Levels
ir Control
itizen
otectors Sec
ore

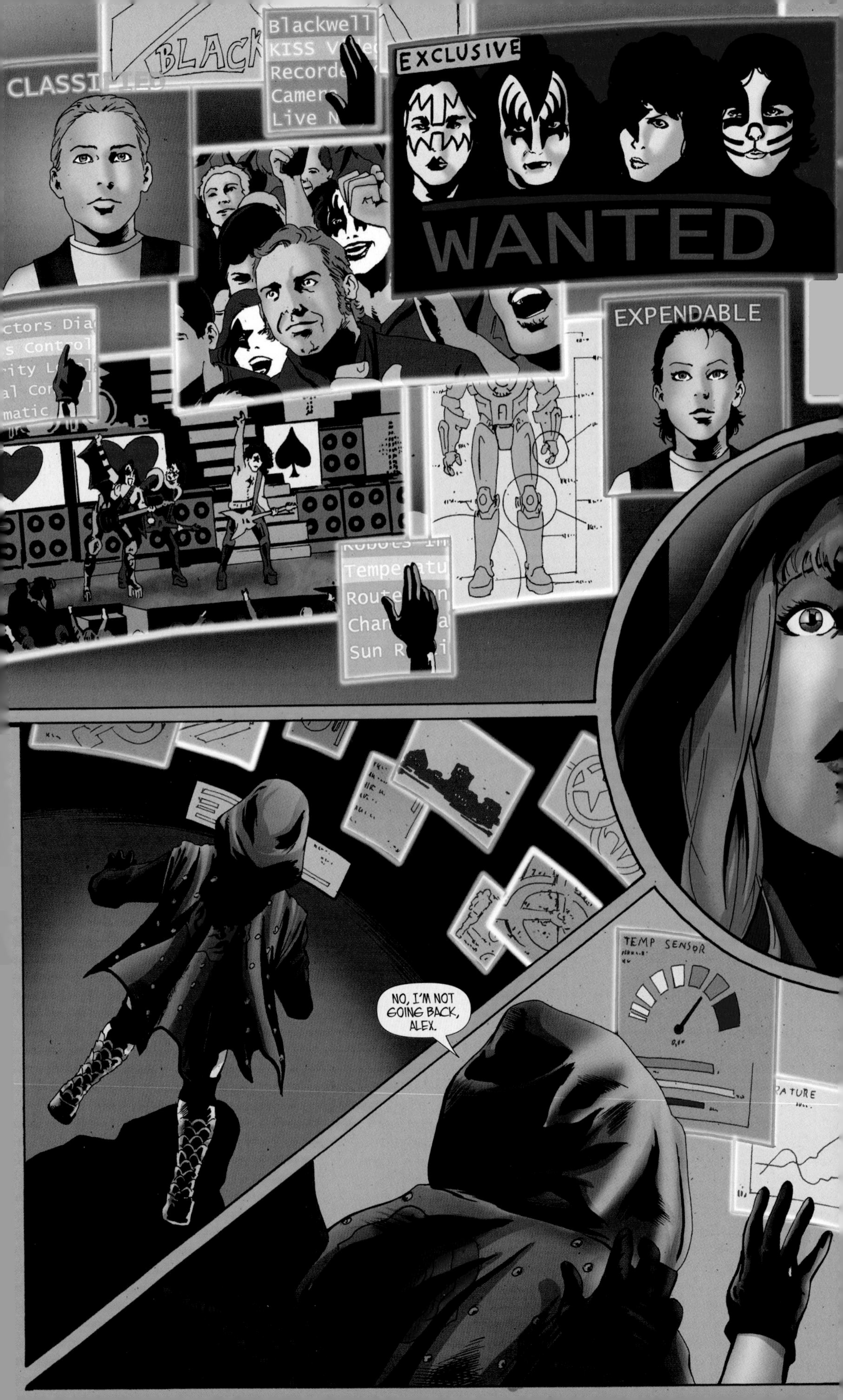
Blackwell
EXCLUSIVE
WANTED
EXPENDABLE
TEMP SENSOR
NO, I'M NOT GOING BACK, ALEX.

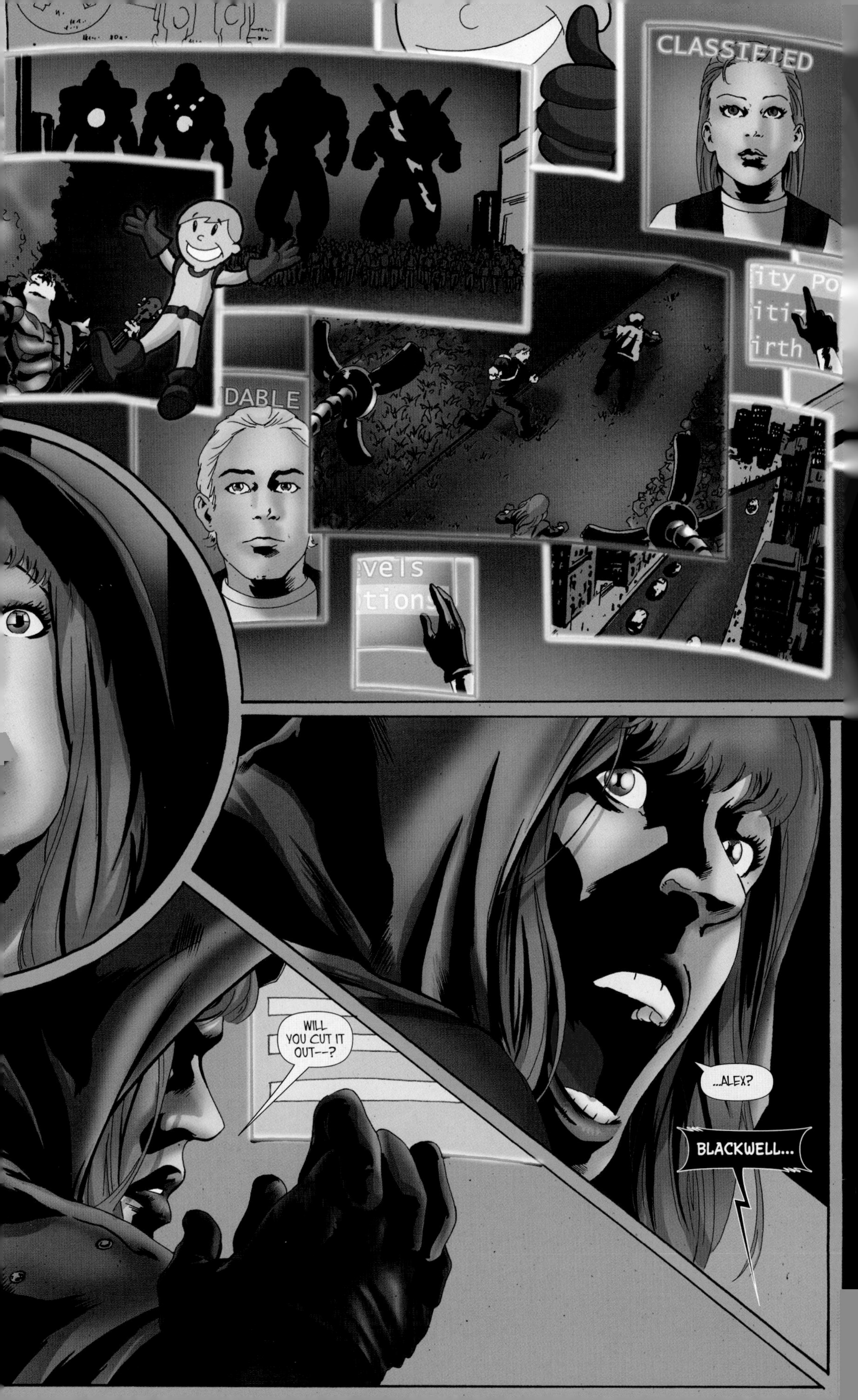
CLASSIFIED
DABLE
WILL YOU CUT IT OUT--?
...ALEX?
BLACKWELL...

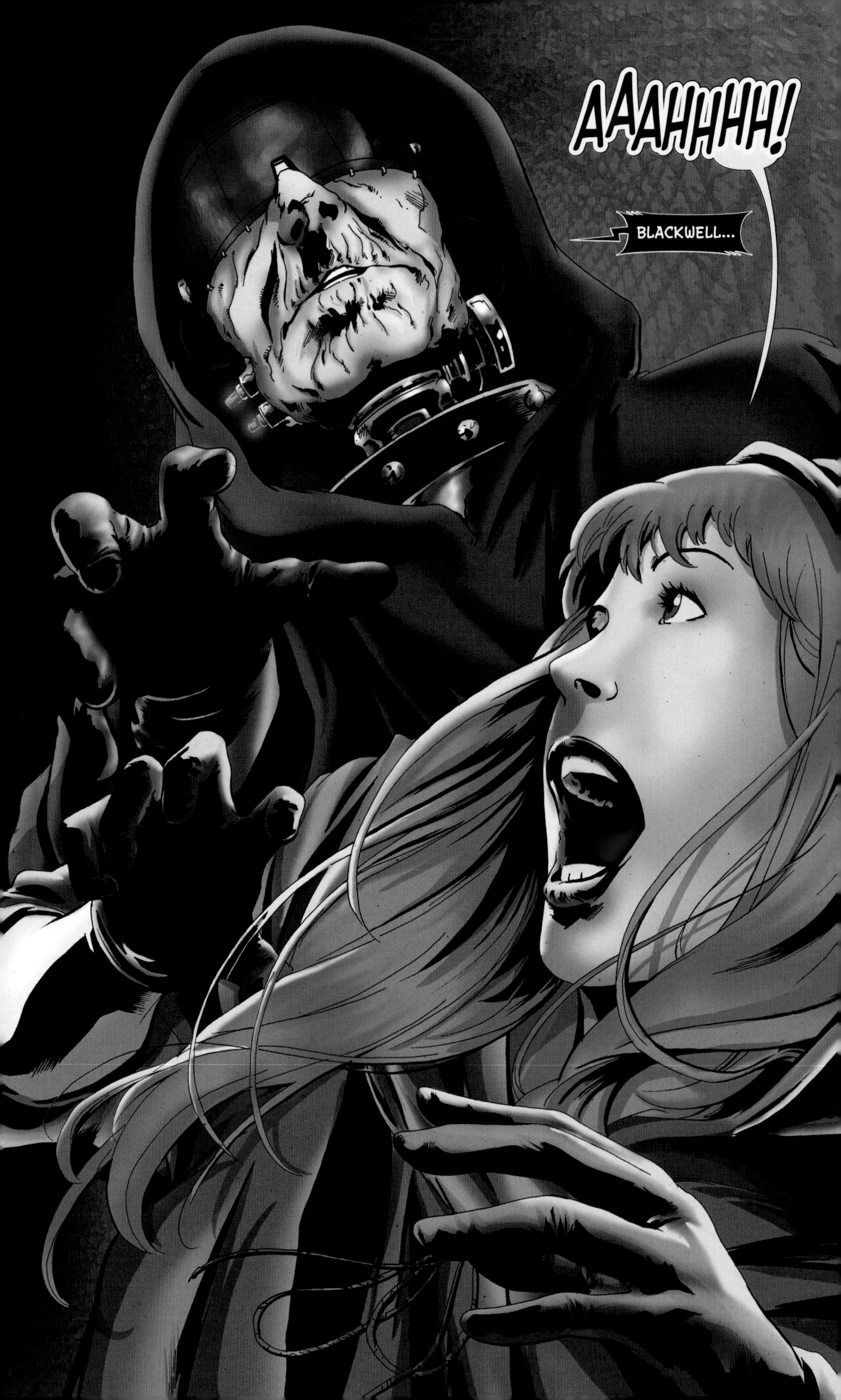
AAAHHHH!
BLACKWELL...

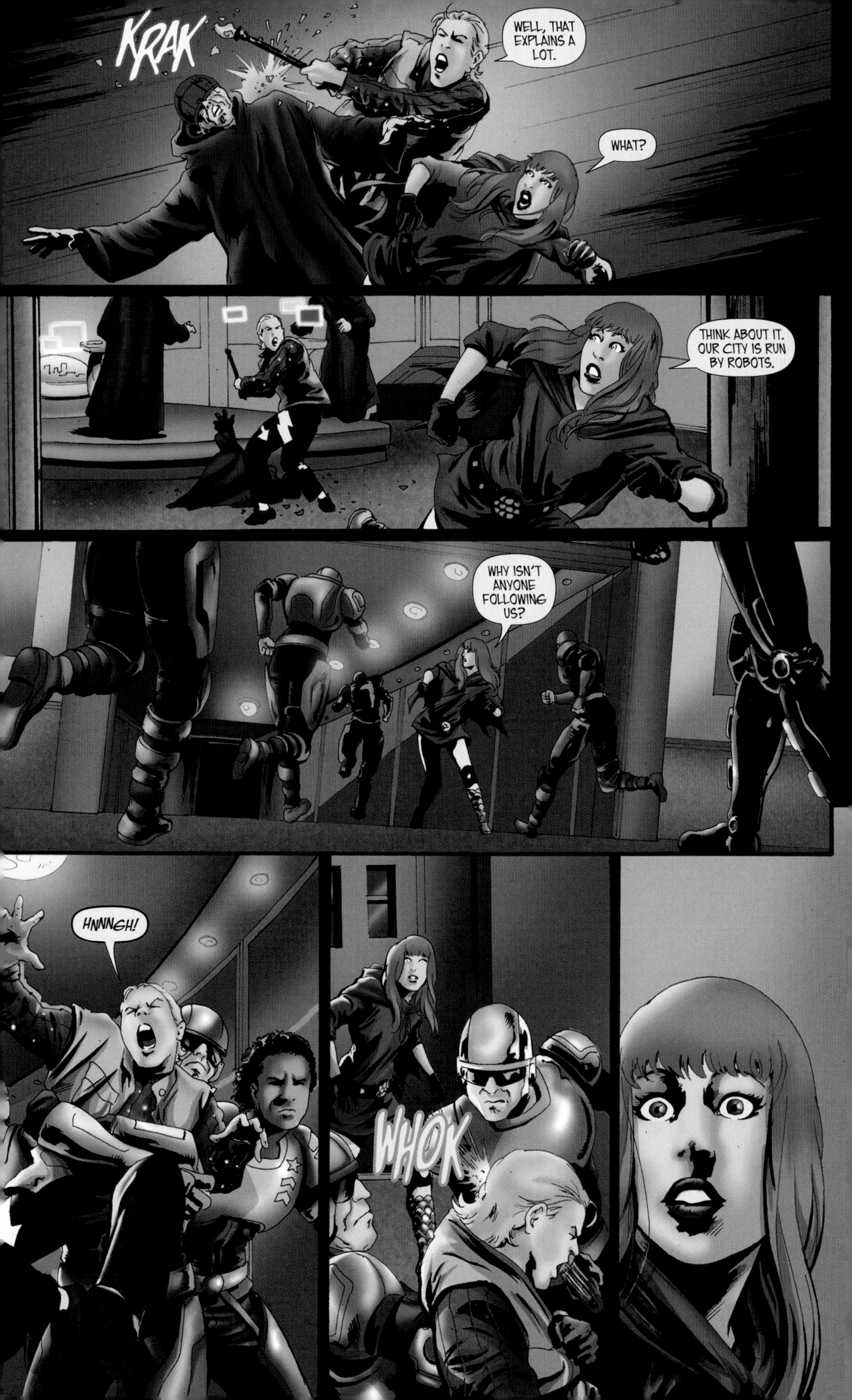
KRAK
WELL, THAT EXPLAINS A LOT.
WHAT?
THINK ABOUT IT. OUR CITY IS RUN BY ROBOTS.
WHY ISN'T ANYONE FOLLOWING US?
HNNNGH!
WHOK

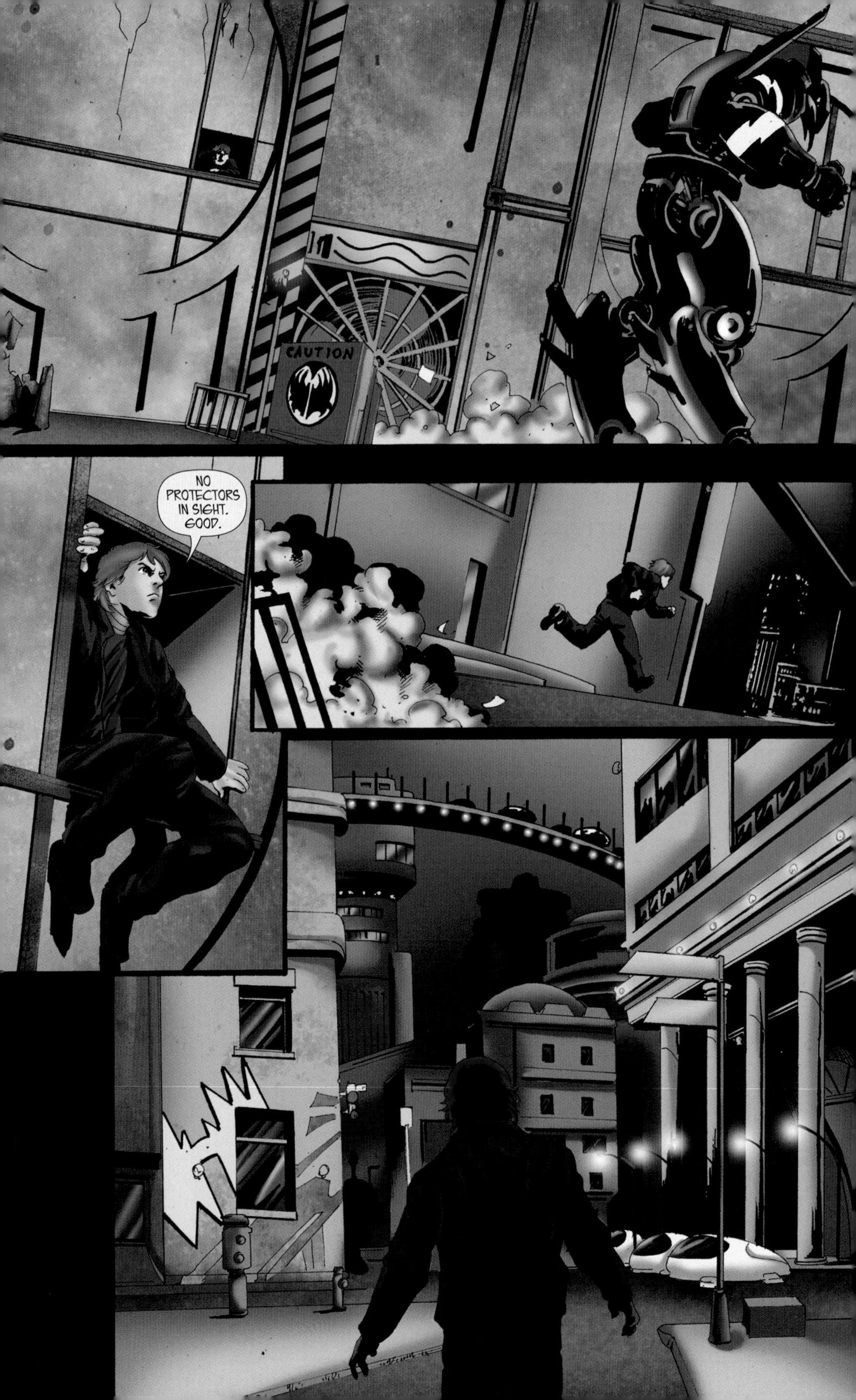
CAUTION
NO PROTECTORS IN SIGHT. GOOD.

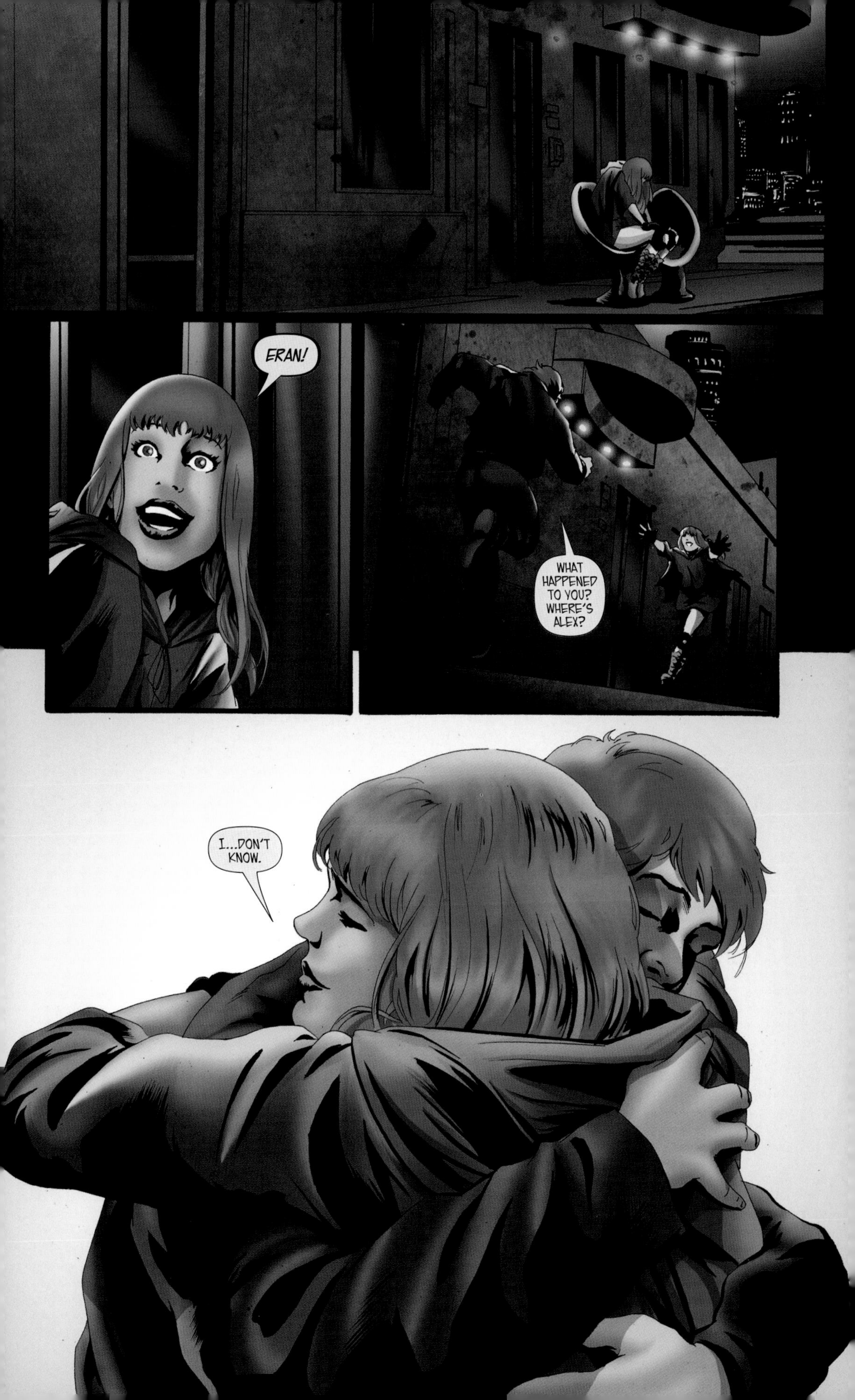
ERAN!
WHAT HAPPENED TO YOU? WHERE'S ALEX?
I...DON'T KNOW.

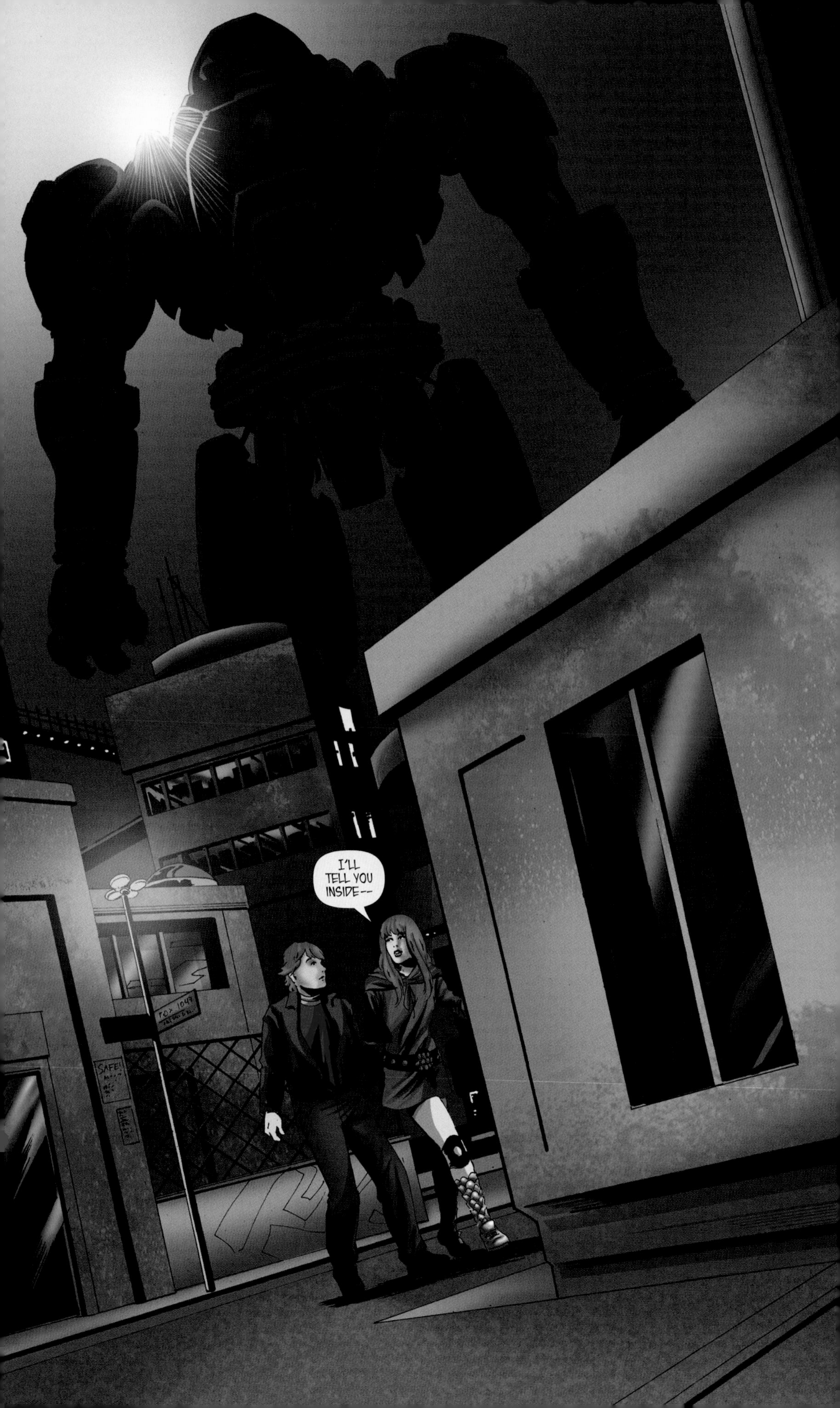
I'LL TELL YOU INSIDE--

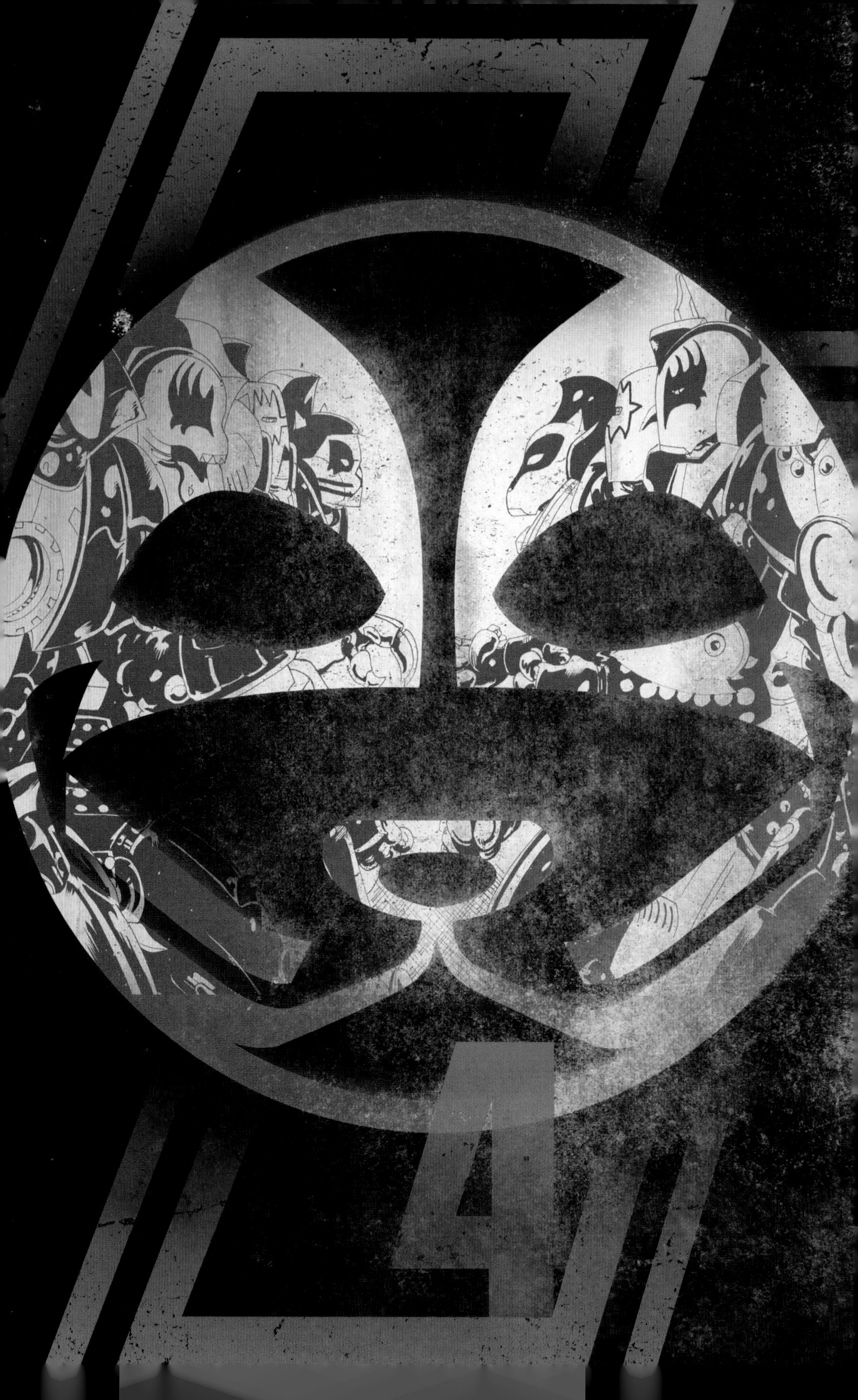

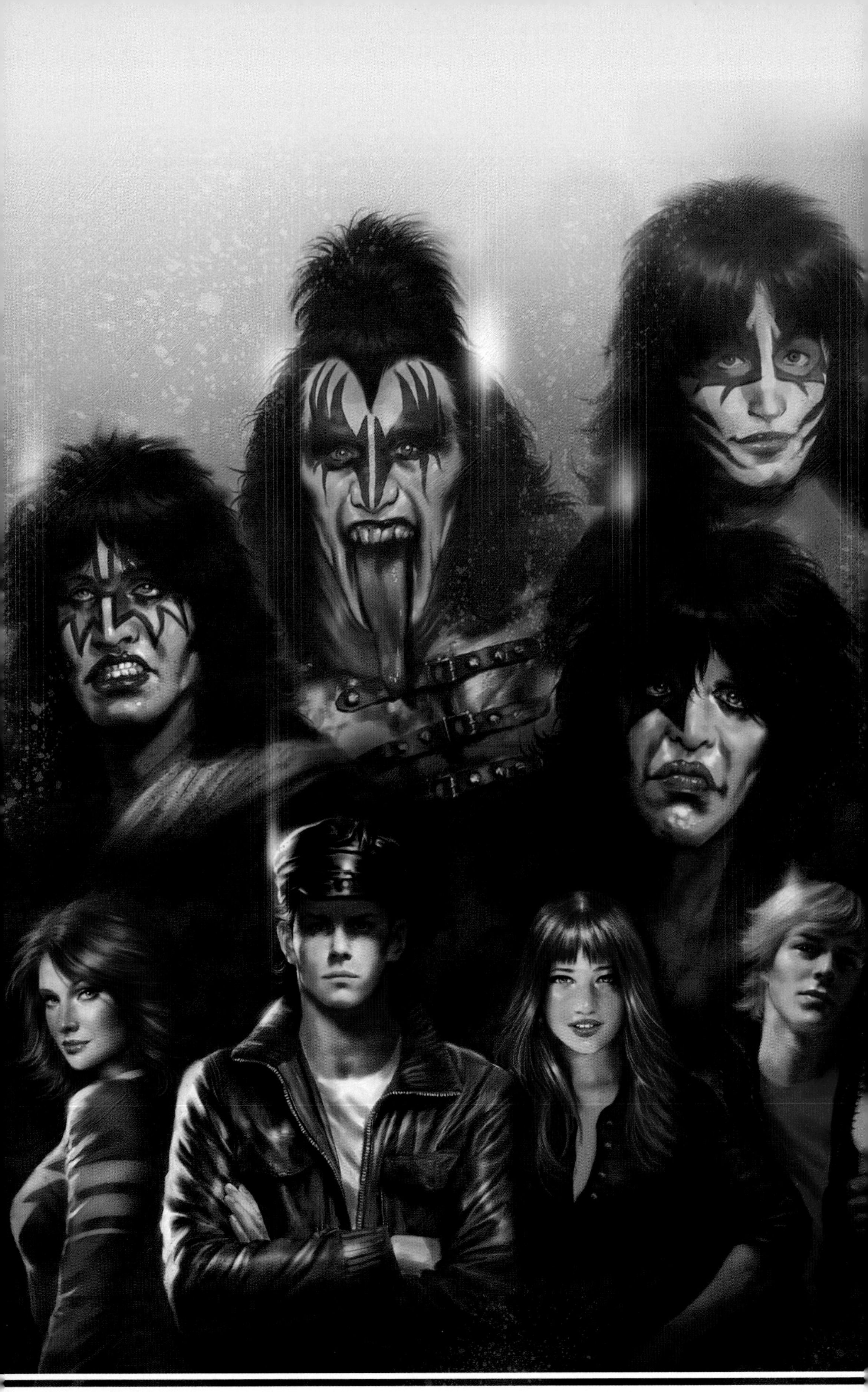

ISSUE 4, MAIN COVER: Art by Lucio Parrillo

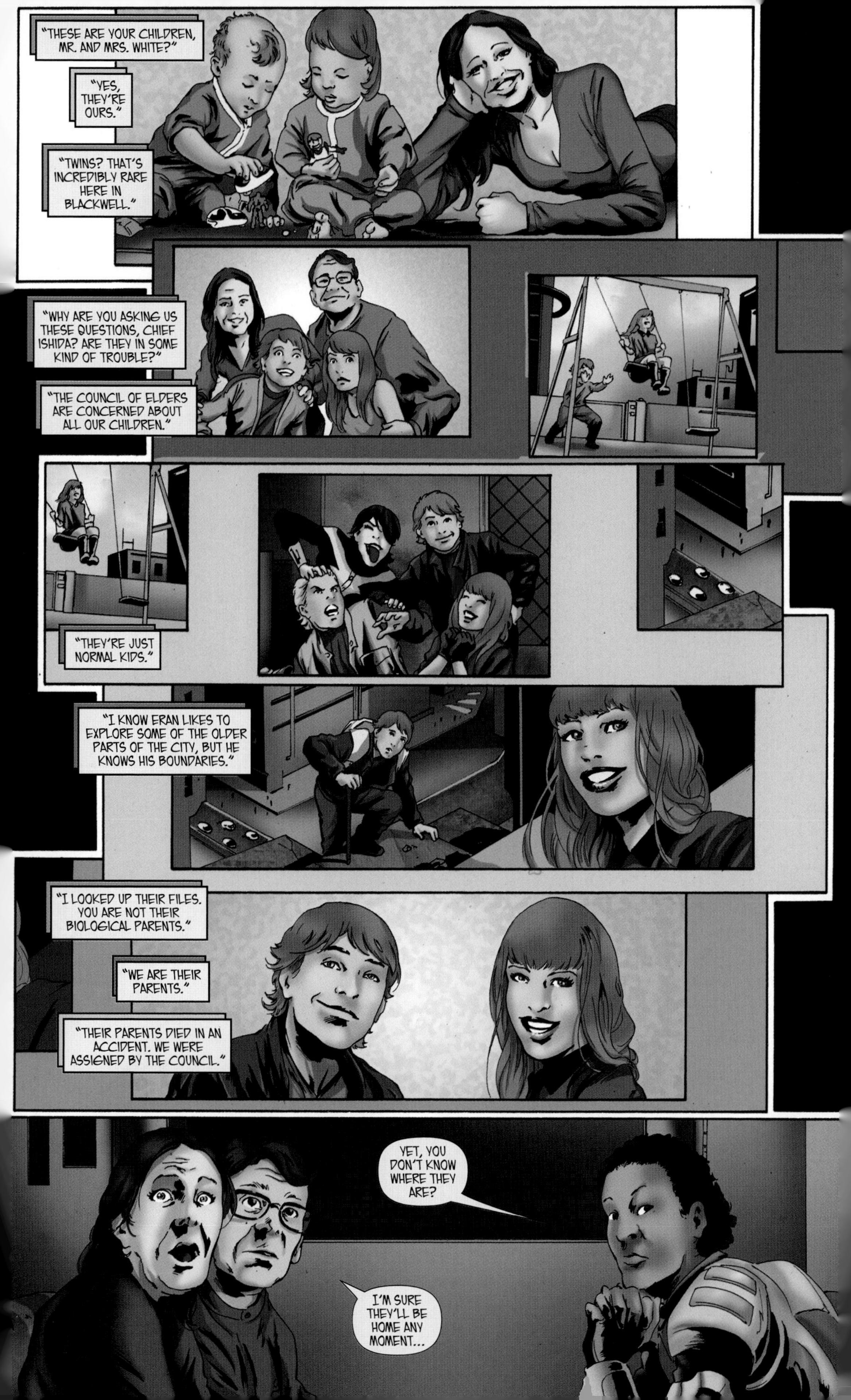

"THESE ARE YOUR CHILDREN, MR. AND MRS. WHITE?"
"YES, THEY'RE OURS."
"TWINS? THAT'S INCREDIBLY RARE HERE IN BLACKWELL."
"WHY ARE YOU ASKING US THESE QUESTIONS, CHIEF ISHIDA? ARE THEY IN SOME KIND OF TROUBLE?"
"THE COUNCIL OF ELDERS ARE CONCERNED ABOUT ALL OUR CHILDREN."
"THEY'RE JUST NORMAL KIDS."
"I KNOW ERAN LIKES TO EXPLORE SOME OF THE OLDER PARTS OF THE CITY, BUT HE KNOWS HIS BOUNDARIES."
"I LOOKED UP THEIR FILES. YOU ARE NOT THEIR BIOLOGICAL PARENTS."
"WE ARE THEIR PARENTS."
"THEIR PARENTS DIED IN AN ACCIDENT. WE WERE ASSIGNED BY THE COUNCIL."
YET, YOU DON'T KNOW WHERE THEY ARE?
I'M SURE THEY'LL BE HOME ANY MOMENT...

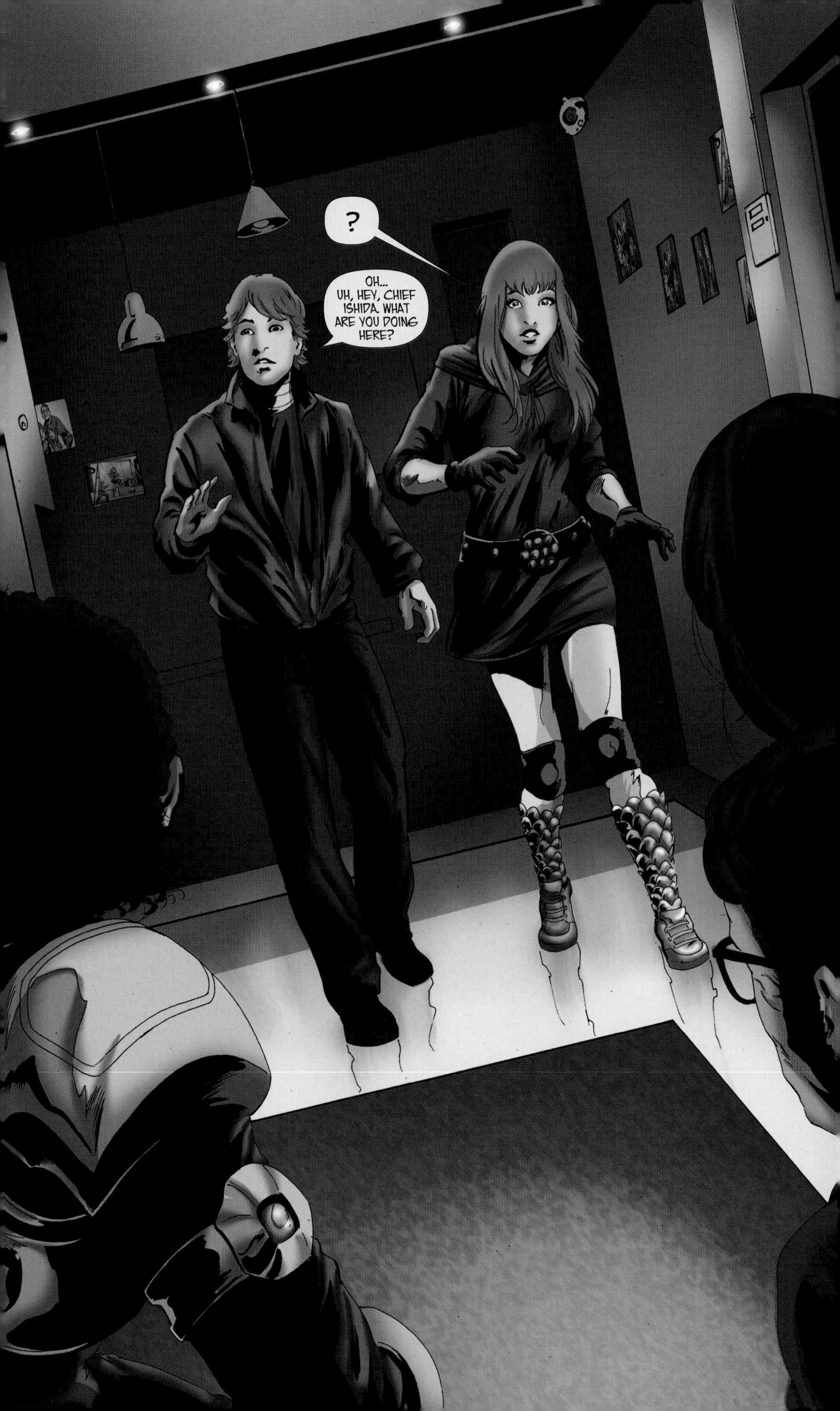
?
OH... UH, HEY, CHIEF ISHIDA. WHAT ARE YOU DOING HERE?

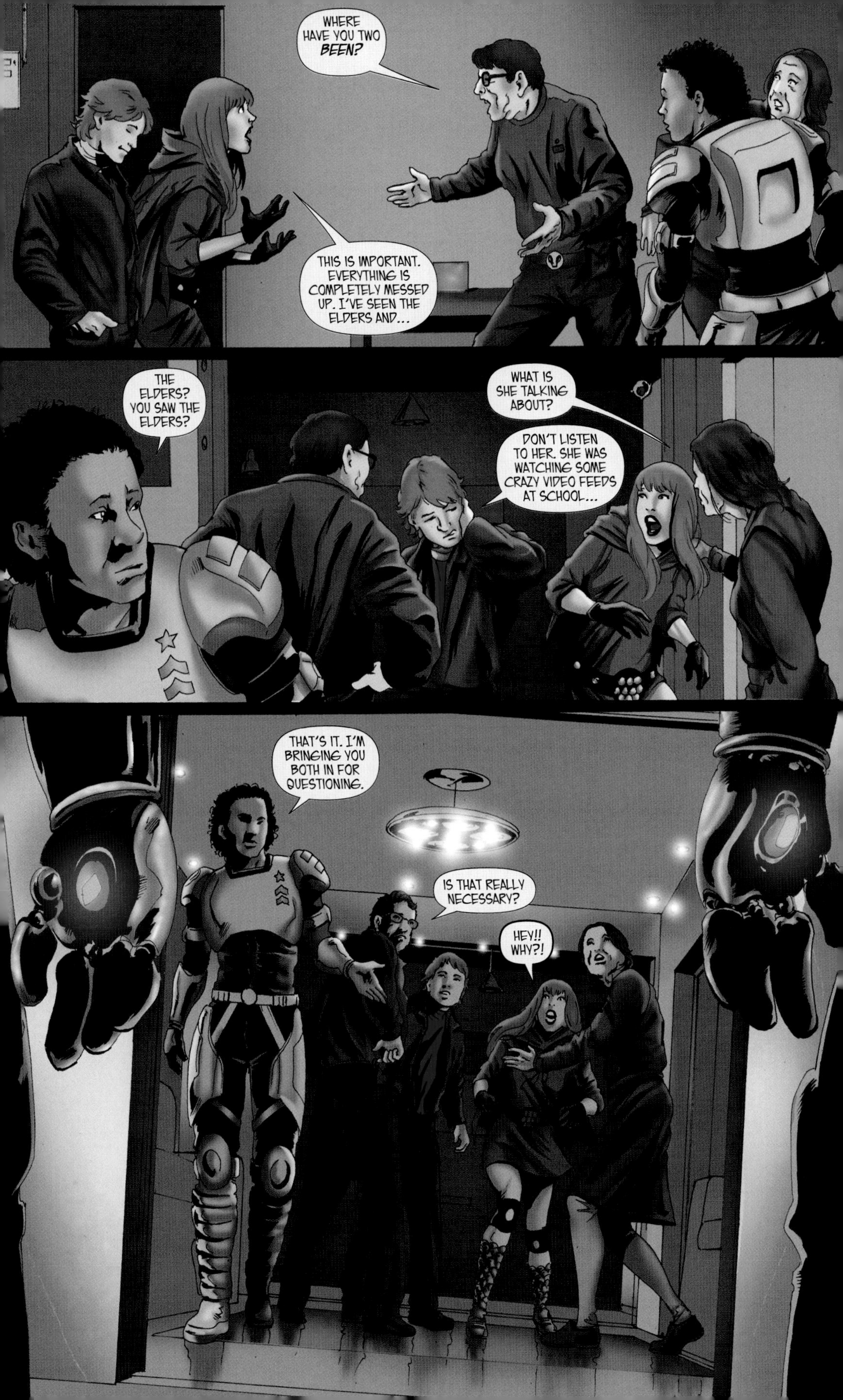
WHERE HAVE YOU TWO BEEN?
THIS IS IMPORTANT. EVERYTHING IS COMPLETELY MESSED UP. I'VE SEEN THE ELDERS AND...
THE ELDERS? YOU SAW THE ELDERS?
WHAT IS SHE TALKING ABOUT?
DON'T LISTEN TO HER. SHE WAS WATCHING SOME CRAZY VIDEO FEEDS AT SCHOOL...
THAT'S IT. I'M BRINGING YOU BOTH IN FOR QUESTIONING.
IS THAT REALLY NECESSARY?
HEY!! WHY?!

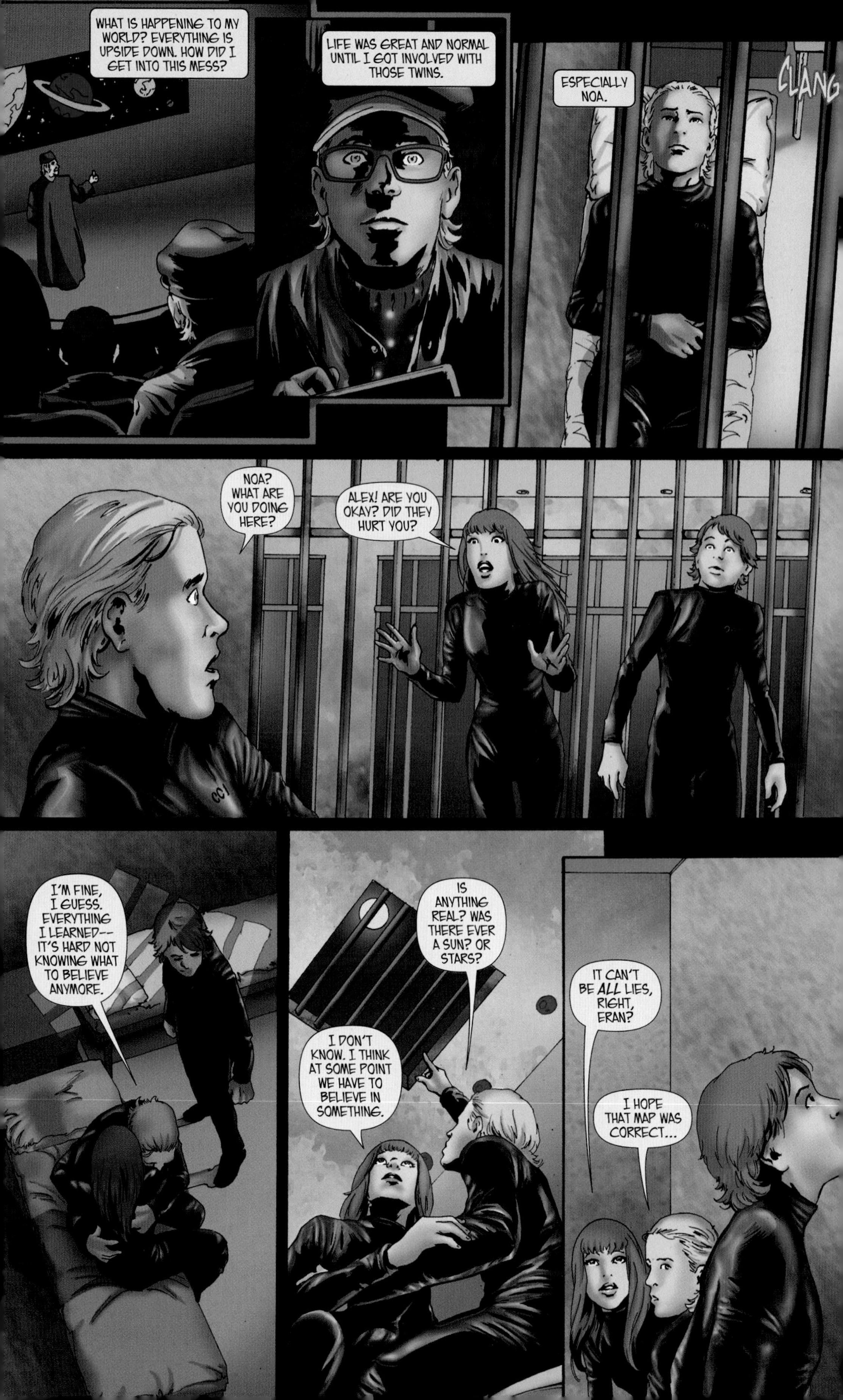
WHAT IS HAPPENING TO MY WORLD? EVERYTHING IS UPSIDE DOWN. HOW DID I GET INTO THIS MESS?
LIFE WAS GREAT AND NORMAL UNTIL I GOT INVOLVED WITH THOSE TWINS.
ESPECIALLY NOA.
CLANG
NOA? WHAT ARE YOU DOING HERE?
ALEX! ARE YOU OKAY? DID THEY HURT YOU?
I'M FINE, I GUESS. EVERYTHING I LEARNED-- IT'S HARD NOT KNOWING WHAT TO BELIEVE ANYMORE.
IS ANYTHING REAL? WAS THERE EVER A SUN? OR STARS?
I DON'T KNOW. I THINK AT SOME POINT WE HAVE TO BELIEVE IN SOMETHING.
IT CAN'T BE ALL LIES, RIGHT, ERAN?
I HOPE THAT MAP WAS CORRECT...

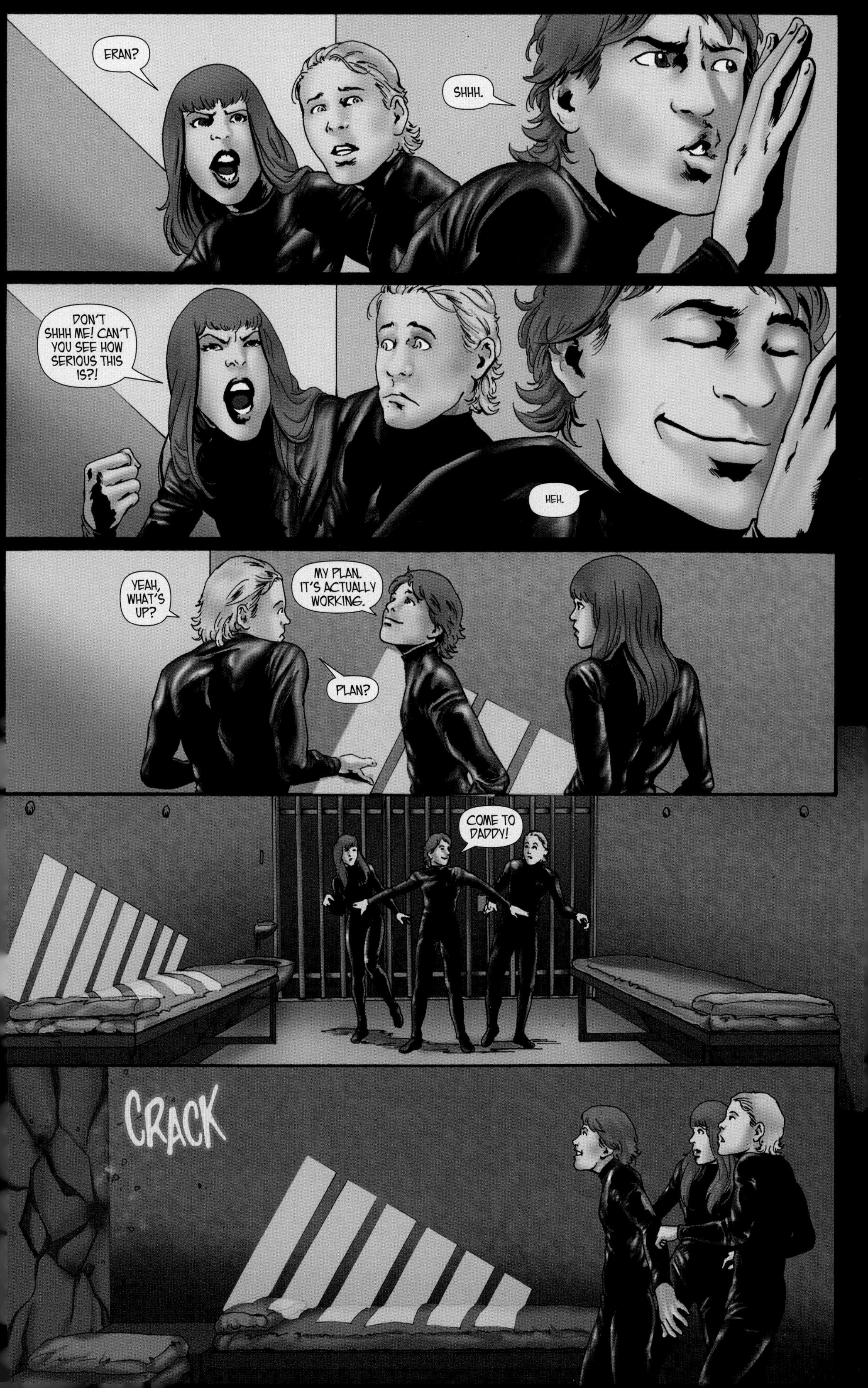
ERAN?
SHHH.
DON'T SHHH ME! CAN'T YOU SEE HOW SERIOUS THIS IS?!
HEH.
YEAH, WHAT'S UP?
MY PLAN. IT'S ACTUALLY WORKING.
PLAN?
COME TO DADDY!
CRACK

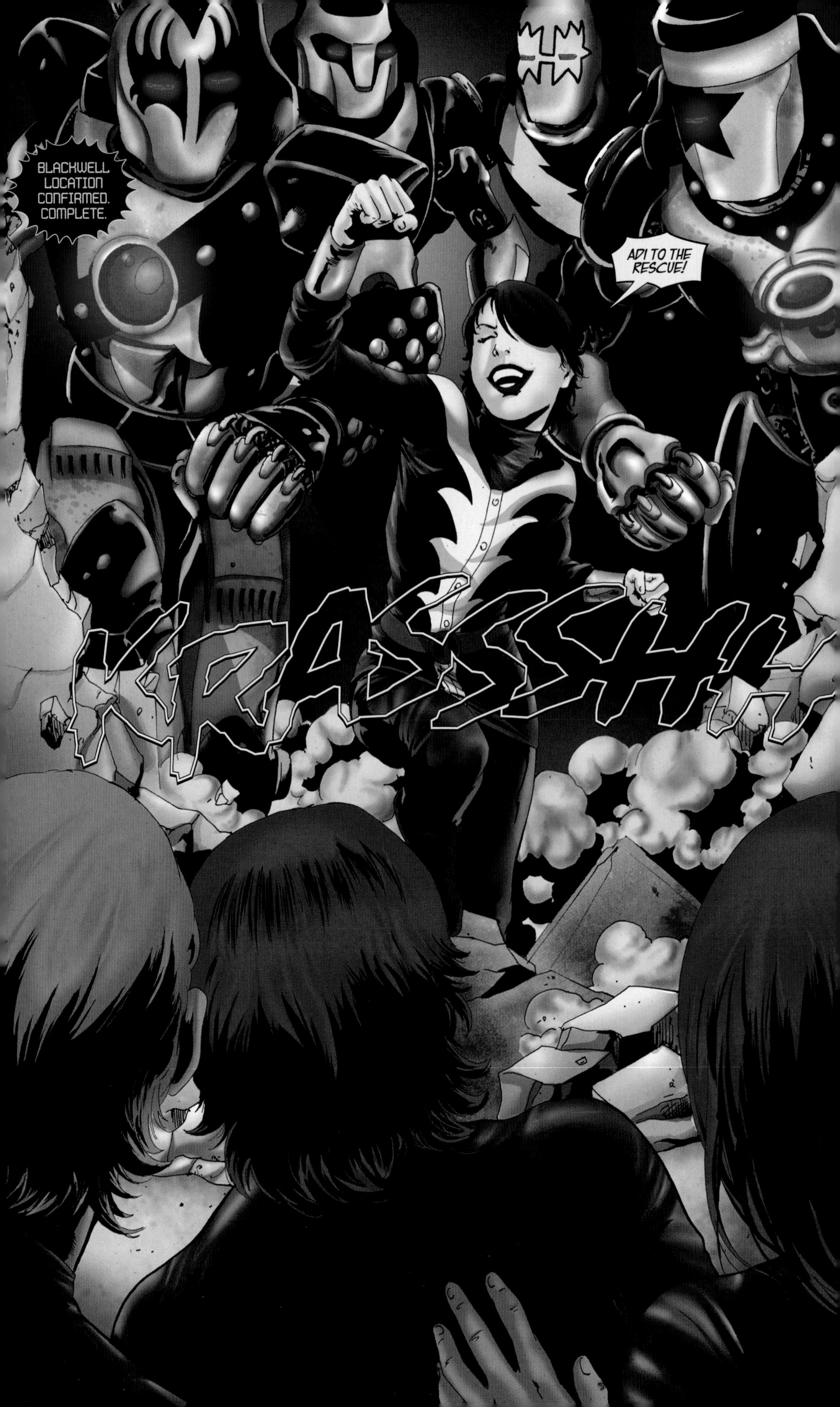

BLACKWELL LOCATION CONFIRMED. COMPLETE.
ADI TO THE RESCUE!
KRASSH!

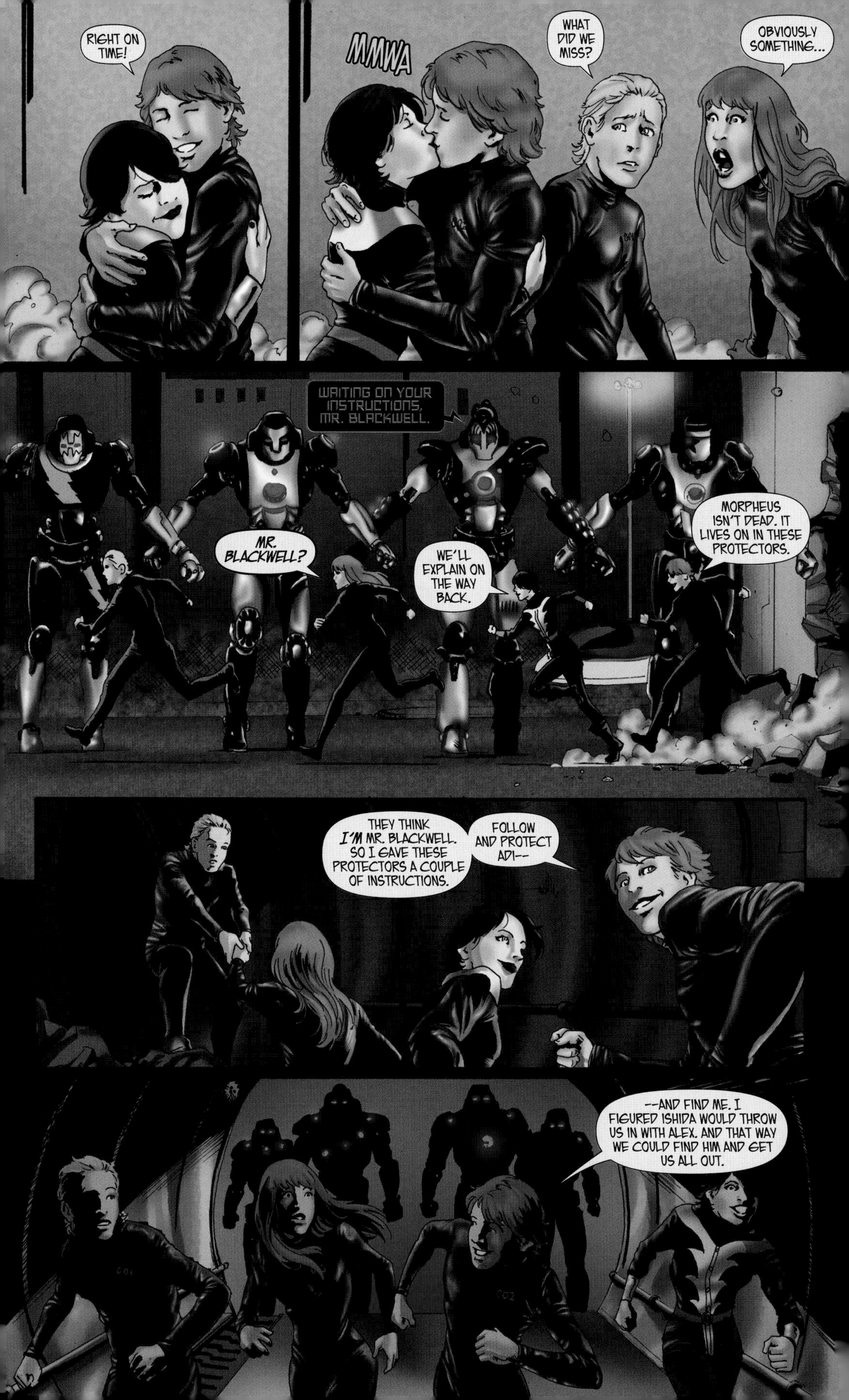
RIGHT ON TIME!
MMWA
WHAT DID WE MISS?
OBVIOUSLY SOMETHING...
WAITING ON YOUR INSTRUCTIONS, MR. BLACKWELL.
MR. BLACKWELL?
WE'LL EXPLAIN ON THE WAY BACK.
MORPHEUS ISN'T DEAD. IT LIVES ON IN THESE PROTECTORS.
THEY THINK I'M MR. BLACKWELL. SO I GAVE THESE PROTECTORS A COUPLE OF INSTRUCTIONS.
FOLLOW AND PROTECT ADI--
--AND FIND ME. I FIGURED ISHIDA WOULD THROW US IN WITH ALEX. AND THAT WAY WE COULD FIND HIM AND GET US ALL OUT.

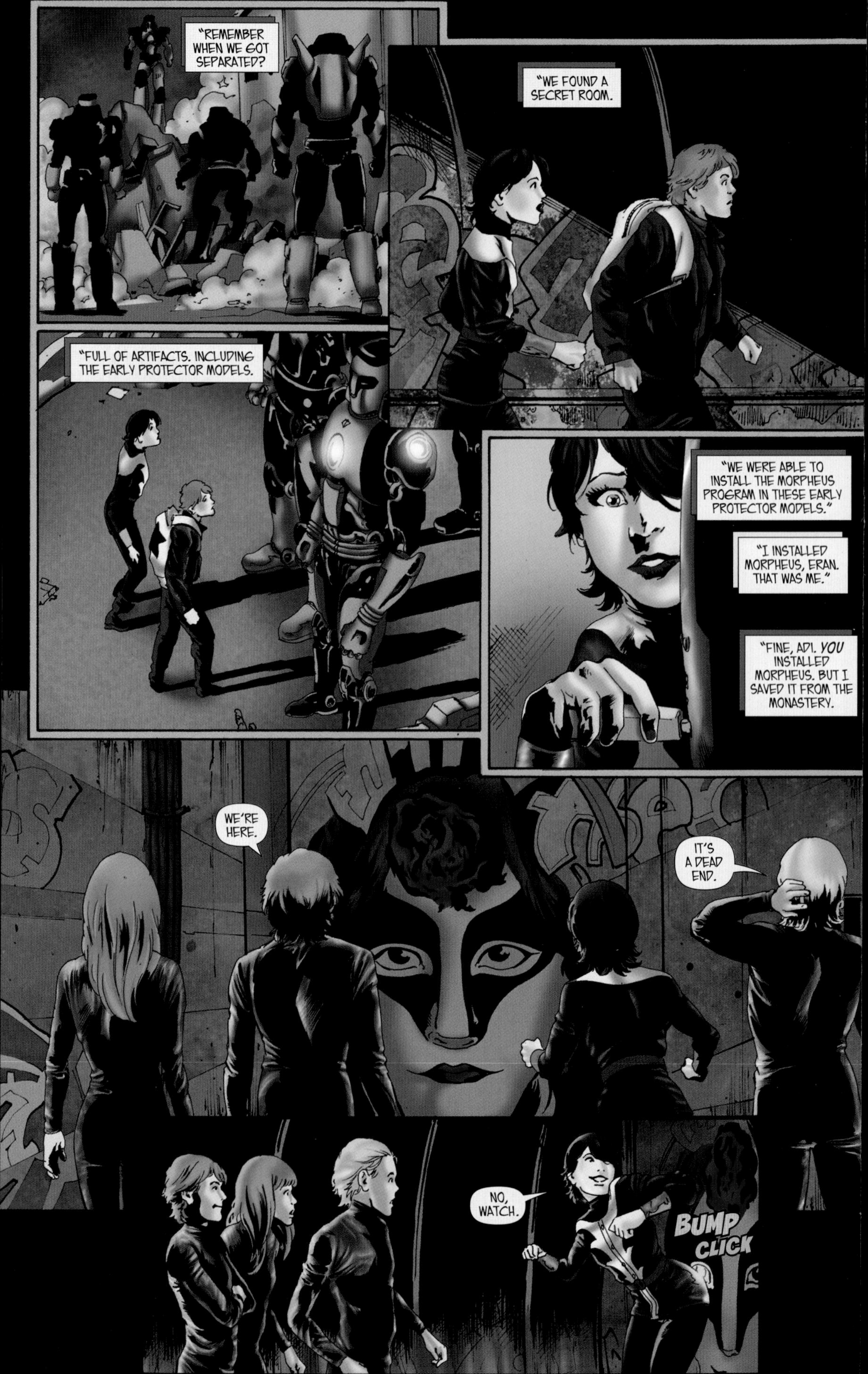
"REMEMBER WHEN WE GOT SEPARATED?
"WE FOUND A SECRET ROOM.
"FULL OF ARTIFACTS. INCLUDING THE EARLY PROTECTOR MODELS.
"WE WERE ABLE TO INSTALL THE MORPHEUS PROGRAM IN THESE EARLY PROTECTOR MODELS."
"I INSTALLED MORPHEUS, ERAN. THAT WAS ME."
"FINE, ADI. YOU INSTALLED MORPHEUS. BUT I SAVED IT FROM THE MONASTERY.
WE'RE HERE.
IT'S A DEAD END.
NO, WATCH.
BUMP
CLICK

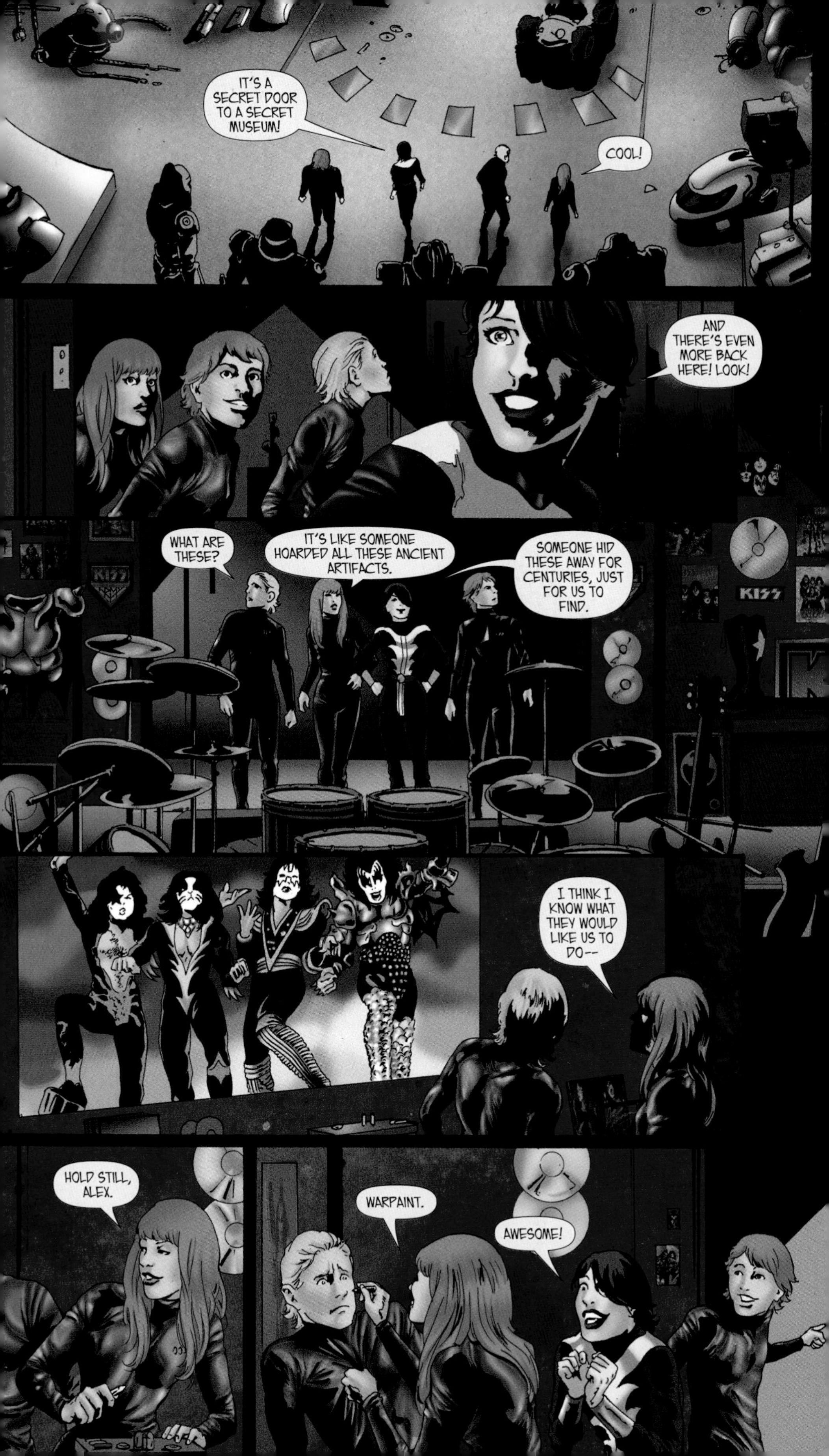
IT'S A SECRET DOOR TO A SECRET MUSEUM!
COOL!
AND THERE'S EVEN MORE BACK HERE! LOOK!
KISS
WHAT ARE THESE?
IT'S LIKE SOMEONE HOARDED ALL THESE ANCIENT ARTIFACTS.
SOMEONE HID THESE AWAY FOR CENTURIES, JUST FOR US TO FIND.
KISS
I THINK I KNOW WHAT THEY WOULD LIKE US TO DO--
HOLD STILL, ALEX.
WARPAINT.
AWESOME!

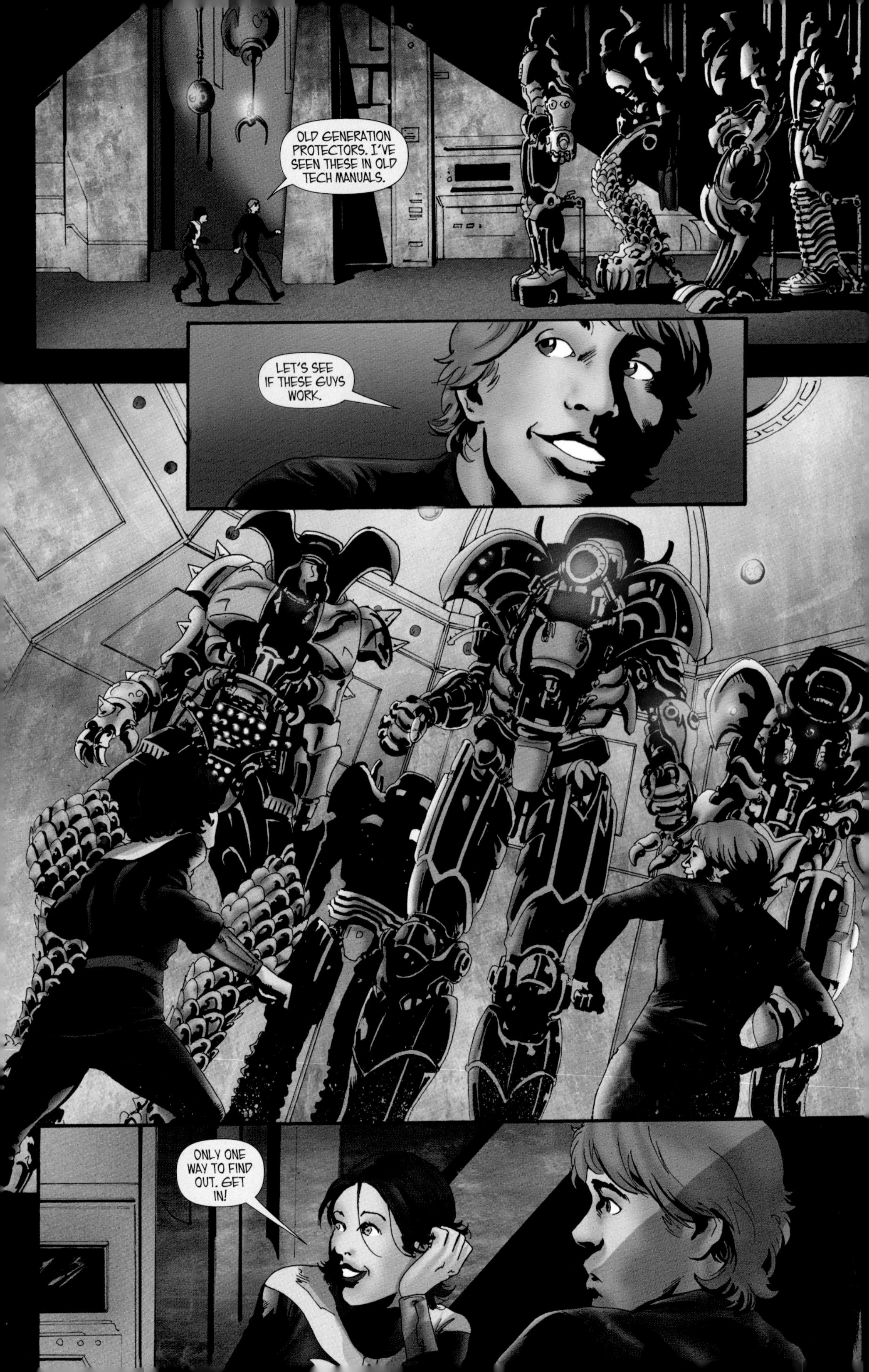
OLD GENERATION PROTECTORS. I'VE SEEN THESE IN OLD TECH MANUALS.
LET'S SEE IF THESE GUYS WORK.
ONLY ONE WAY TO FIND OUT. GET IN!

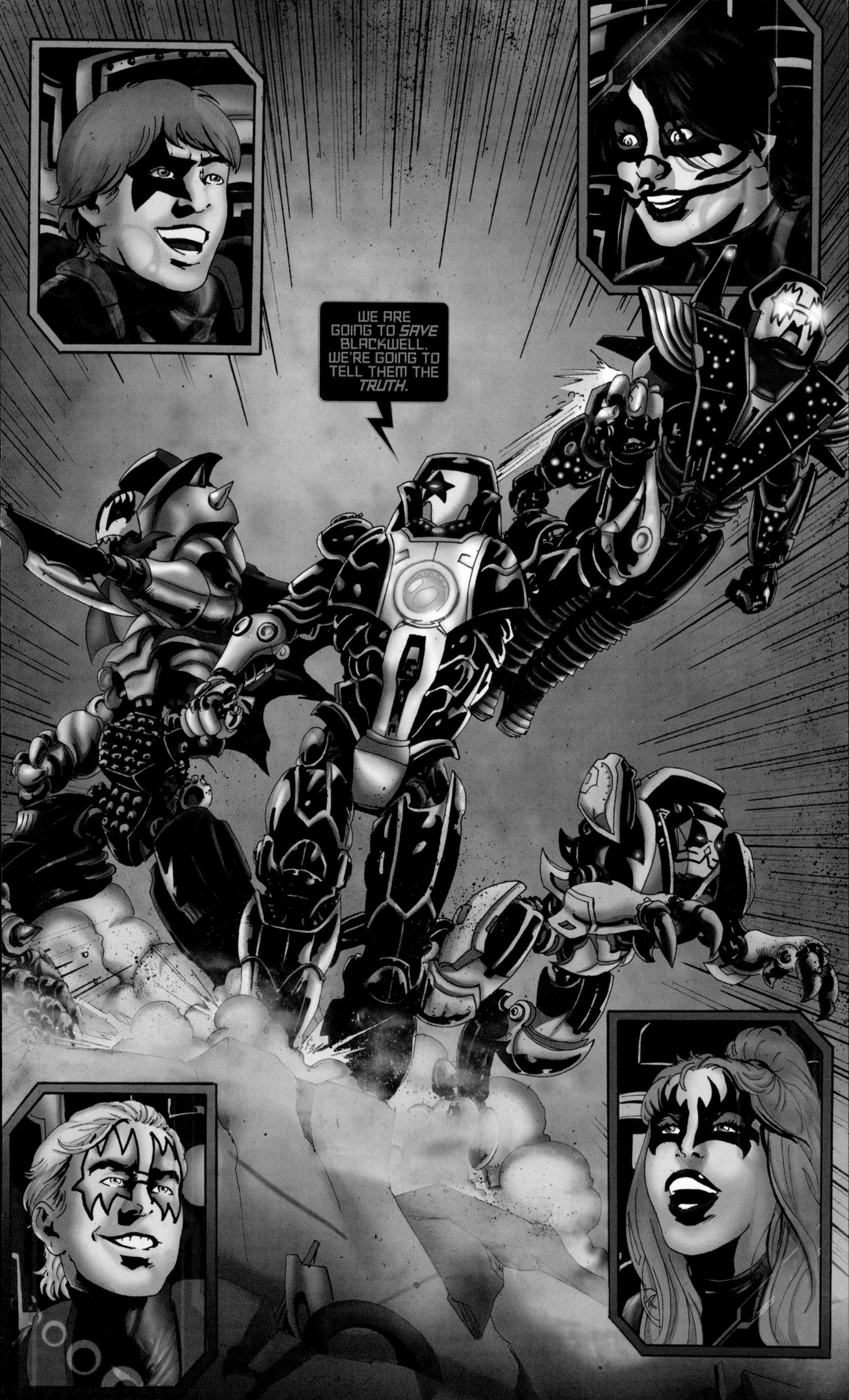
WE ARE GOING TO *SAVE* BLACKWELL. WE'RE GOING TO TELL THEM THE *TRUTH.*

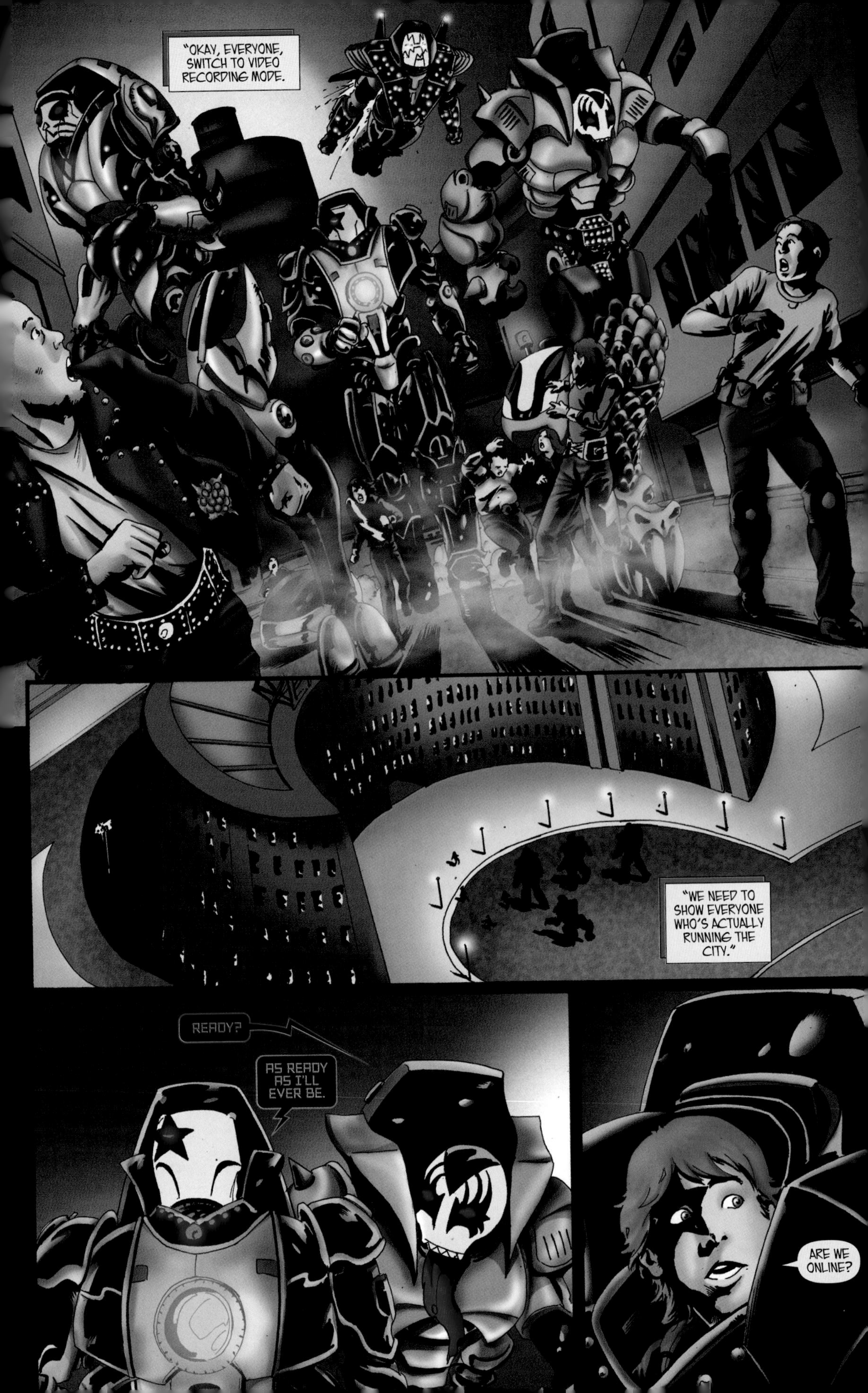
"OKAY, EVERYONE, SWITCH TO VIDEO RECORDING MODE.
"WE NEED TO SHOW EVERYONE WHO'S ACTUALLY RUNNING THE CITY."
READY?
AS READY AS I'LL EVER BE.
ARE WE ONLINE?

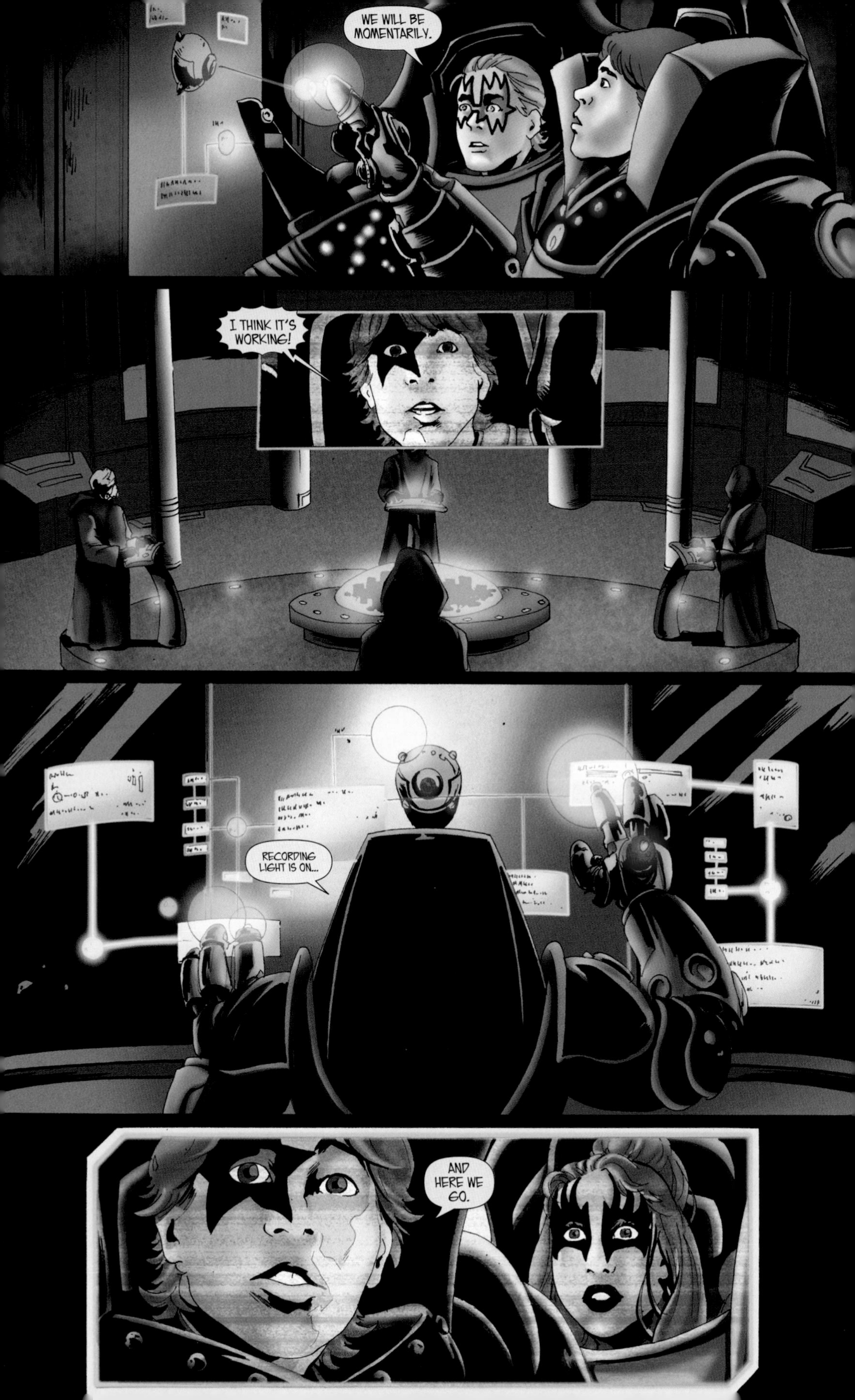
WE WILL BE MOMENTARILY.
I THINK IT'S WORKING!
RECORDING LIGHT IS ON...
AND HERE WE GO.

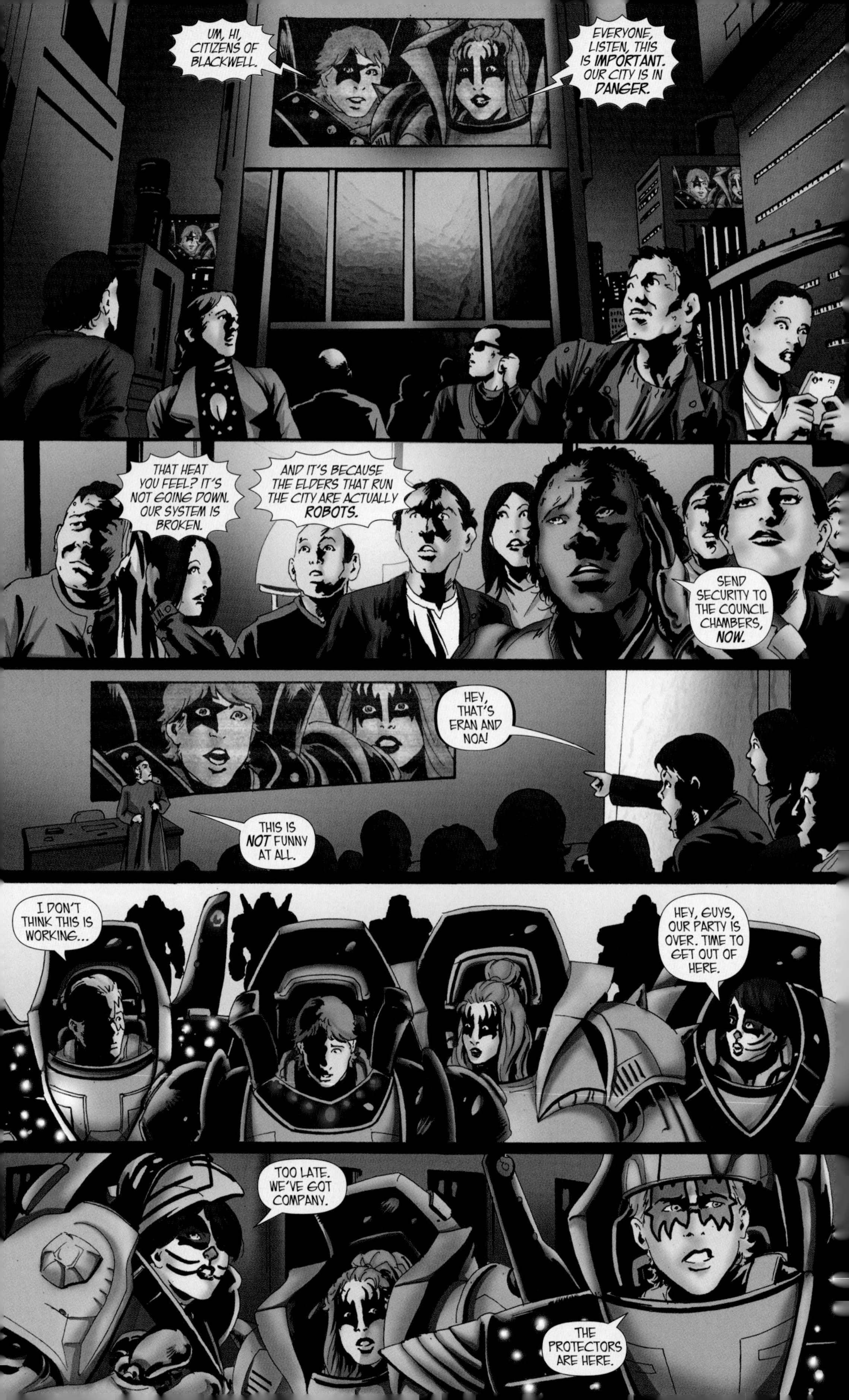
UM, HI, CITIZENS OF BLACKWELL.
EVERYONE, LISTEN, THIS IS IMPORTANT. OUR CITY IS IN DANGER.
THAT HEAT YOU FEEL? IT'S NOT GOING DOWN. OUR SYSTEM IS BROKEN.
AND IT'S BECAUSE THE ELDERS THAT RUN THE CITY ARE ACTUALLY ROBOTS.
SEND SECURITY TO THE COUNCIL CHAMBERS, NOW.
HEY, THAT'S ERAN AND NOA!
THIS IS NOT FUNNY AT ALL.
I DON'T THINK THIS IS WORKING...
HEY, GUYS, OUR PARTY IS OVER. TIME TO GET OUT OF HERE.
TOO LATE. WE'VE GOT COMPANY.
THE PROTECTORS ARE HERE.

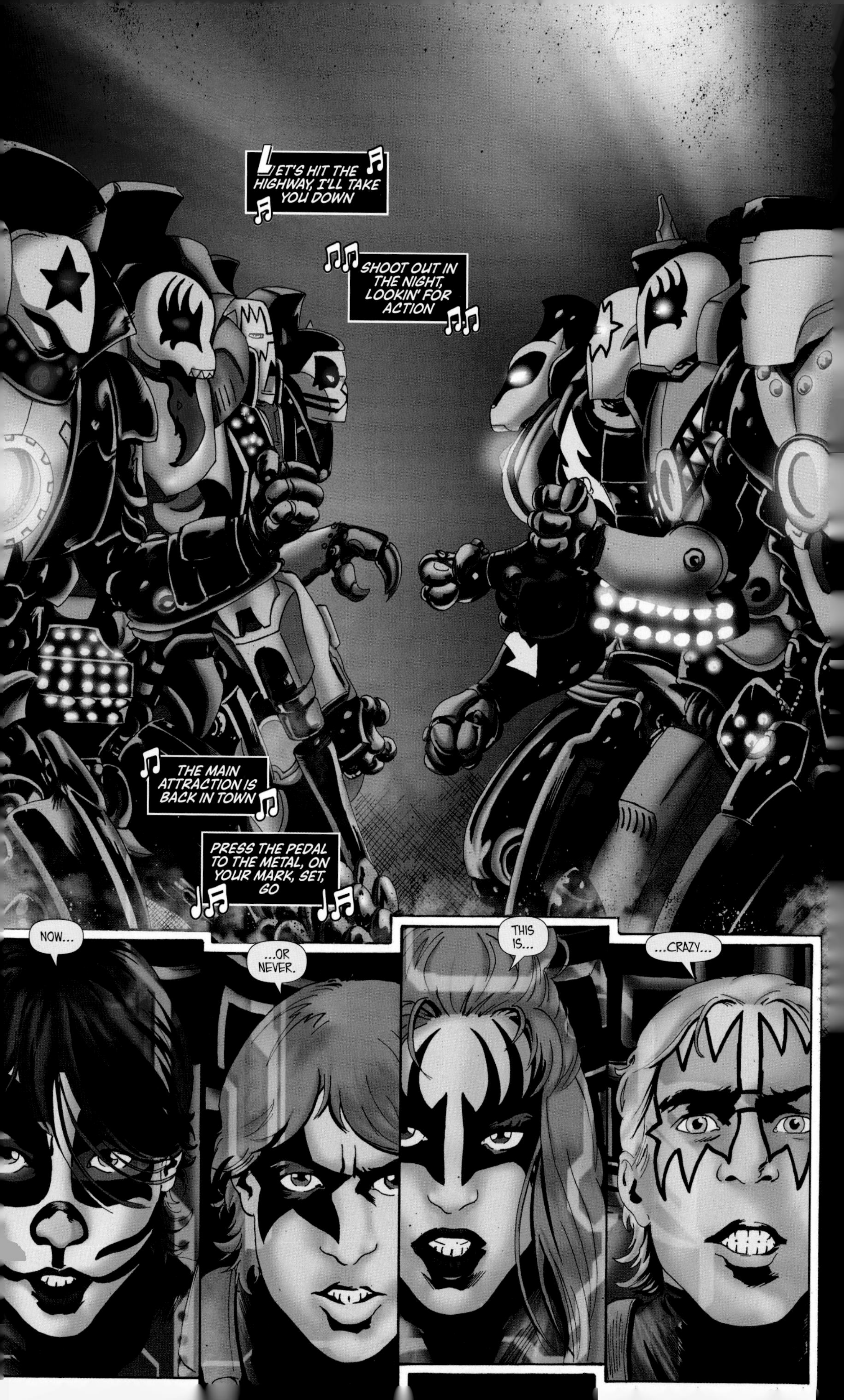
LET'S HIT THE HIGHWAY, I'LL TAKE YOU DOWN
SHOOT OUT IN THE NIGHT, LOOKIN' FOR ACTION
THE MAIN ATTRACTION IS BACK IN TOWN
PRESS THE PEDAL TO THE METAL, ON YOUR MARK, SET, GO
NOW...
...OR NEVER.
THIS IS...
...CRAZY...

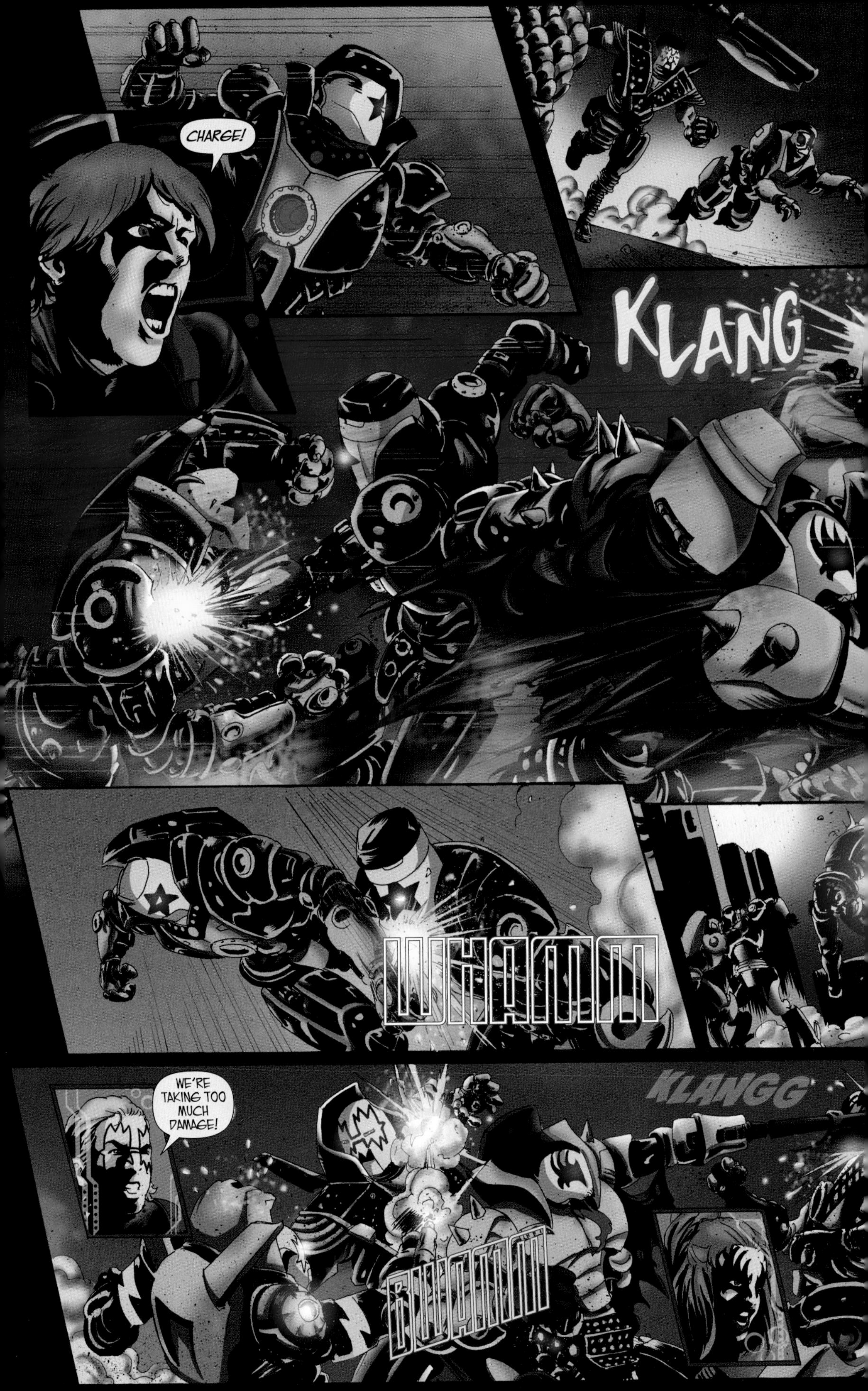
CHARGE!
KLANG
WHAMM
WE'RE TAKING TOO MUCH DAMAGE!
KLANGG

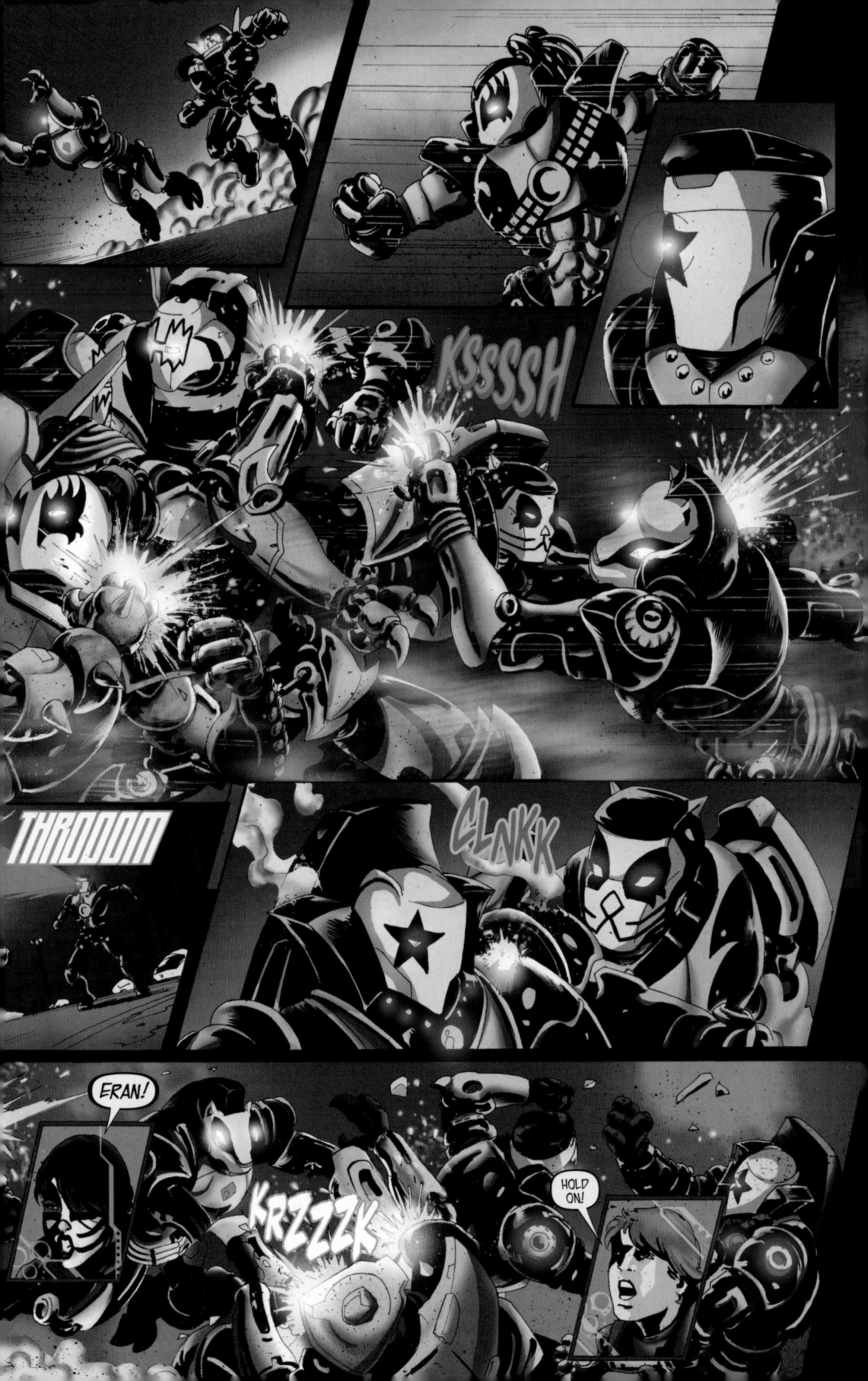
KSSSSH
THROOOM
CLNKK
ERAN!
KRZZZK
HOLD ON!

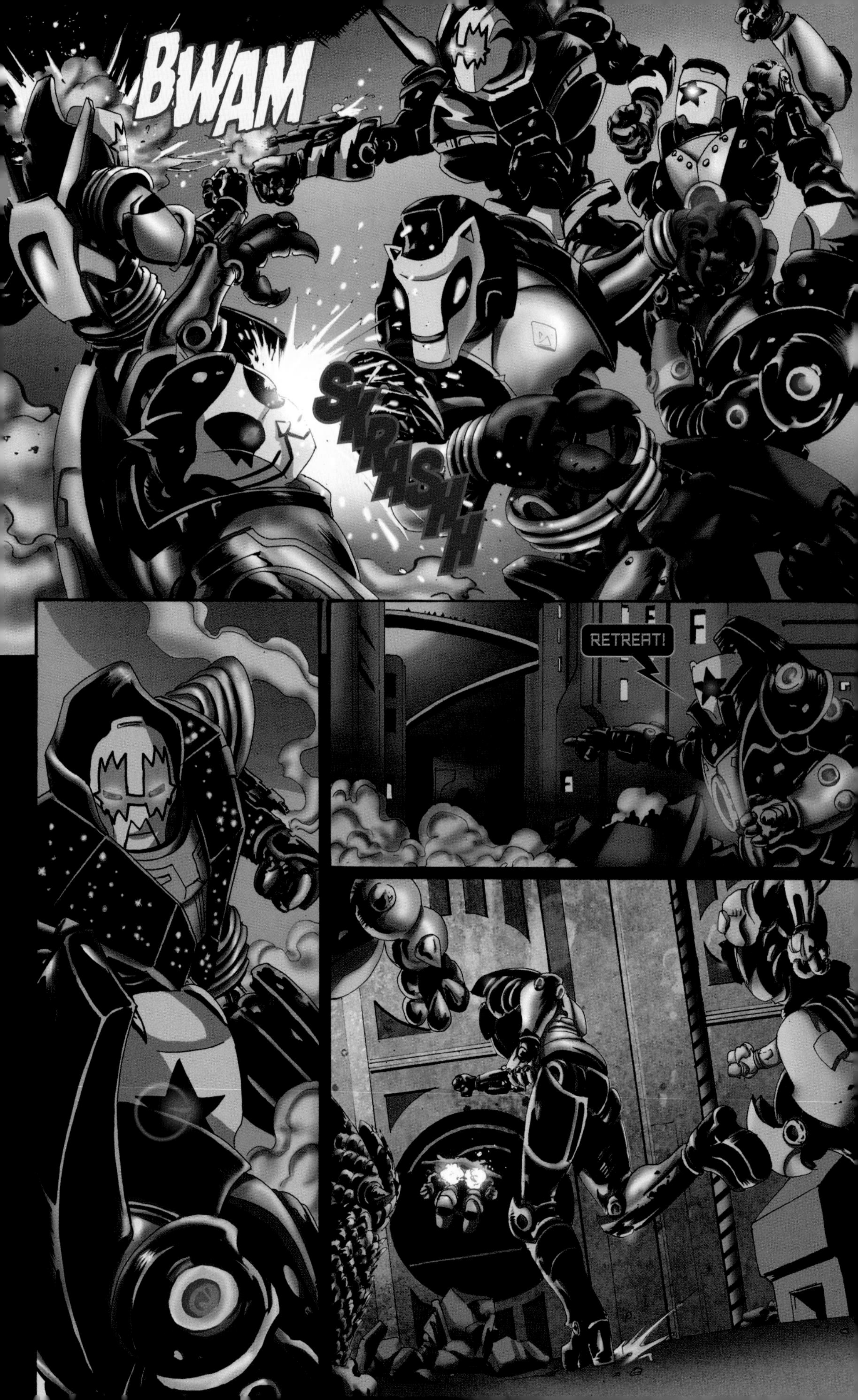
BWAM
SKRASHH
RETREAT!

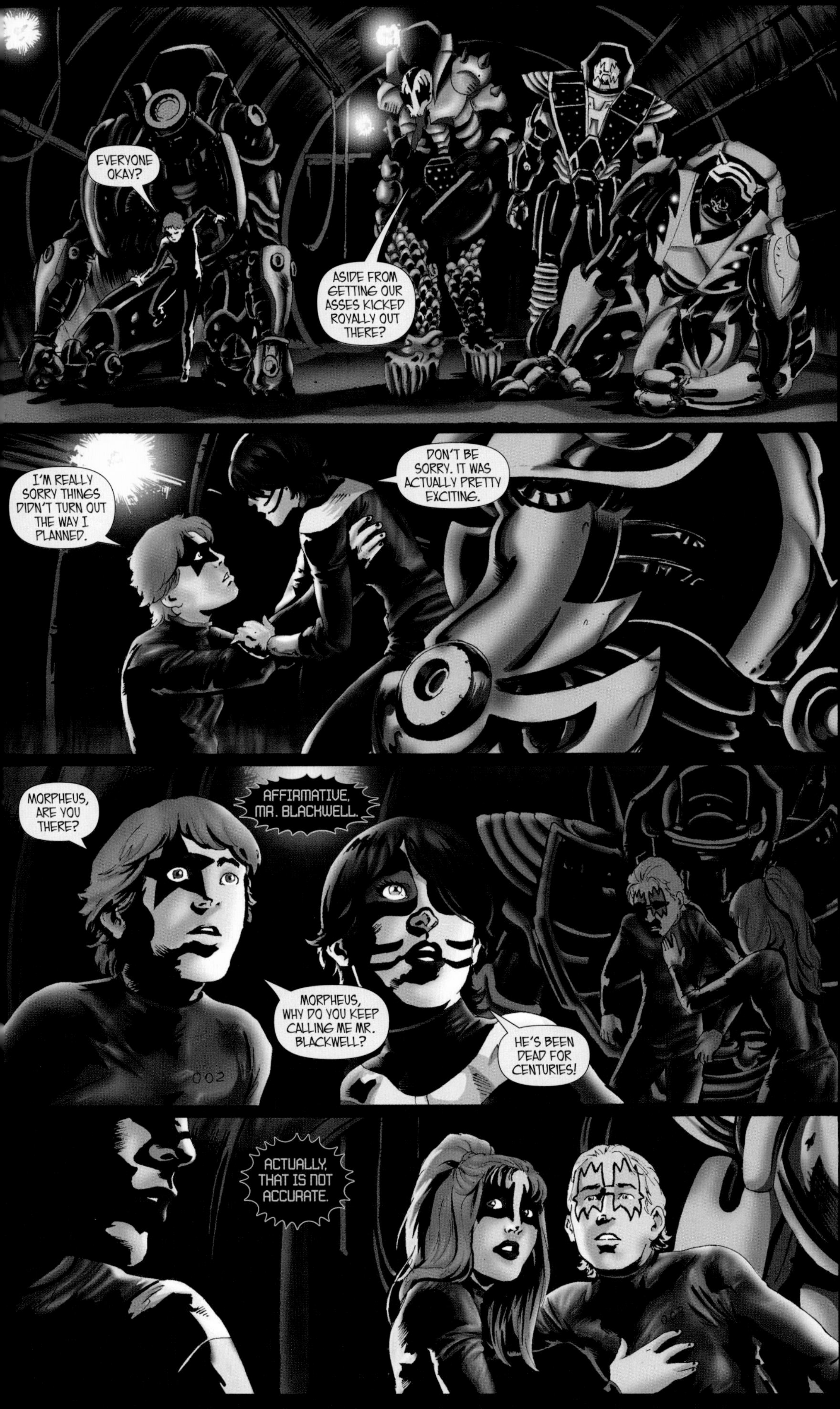
EVERYONE OKAY?
ASIDE FROM GETTING OUR ASSES KICKED ROYALLY OUT THERE?
I'M REALLY SORRY THINGS DIDN'T TURN OUT THE WAY I PLANNED.
DON'T BE SORRY. IT WAS ACTUALLY PRETTY EXCITING.
MORPHEUS, ARE YOU THERE?
AFFIRMATIVE, MR. BLACKWELL.
MORPHEUS, WHY DO YOU KEEP CALLING ME MR. BLACKWELL?
HE'S BEEN DEAD FOR CENTURIES!
ACTUALLY, THAT IS NOT ACCURATE.

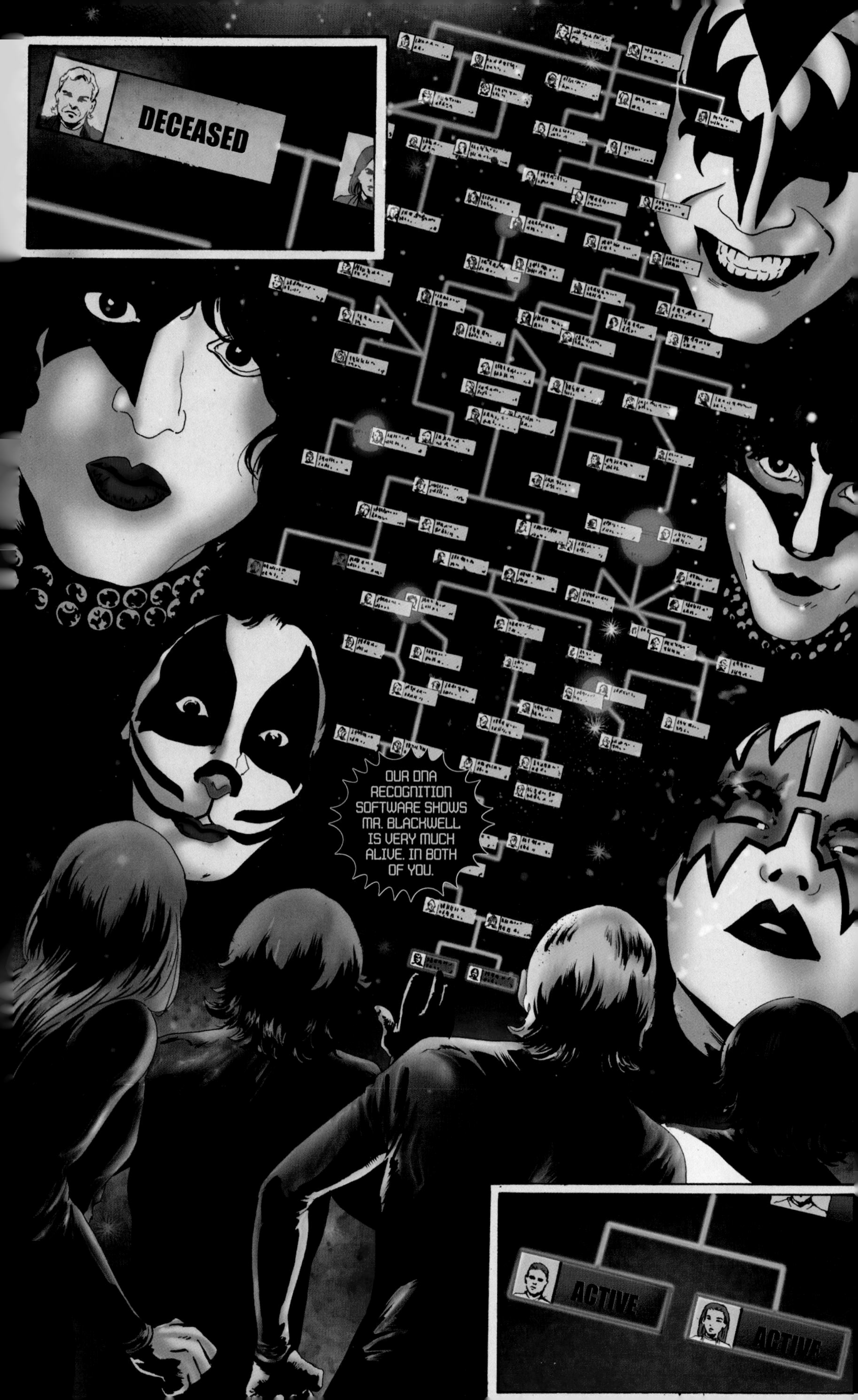
DECEASED
OUR DNA RECOGNITION SOFTWARE SHOWS MR. BLACKWELL IS VERY MUCH ALIVE. IN BOTH OF YOU.
ACTIVE
ACTIVE

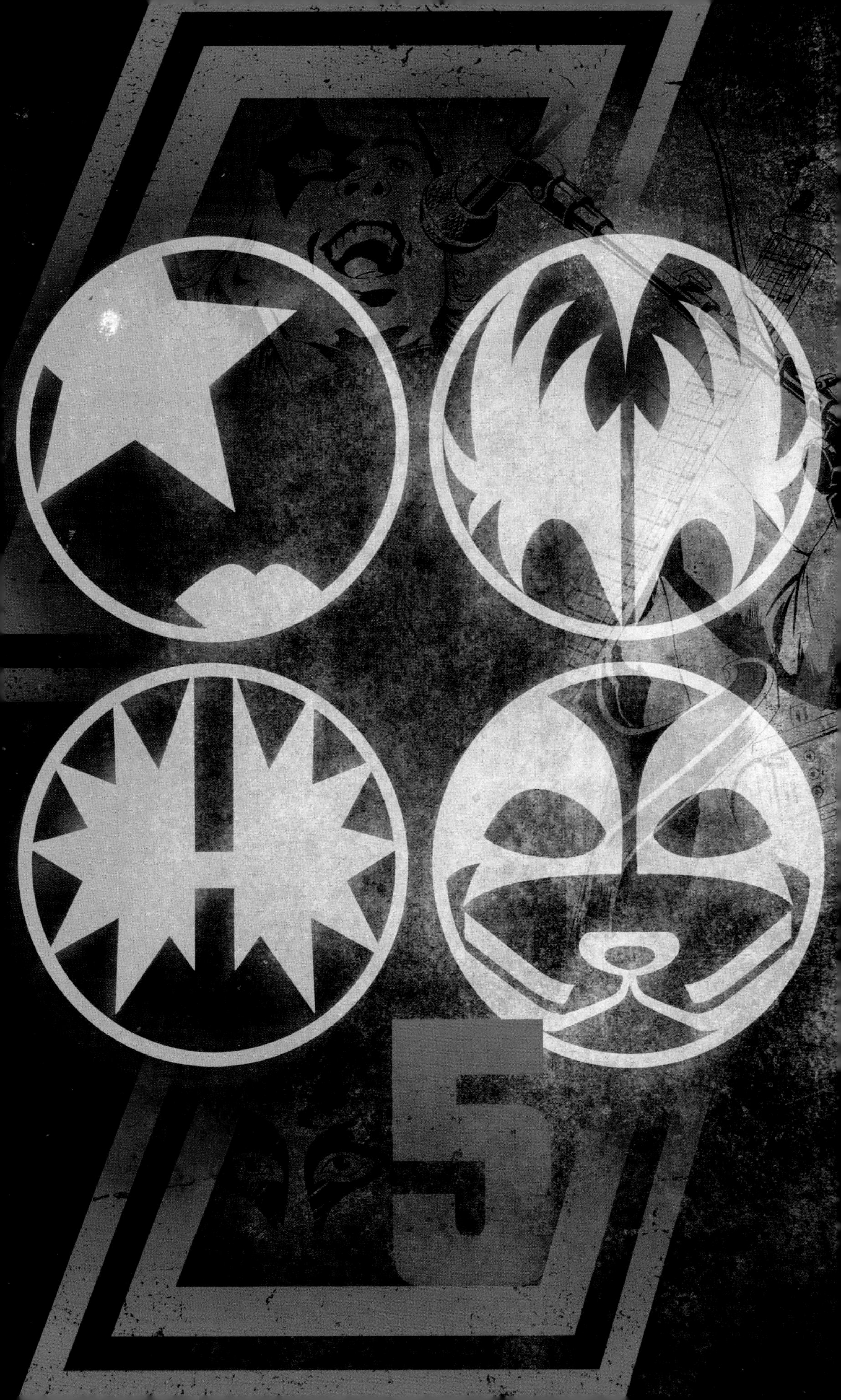
5

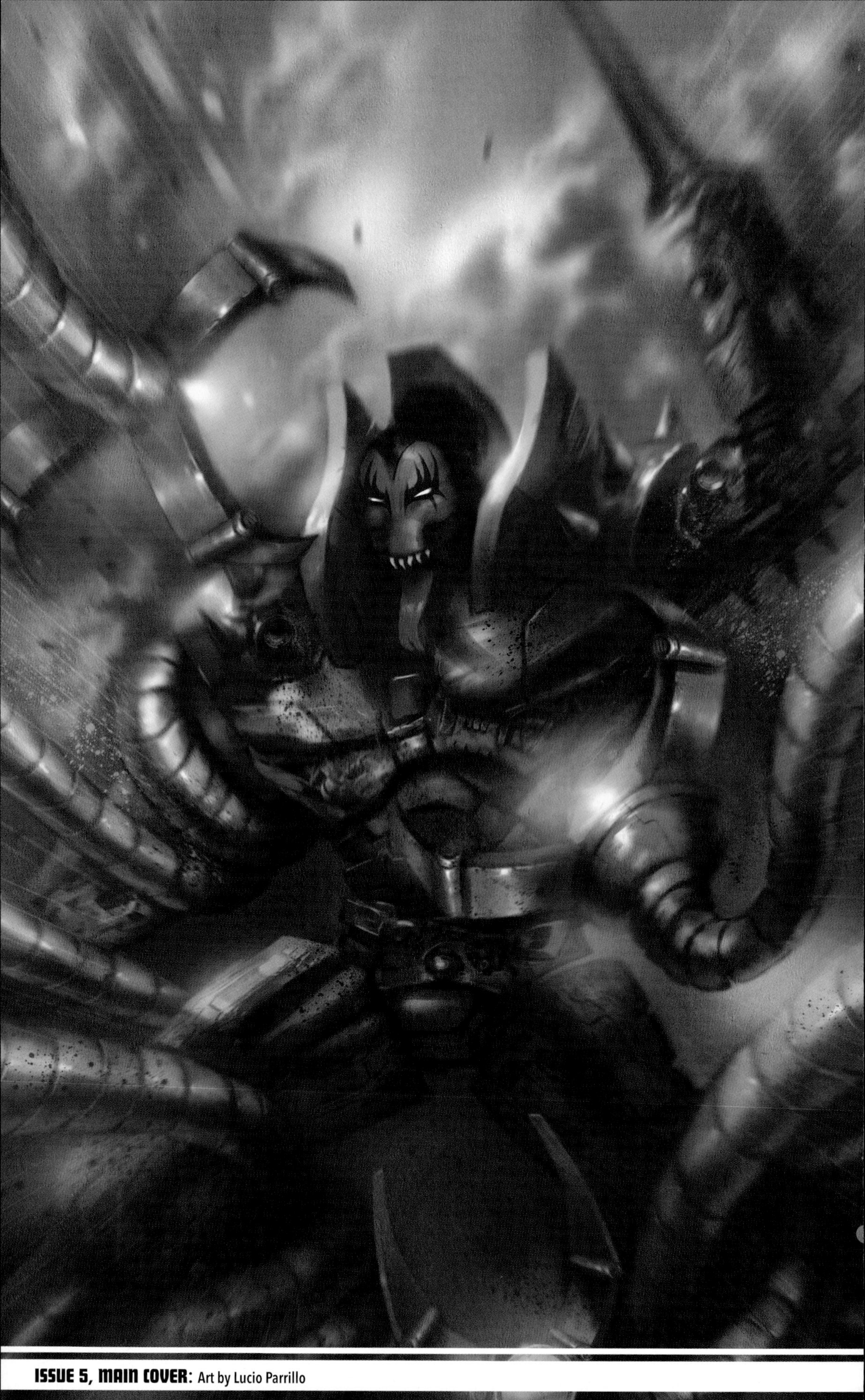

ISSUE 5, MAIN COVER: Art by Lucio Parrillo

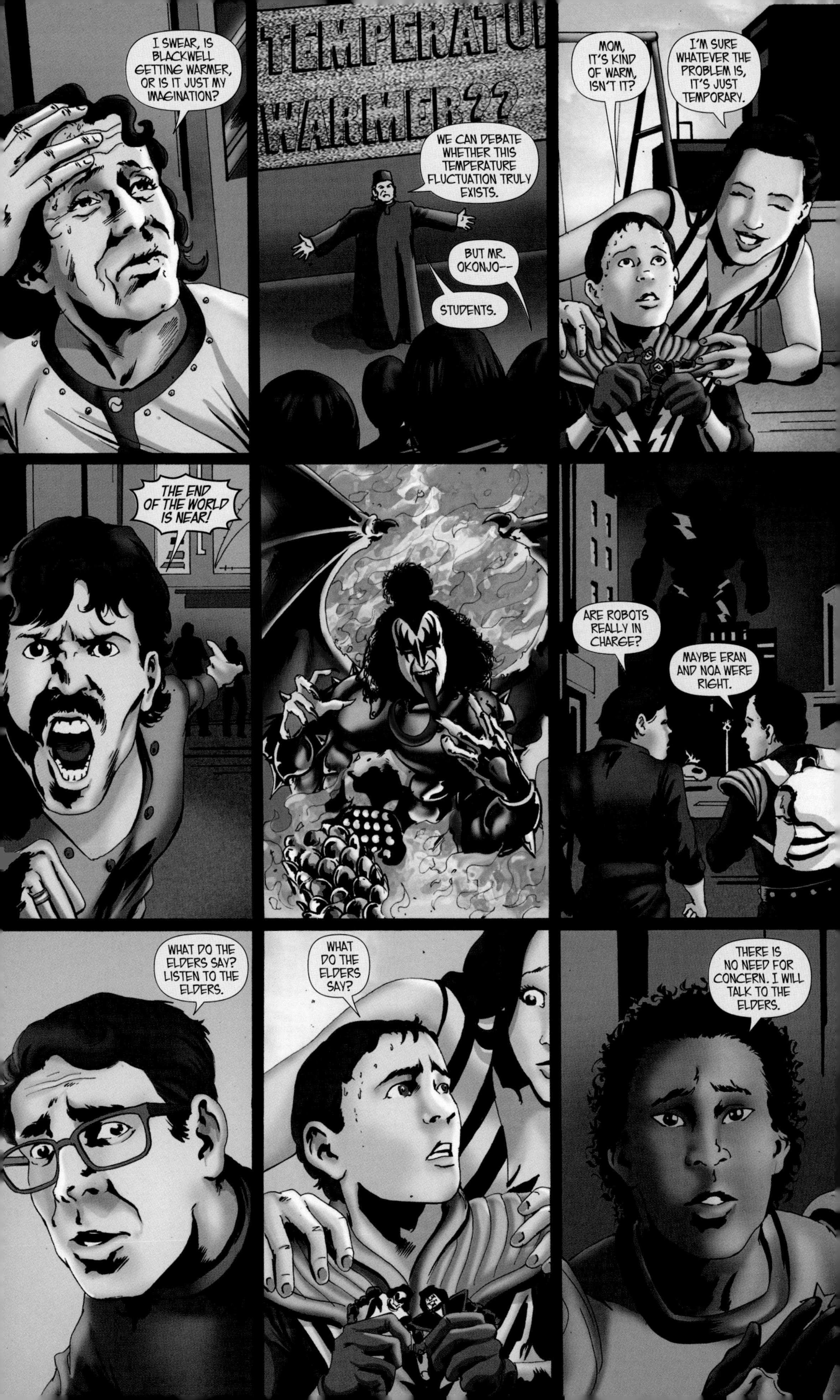

I SWEAR, IS BLACKWELL GETTING WARMER, OR IS IT JUST MY IMAGINATION?
TEMPERATU
WARMER??
WE CAN DEBATE WHETHER THIS TEMPERATURE FLUCTUATION TRULY EXISTS.
BUT MR. OKONJO--
STUDENTS.
MOM, IT'S KIND OF WARM, ISN'T IT?
I'M SURE WHATEVER THE PROBLEM IS, IT'S JUST TEMPORARY.
THE END OF THE WORLD IS NEAR!
ARE ROBOTS REALLY IN CHARGE?
MAYBE ERAN AND NOA WERE RIGHT.
WHAT DO THE ELDERS SAY? LISTEN TO THE ELDERS.
WHAT DO THE ELDERS SAY?
THERE IS NO NEED FOR CONCERN. I WILL TALK TO THE ELDERS.

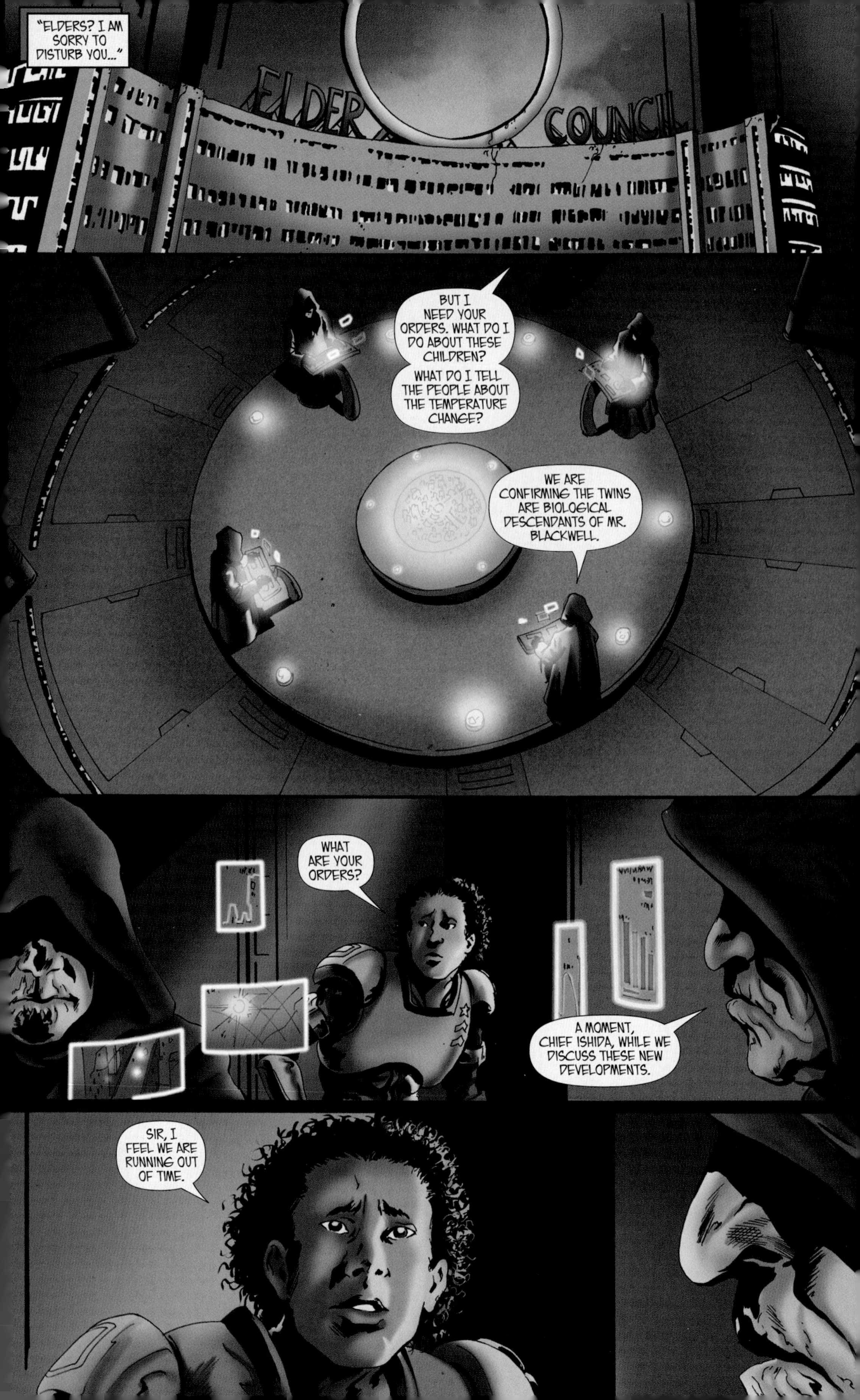
"ELDERS? I AM SORRY TO DISTURB YOU..."
ELDER COUNCIL
BUT I NEED YOUR ORDERS. WHAT DO I DO ABOUT THESE CHILDREN?
WHAT DO I TELL THE PEOPLE ABOUT THE TEMPERATURE CHANGE?
WE ARE CONFIRMING THE TWINS ARE BIOLOGICAL DESCENDANTS OF MR. BLACKWELL.
WHAT ARE YOUR ORDERS?
A MOMENT, CHIEF ISHIDA, WHILE WE DISCUSS THESE NEW DEVELOPMENTS.
SIR, I FEEL WE ARE RUNNING OUT OF TIME.

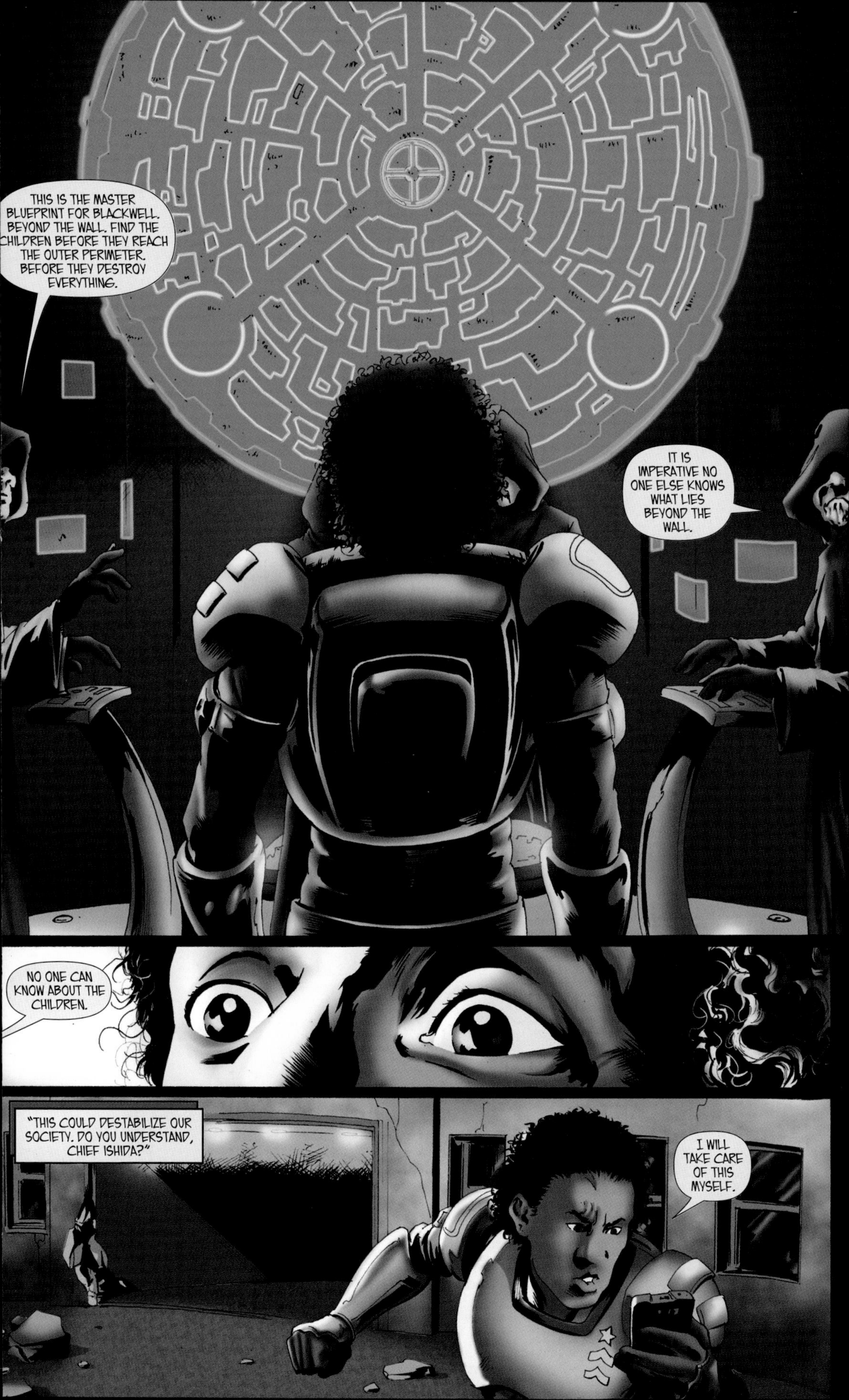
THIS IS THE MASTER BLUEPRINT FOR BLACKWELL. BEYOND THE WALL. FIND THE CHILDREN BEFORE THEY REACH THE OUTER PERIMETER. BEFORE THEY DESTROY EVERYTHING.
IT IS IMPERATIVE NO ONE ELSE KNOWS WHAT LIES BEYOND THE WALL.
NO ONE CAN KNOW ABOUT THE CHILDREN.
"THIS COULD DESTABILIZE OUR SOCIETY. DO YOU UNDERSTAND, CHIEF ISHIDA?"
I WILL TAKE CARE OF THIS MYSELF.

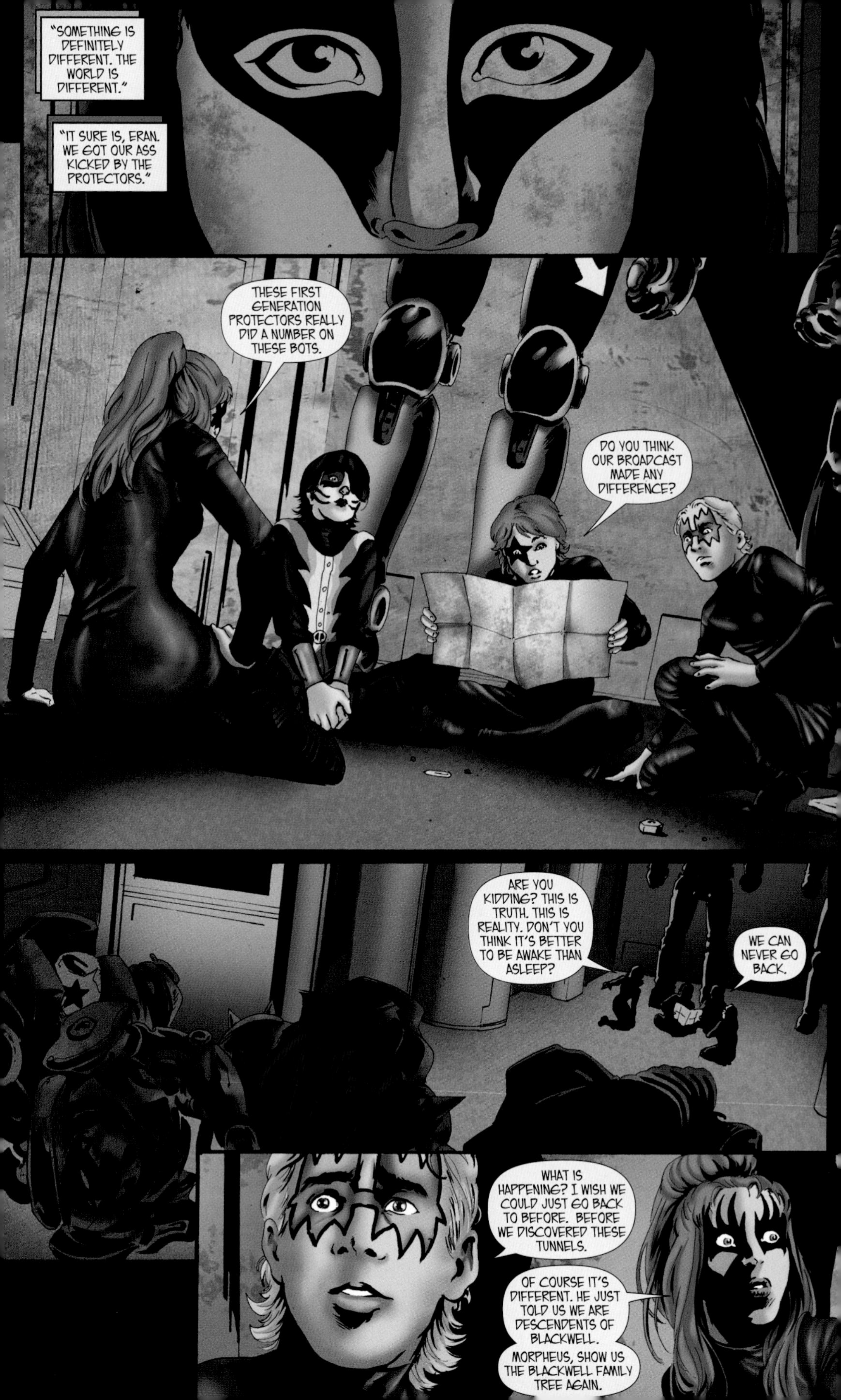
"SOMETHING IS DEFINITELY DIFFERENT. THE WORLD IS DIFFERENT."
"IT SURE IS, ERAN. WE GOT OUR ASS KICKED BY THE PROTECTORS."
THESE FIRST GENERATION PROTECTORS REALLY DID A NUMBER ON THESE BOTS.
DO YOU THINK OUR BROADCAST MADE ANY DIFFERENCE?
ARE YOU KIDDING? THIS IS TRUTH. THIS IS REALITY. DON'T YOU THINK IT'S BETTER TO BE AWAKE THAN ASLEEP?
WE CAN NEVER GO BACK.
WHAT IS HAPPENING? I WISH WE COULD JUST GO BACK TO BEFORE. BEFORE WE DISCOVERED THESE TUNNELS.
OF COURSE IT'S DIFFERENT. HE JUST TOLD US WE ARE DESCENDENTS OF BLACKWELL.
MORPHEUS, SHOW US THE BLACKWELL FAMILY TREE AGAIN.

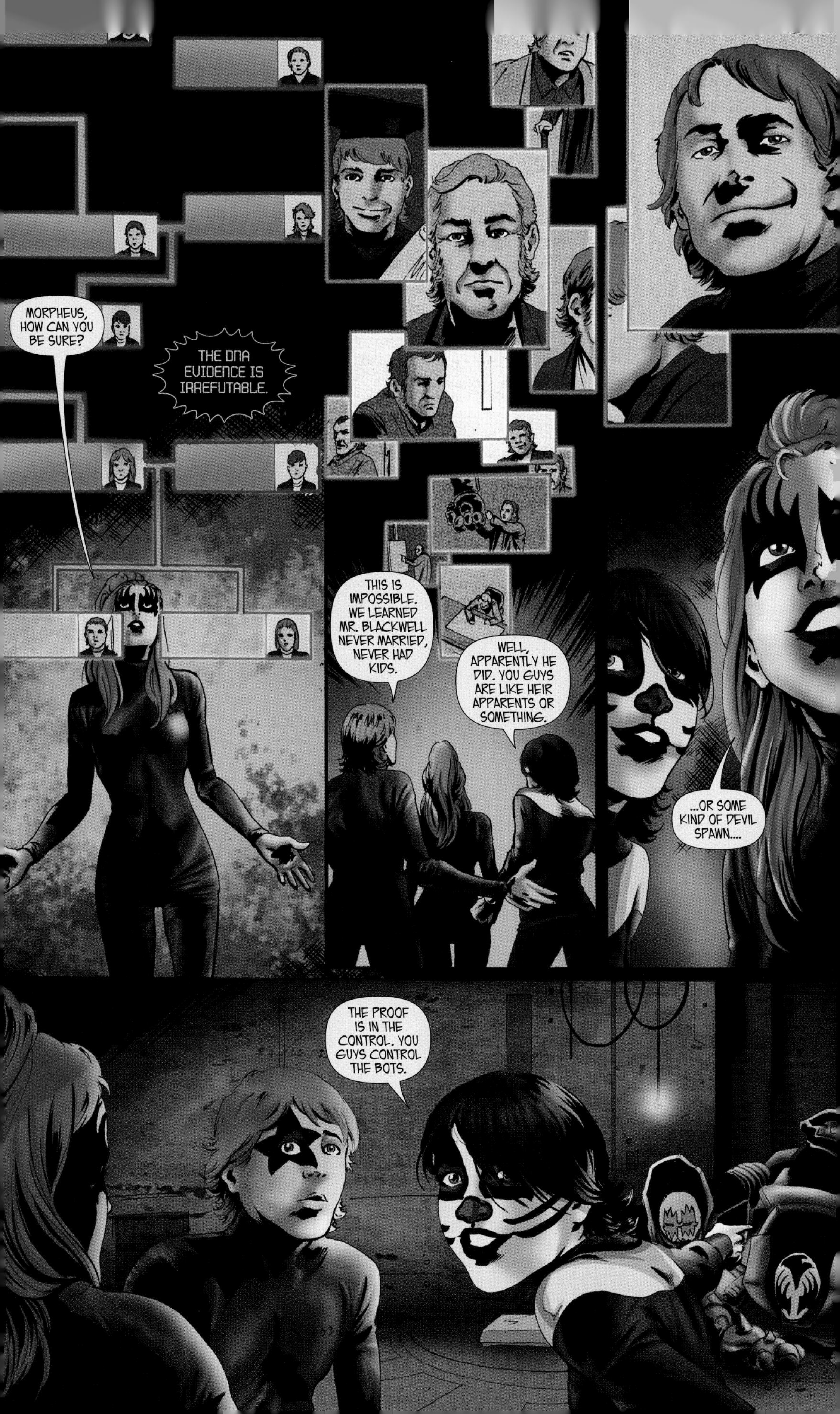
MORPHEUS, HOW CAN YOU BE SURE?
THE DNA EVIDENCE IS IRREFUTABLE.
THIS IS IMPOSSIBLE. WE LEARNED MR. BLACKWELL NEVER MARRIED, NEVER HAD KIDS.
WELL, APPARENTLY HE DID. YOU GUYS ARE LIKE HEIR APPARENTS OR SOMETHING.
...OR SOME KIND OF DEVIL SPAWN....
THE PROOF IS IN THE CONTROL. YOU GUYS CONTROL THE BOTS.

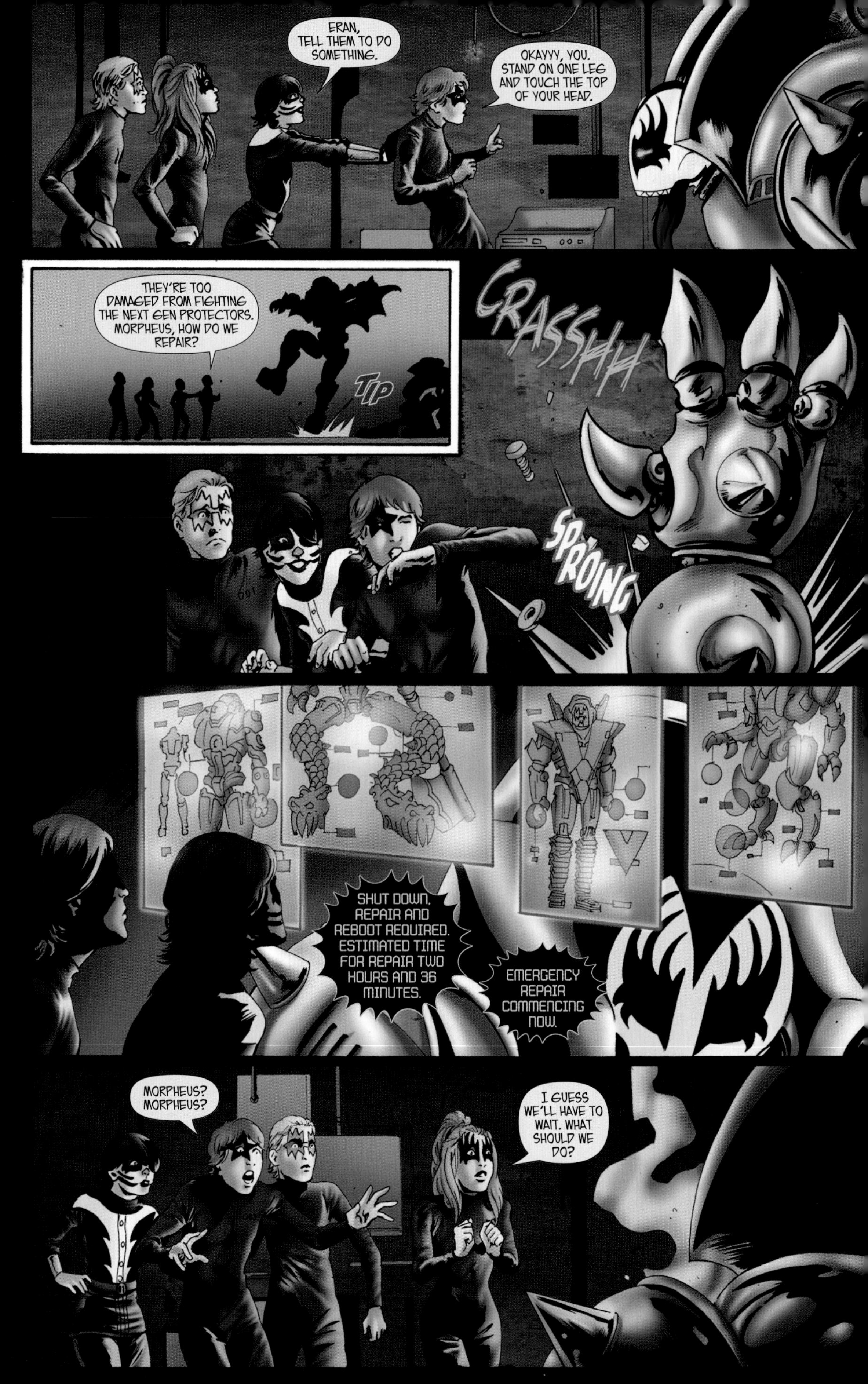

ERAN, TELL THEM TO DO SOMETHING.
OKAYYY, YOU. STAND ON ONE LEG AND TOUCH THE TOP OF YOUR HEAD.
THEY'RE TOO DAMAGED FROM FIGHTING THE NEXT GEN PROTECTORS. MORPHEUS, HOW DO WE REPAIR?
TIP
CRASSHH
SPROING
SHUT DOWN, REPAIR AND REBOOT REQUIRED. ESTIMATED TIME FOR REPAIR TWO HOURS AND 36 MINUTES.
EMERGENCY REPAIR COMMENCING NOW.
MORPHEUS? MORPHEUS?
I GUESS WE'LL HAVE TO WAIT. WHAT SHOULD WE DO?

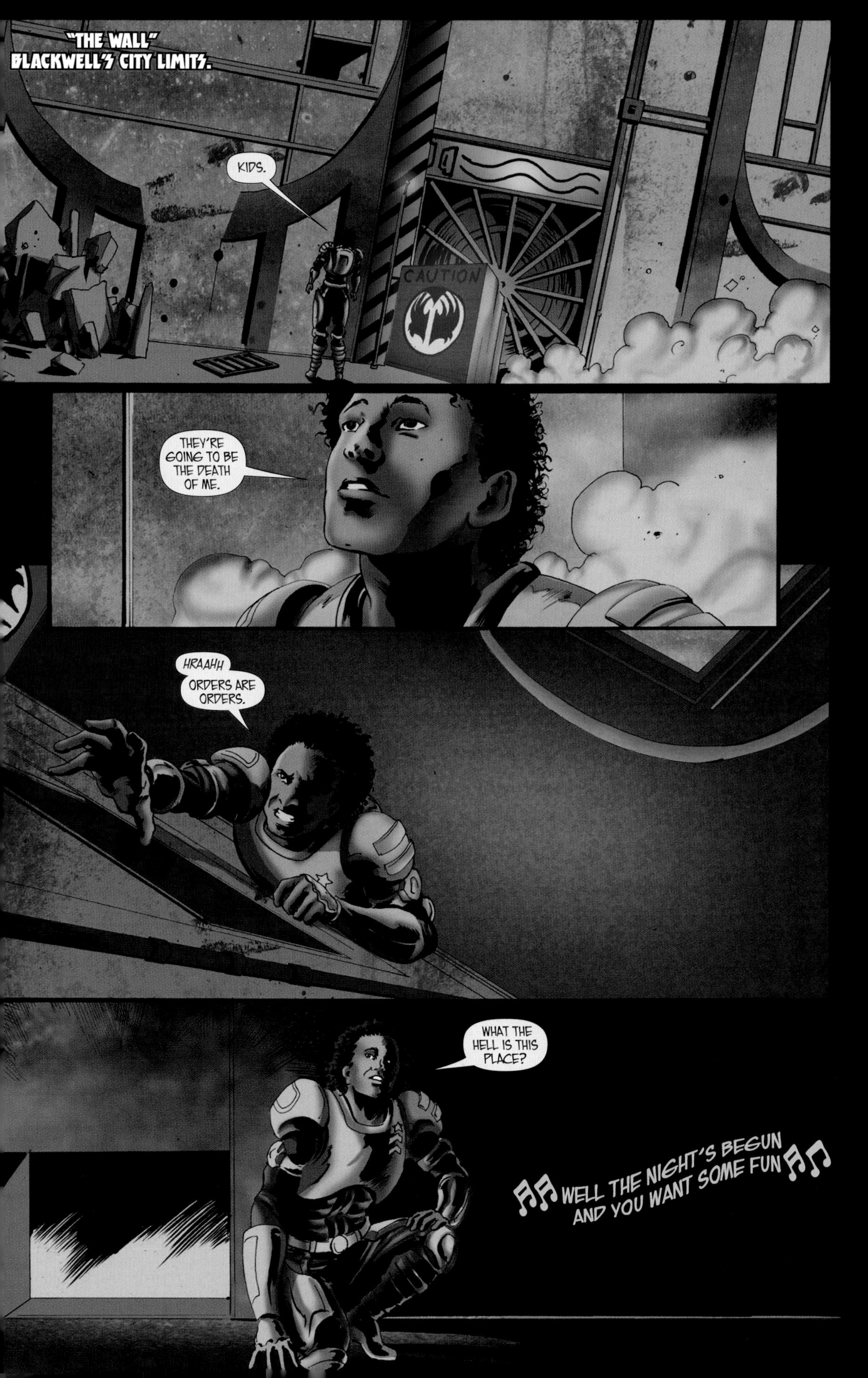
"THE WALL"
BLACKWELL'S CITY LIMITS.
KIDS.
THEY'RE GOING TO BE THE DEATH OF ME.
HRAAHH
ORDERS ARE ORDERS.
WHAT THE HELL IS THIS PLACE?
WELL THE NIGHT'S BEGUN
AND YOU WANT SOME FUN
CAUTION

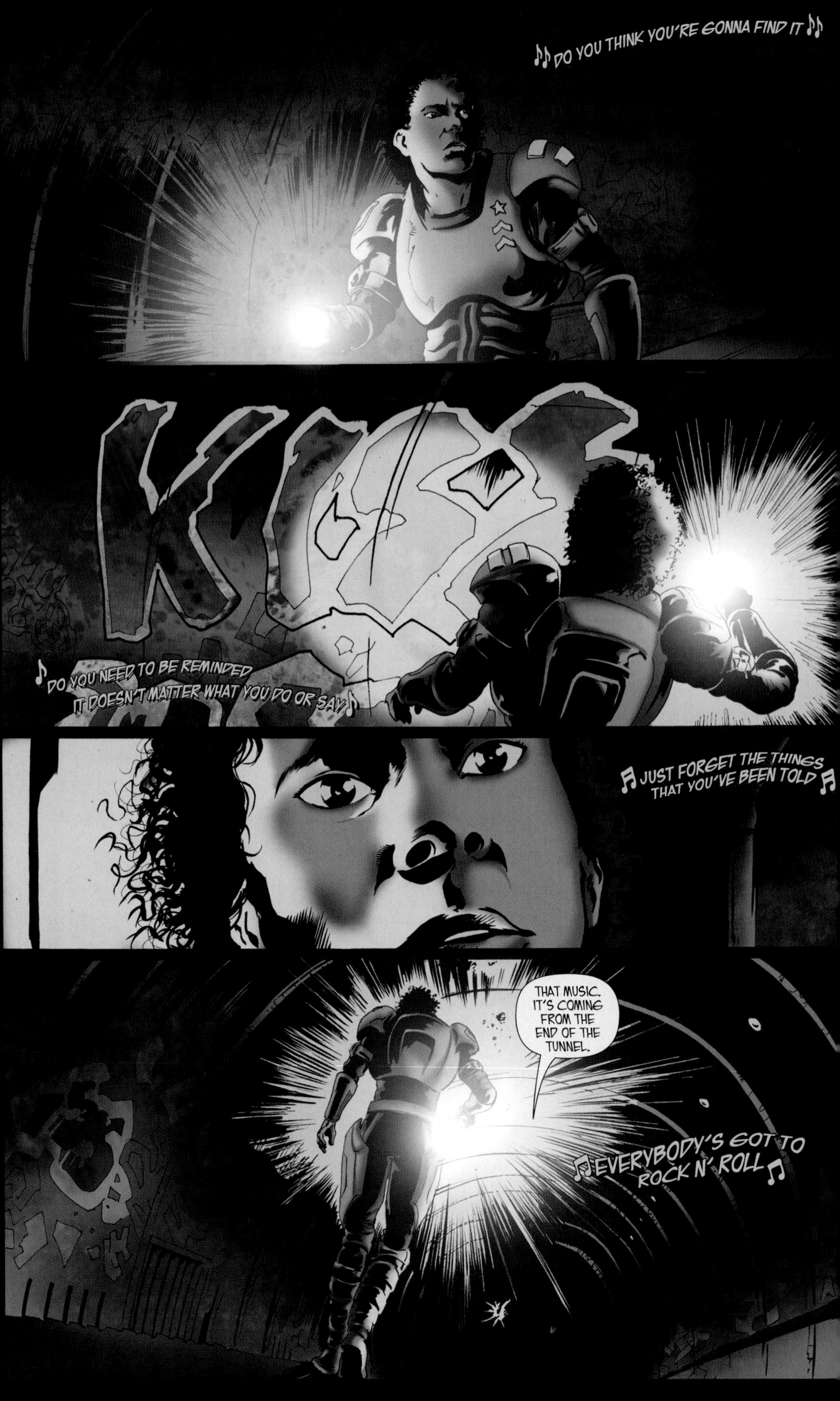
♪♪ DO YOU THINK YOU'RE GONNA FIND IT ♪♪
♪ DO YOU NEED TO BE REMINDED
IT DOESN'T MATTER WHAT YOU DO OR SAY ♪
♫ JUST FORGET THE THINGS
THAT YOU'VE BEEN TOLD ♫
THAT MUSIC. IT'S COMING FROM THE END OF THE TUNNEL.
♫ EVERYBODY'S GOT TO
ROCK N' ROLL ♫

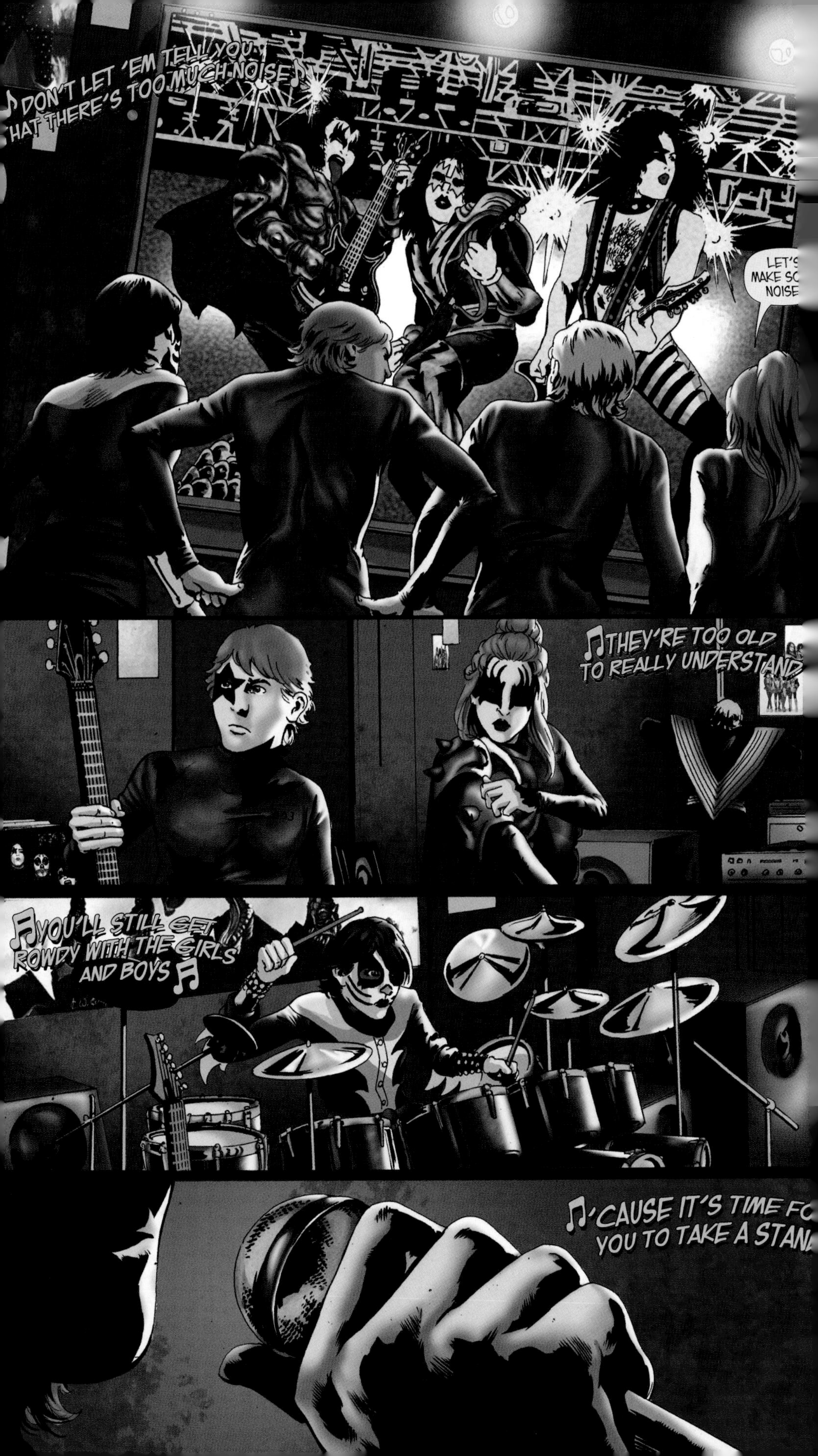
♪DON'T LET 'EM TELL YOU
HAT THERE'S TOO MUCH NOISE♪
LET'S MAKE SO NOISE
♫THEY'RE TOO OLD TO REALLY UNDERSTAND
♫YOU'LL STILL GET ROWDY WITH THE GIRLS AND BOYS♫
♫'CAUSE IT'S TIME FO YOU TO TAKE A STAN

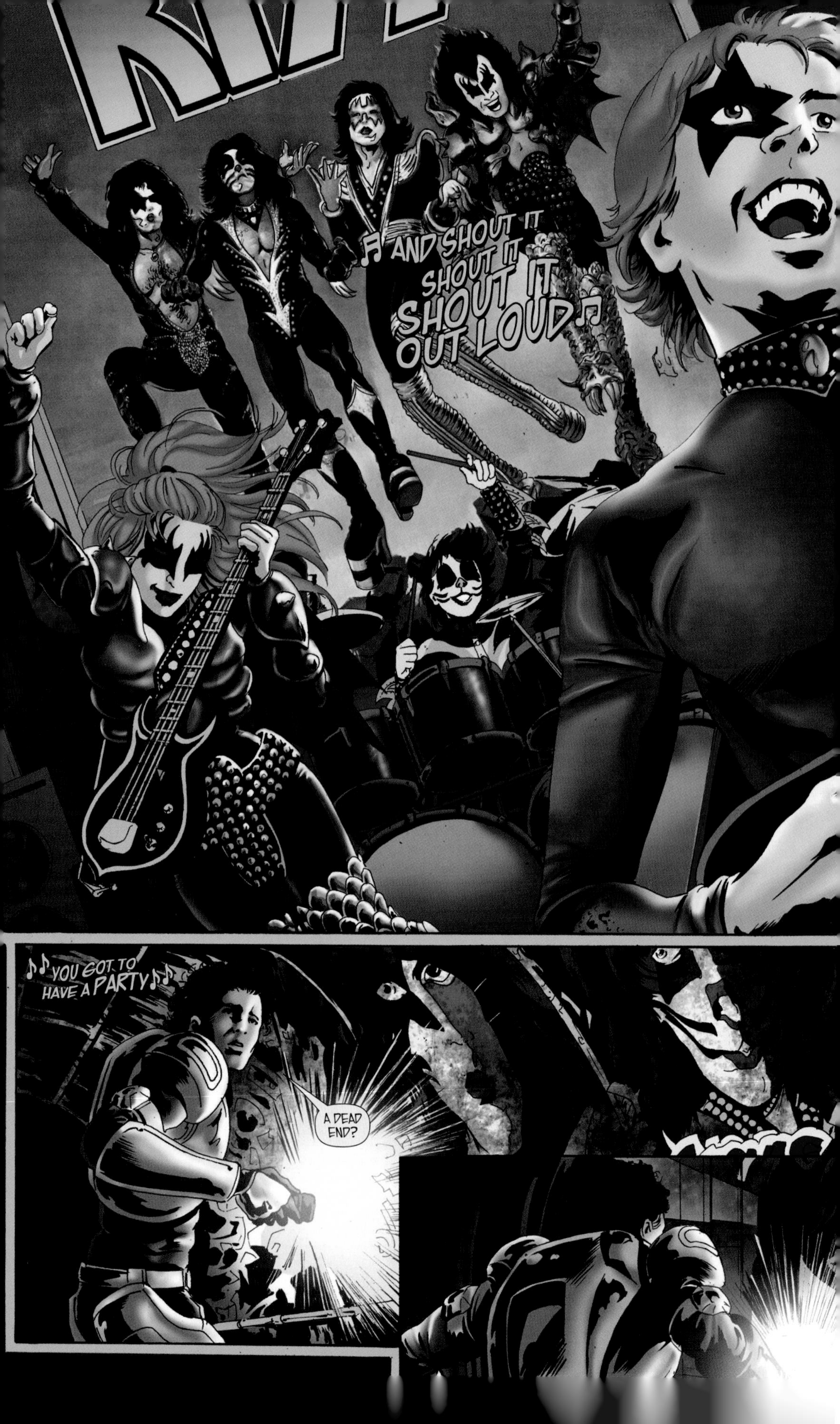
♫ AND SHOUT IT
SHOUT IT
SHOUT IT
OUT LOUD ♫
♪♪ YOU GOT TO HAVE A PARTY ♪♪
A DEAD END?

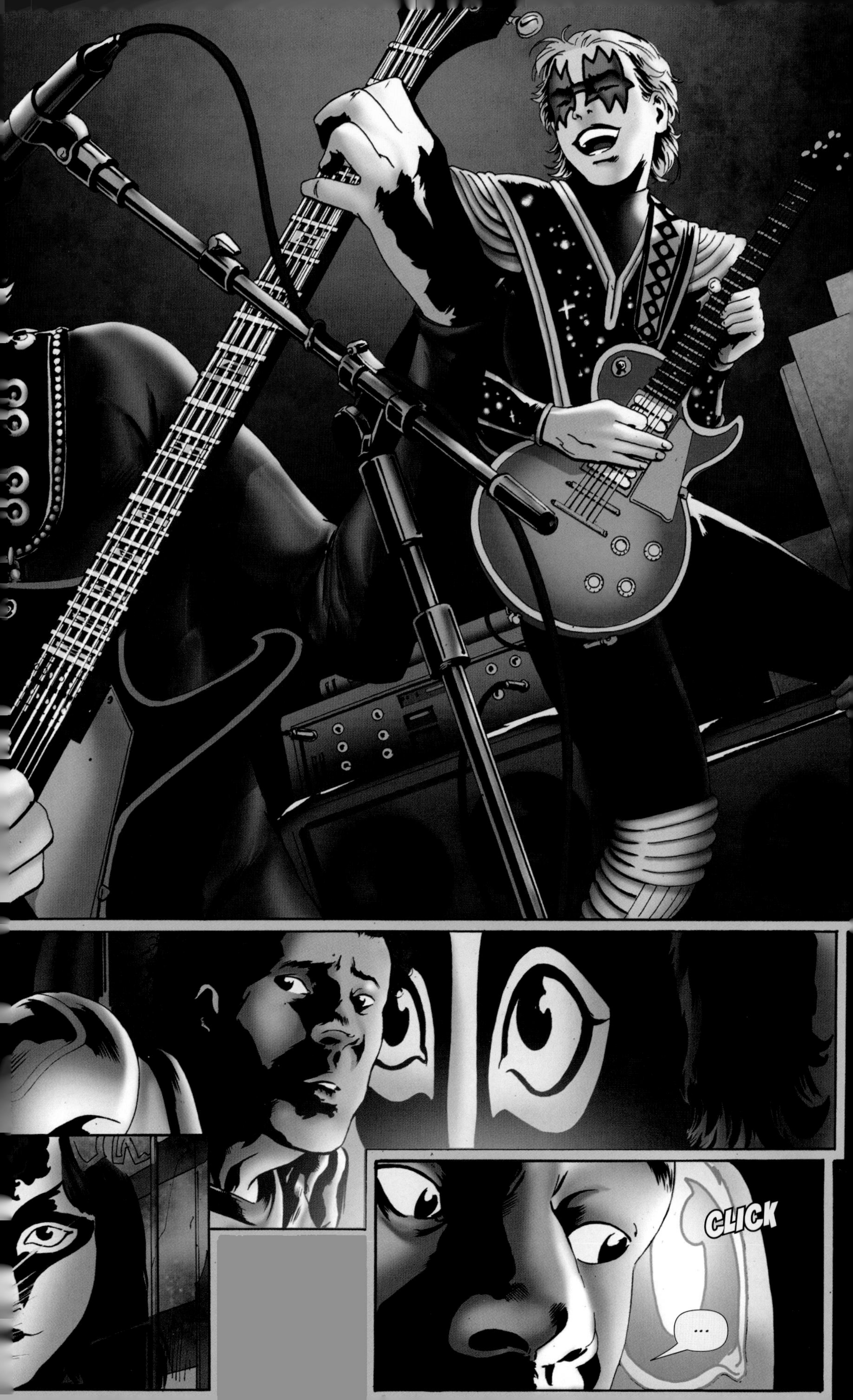
CLICK
...

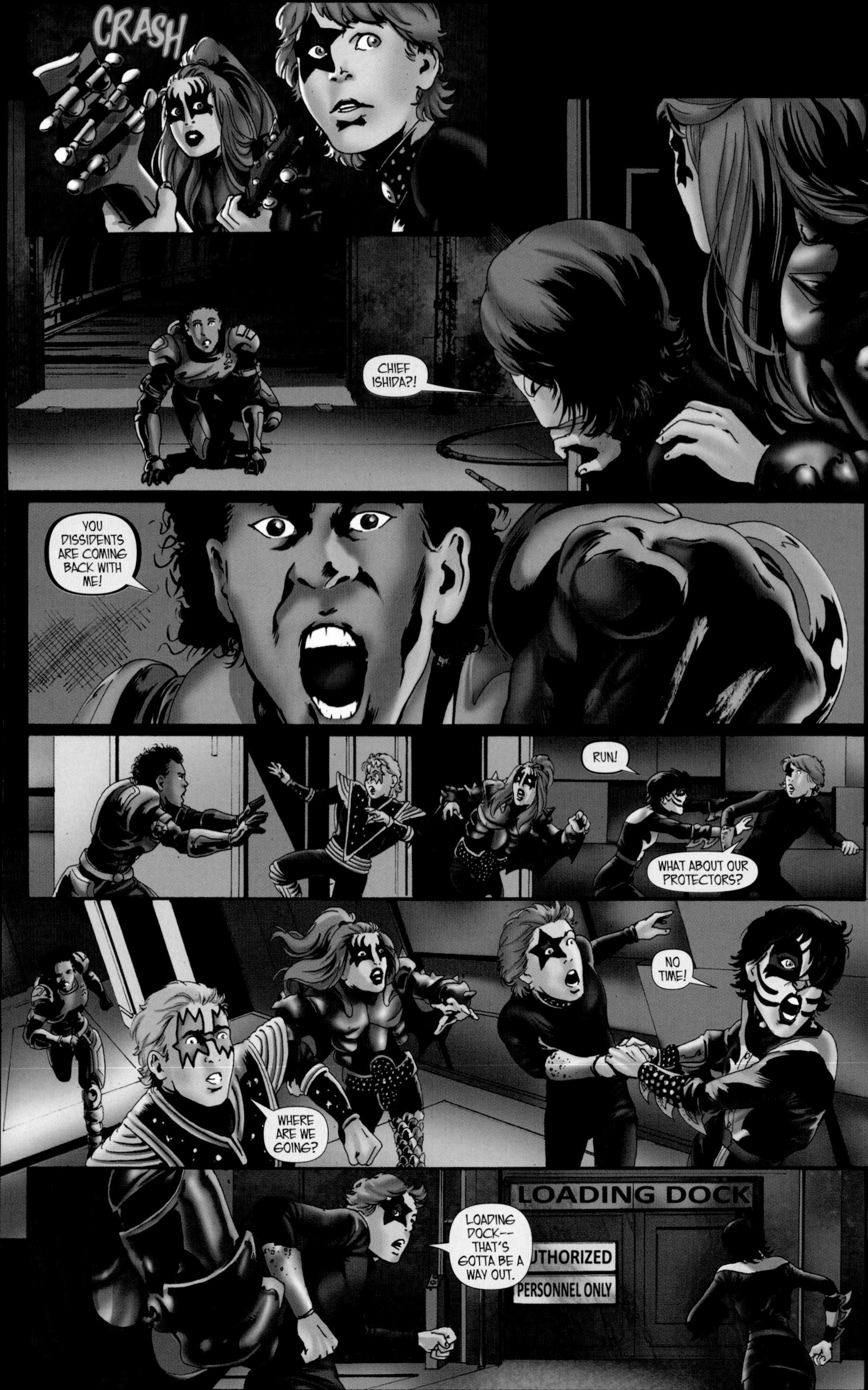
CRASH
CHIEF ISHIDA?!
YOU DISSIDENTS ARE COMING BACK WITH ME!
RUN!
WHAT ABOUT OUR PROTECTORS?
NO TIME!
WHERE ARE WE GOING?
LOADING DOCK
UTHORIZED
PERSONNEL ONLY
LOADING DOCK-- THAT'S GOTTA BE A WAY OUT.

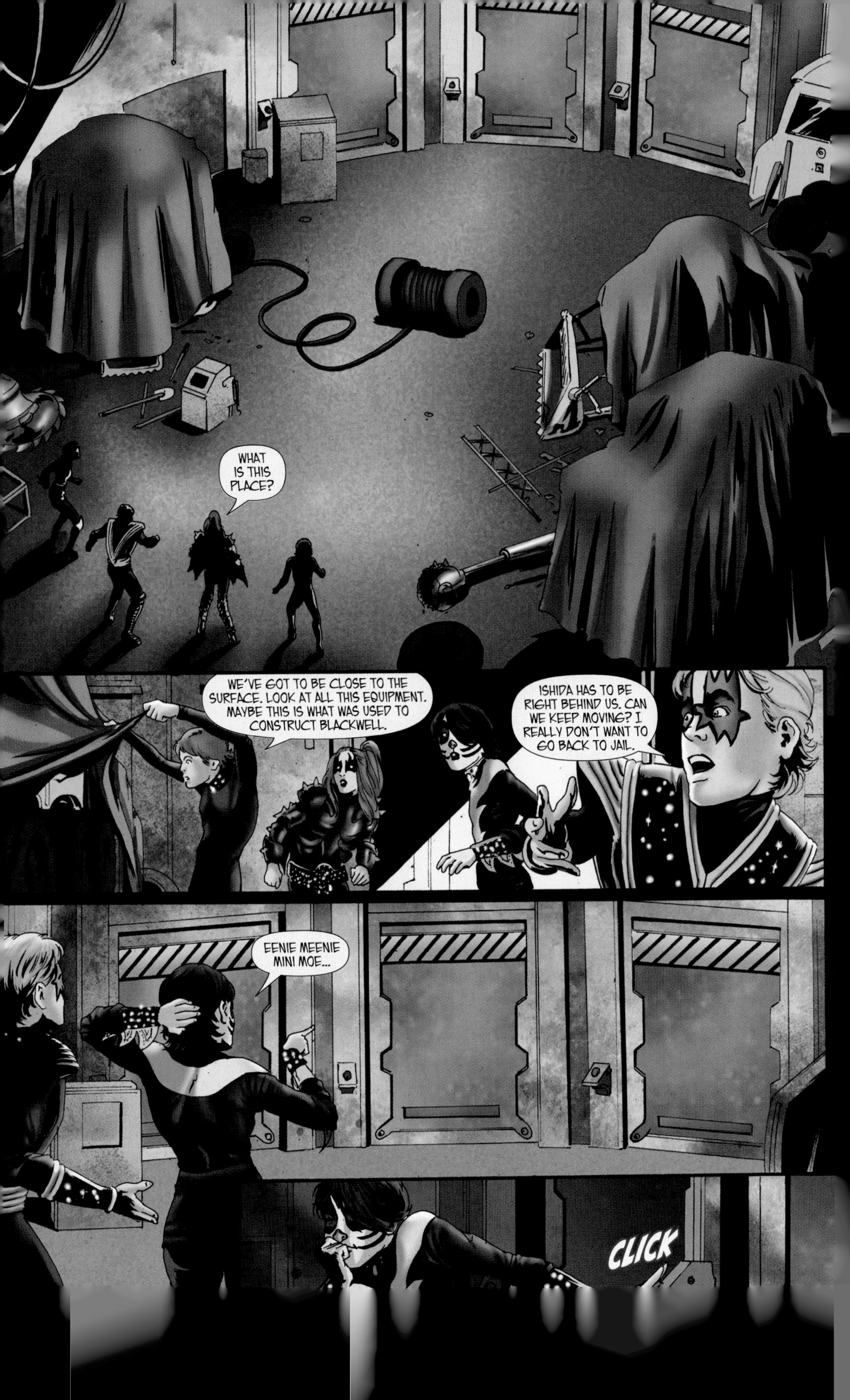
WHAT IS THIS PLACE?
WE'VE GOT TO BE CLOSE TO THE SURFACE. LOOK AT ALL THIS EQUIPMENT. MAYBE THIS IS WHAT WAS USED TO CONSTRUCT BLACKWELL.
ISHIDA HAS TO BE RIGHT BEHIND US. CAN WE KEEP MOVING? I REALLY DON'T WANT TO GO BACK TO JAIL.
EENIE MEENIE MINI MOE...
CLICK

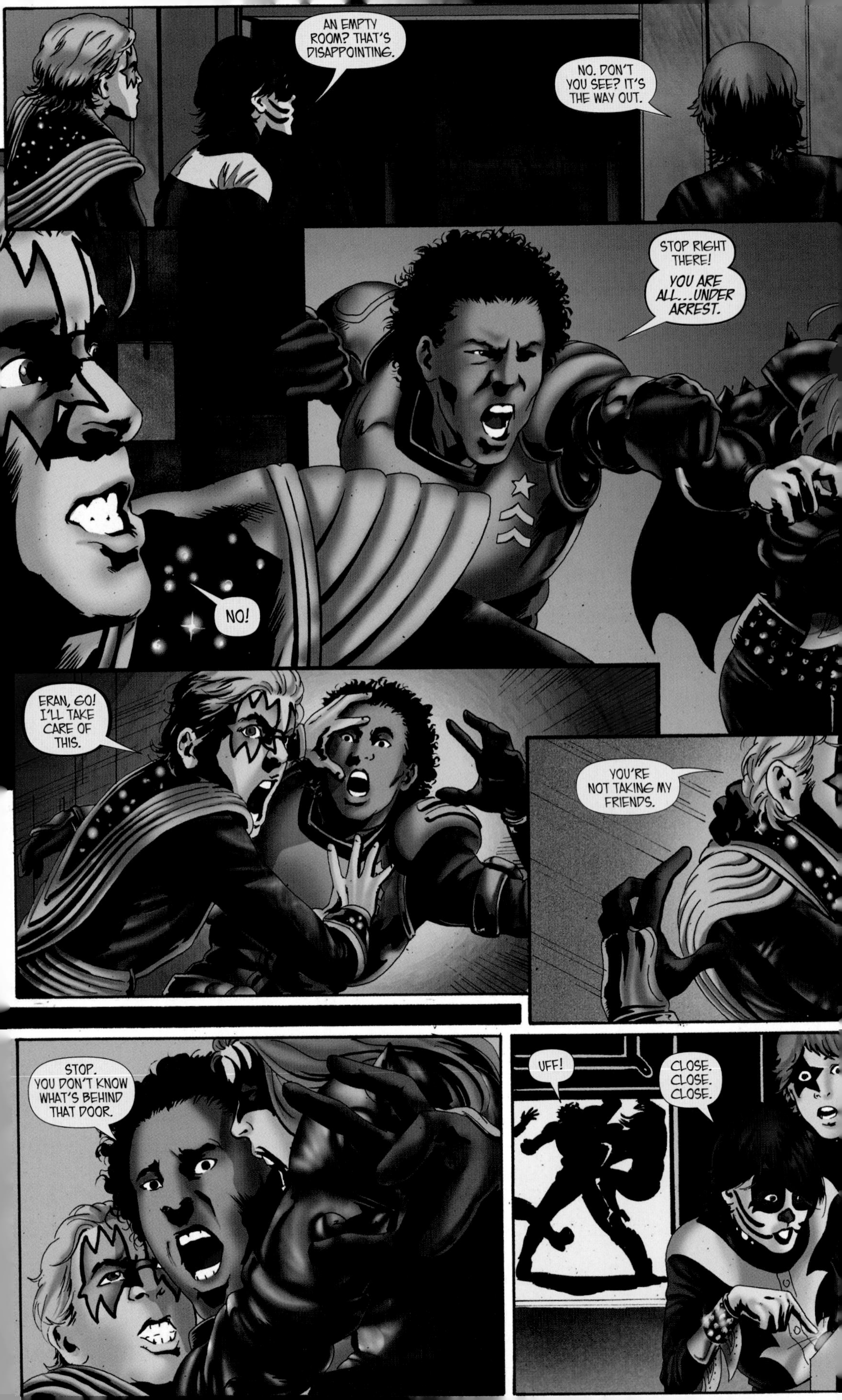
AN EMPTY ROOM? THAT'S DISAPPOINTING.
NO. DON'T YOU SEE? IT'S THE WAY OUT.
STOP RIGHT THERE! YOU ARE ALL...UNDER ARREST.
NO!
ERAN, GO! I'LL TAKE CARE OF THIS.
YOU'RE NOT TAKING MY FRIENDS.
STOP. YOU DON'T KNOW WHAT'S BEHIND THAT DOOR.
UFF!
CLOSE. CLOSE. CLOSE.

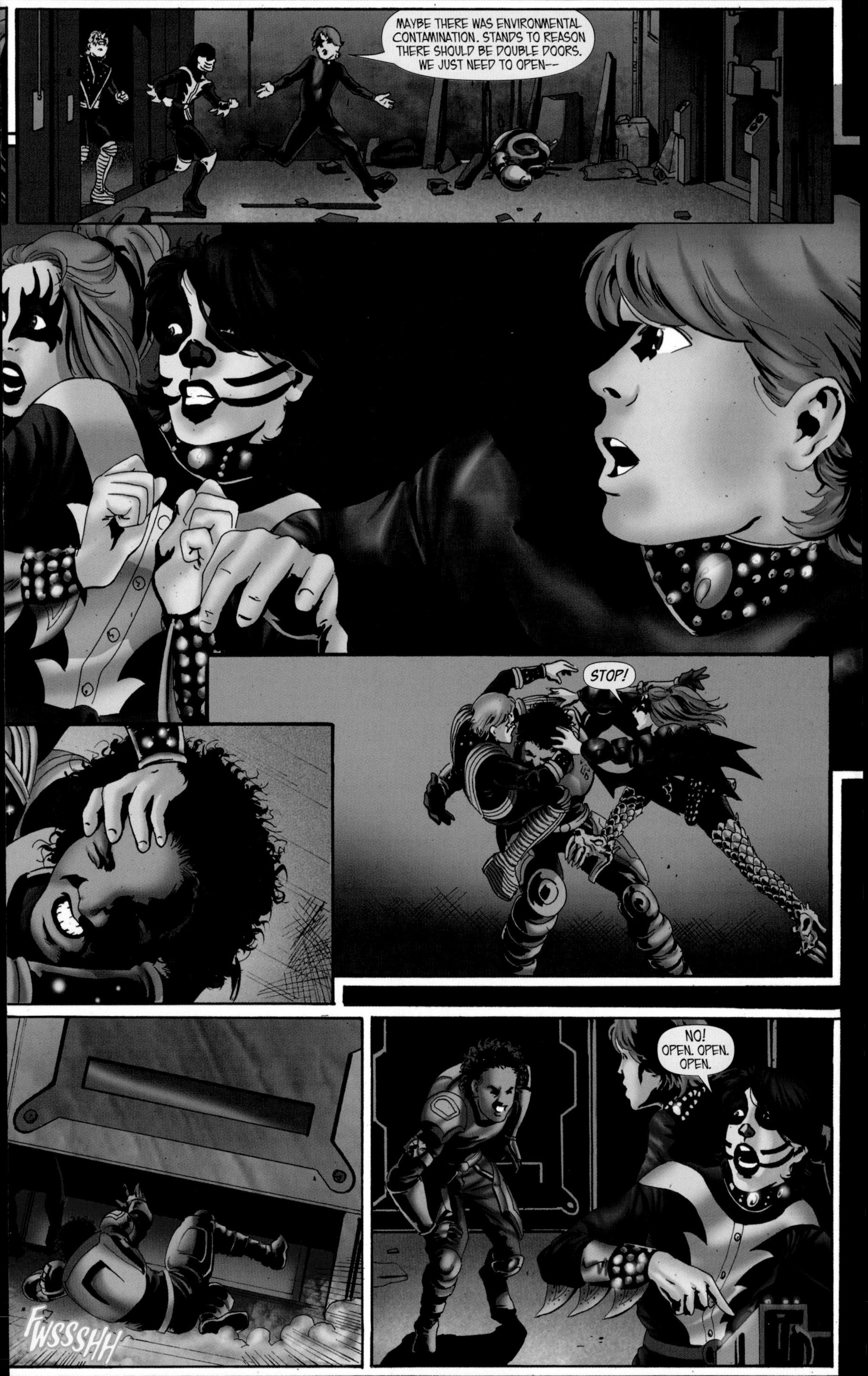
MAYBE THERE WAS ENVIRONMENTAL CONTAMINATION. STANDS TO REASON THERE SHOULD BE DOUBLE DOORS. WE JUST NEED TO OPEN--
STOP!
FWSSSHH
NO! OPEN. OPEN. OPEN.

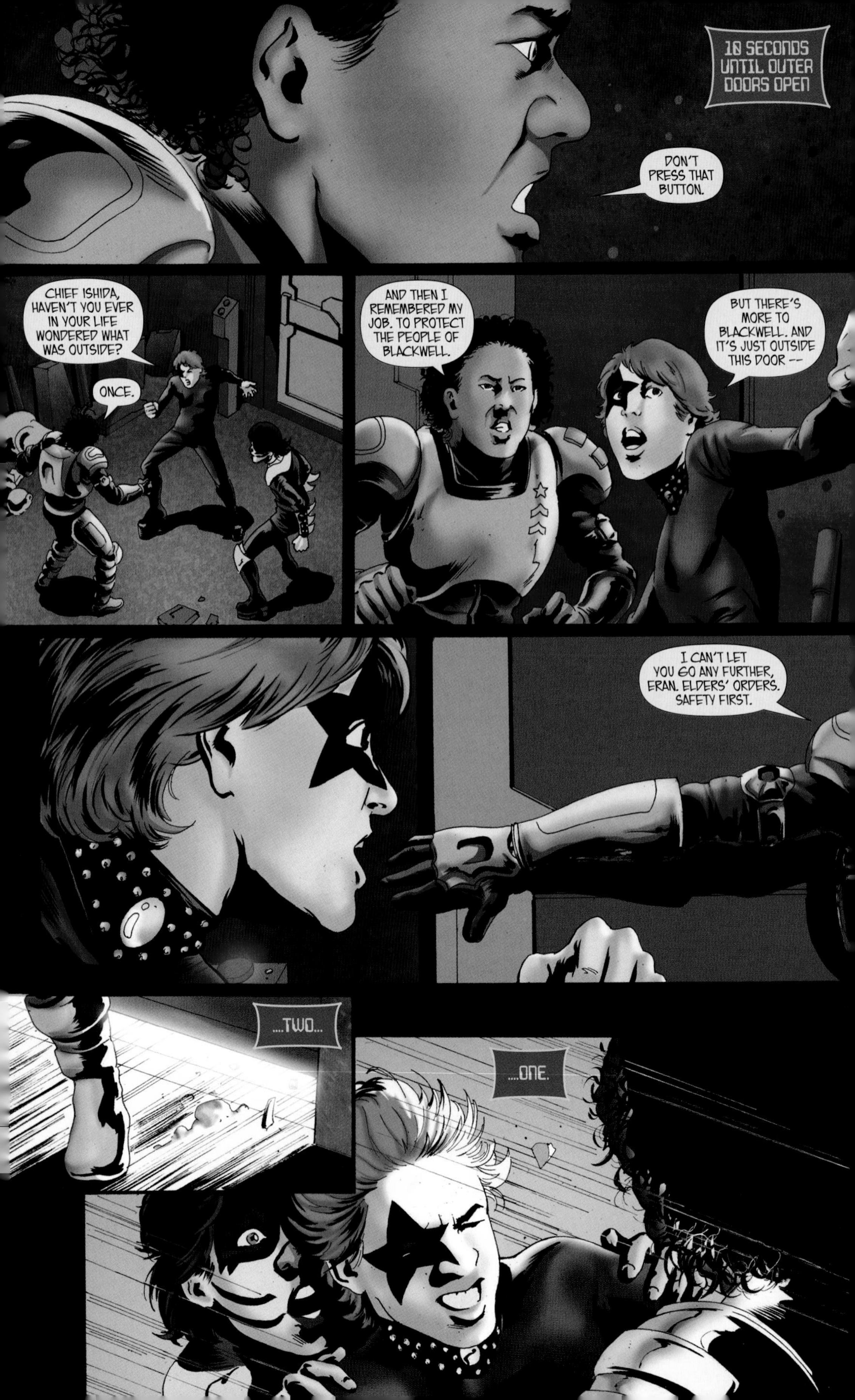
10 SECONDS UNTIL OUTER DOORS OPEN
DON'T PRESS THAT BUTTON.
CHIEF ISHIDA, HAVEN'T YOU EVER IN YOUR LIFE WONDERED WHAT WAS OUTSIDE?
ONCE.
AND THEN I REMEMBERED MY JOB. TO PROTECT THE PEOPLE OF BLACKWELL.
BUT THERE'S MORE TO BLACKWELL. AND IT'S JUST OUTSIDE THIS DOOR --
I CAN'T LET YOU GO ANY FURTHER, ERAN. ELDERS' ORDERS. SAFETY FIRST.
....TWO...
....ONE.

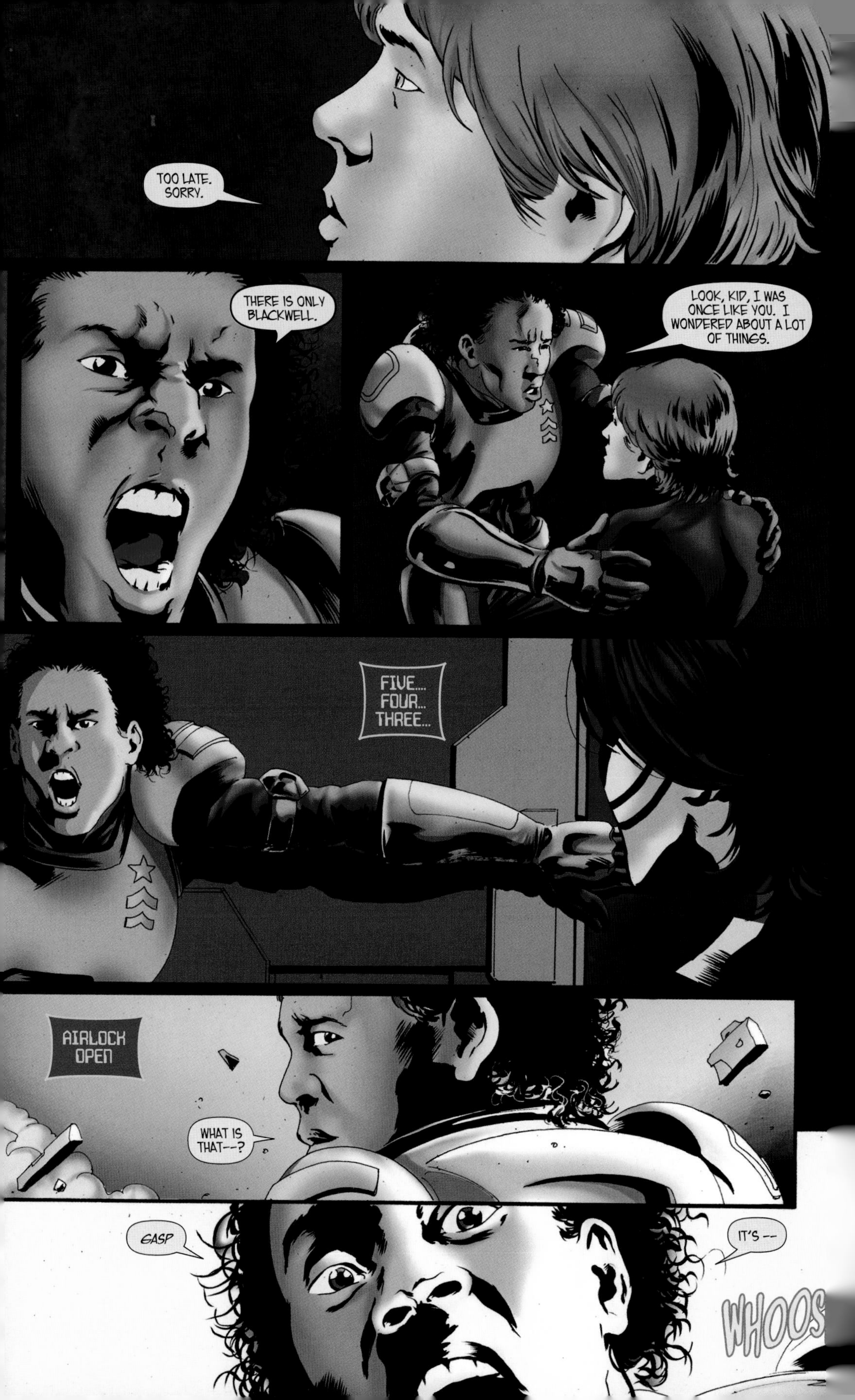

TOO LATE. SORRY.
THERE IS ONLY BLACKWELL.
LOOK, KID, I WAS ONCE LIKE YOU. I WONDERED ABOUT A LOT OF THINGS.
FIVE... FOUR... THREE...
AIRLOCK OPEN
WHAT IS THAT--?
GASP
IT'S --
WHOOS

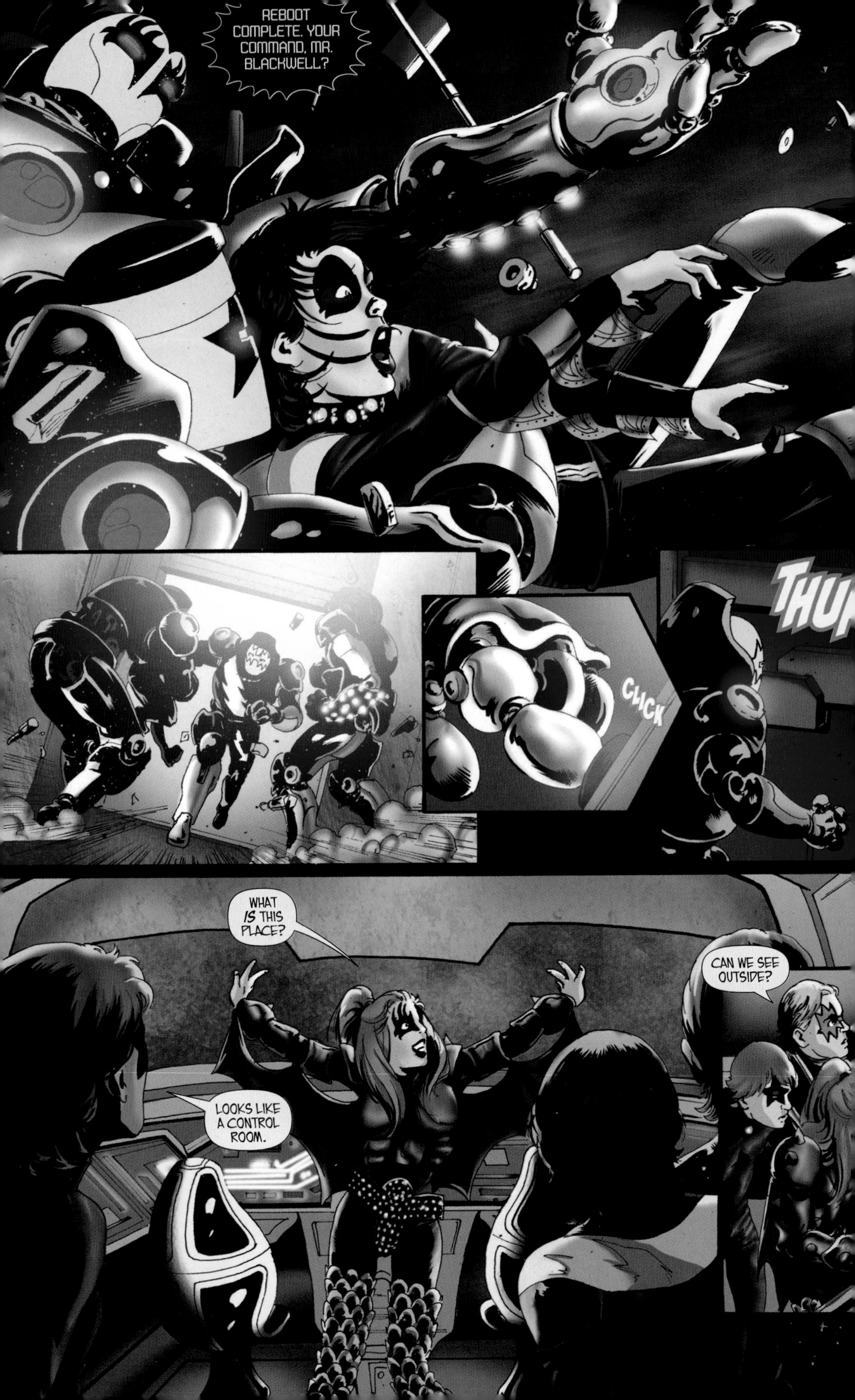
REBOOT COMPLETE. YOUR COMMAND, MR. BLACKWELL?
THUP
CLICK
WHAT IS THIS PLACE?
LOOKS LIKE A CONTROL ROOM.
CAN WE SEE OUTSIDE?

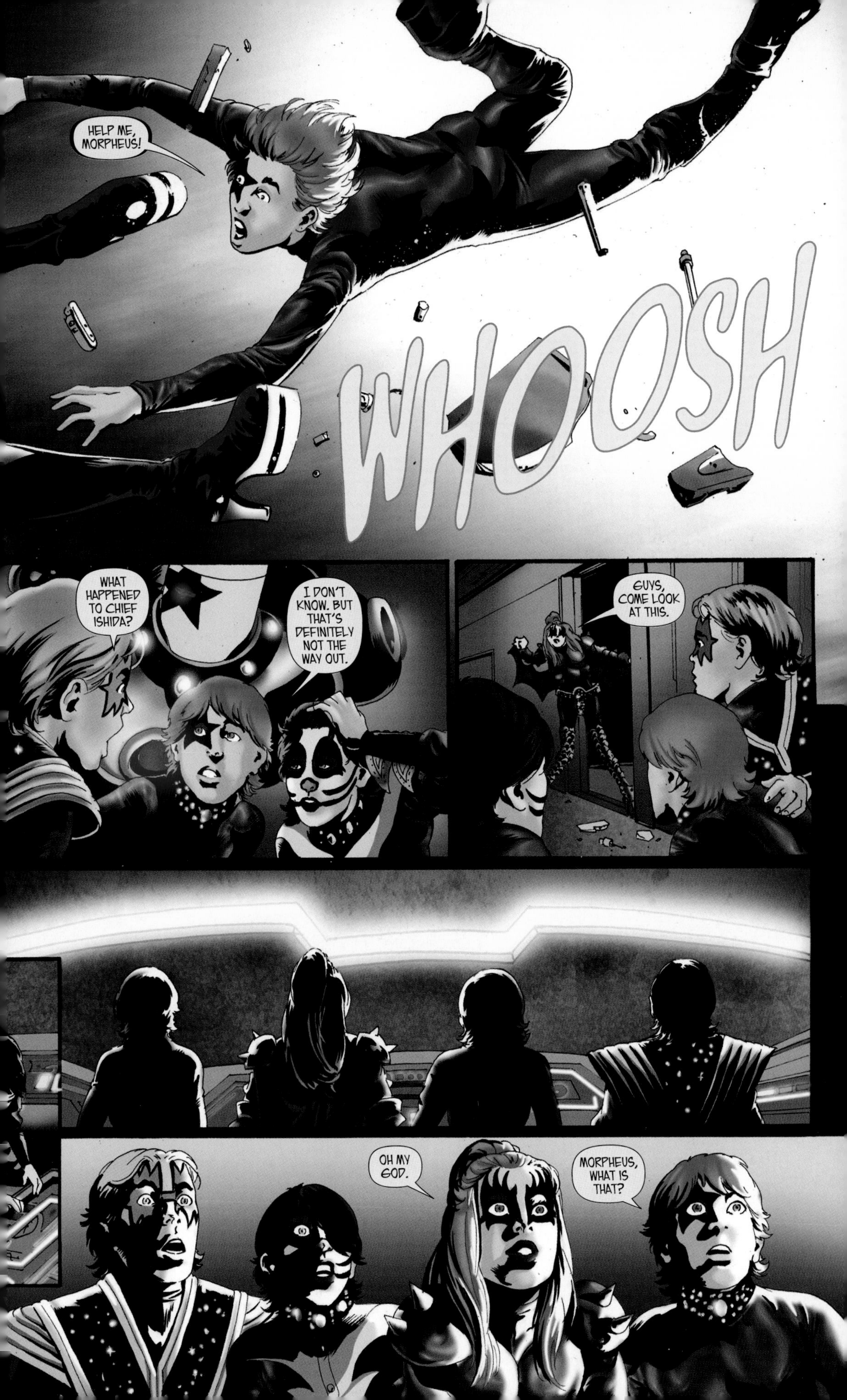
HELP ME, MORPHEUS!
WHOOSH
WHAT HAPPENED TO CHIEF ISHIDA?
I DON'T KNOW. BUT THAT'S DEFINITELY NOT THE WAY OUT.
GUYS, COME LOOK AT THIS.
OH MY GOD.
MORPHEUS, WHAT IS THAT?

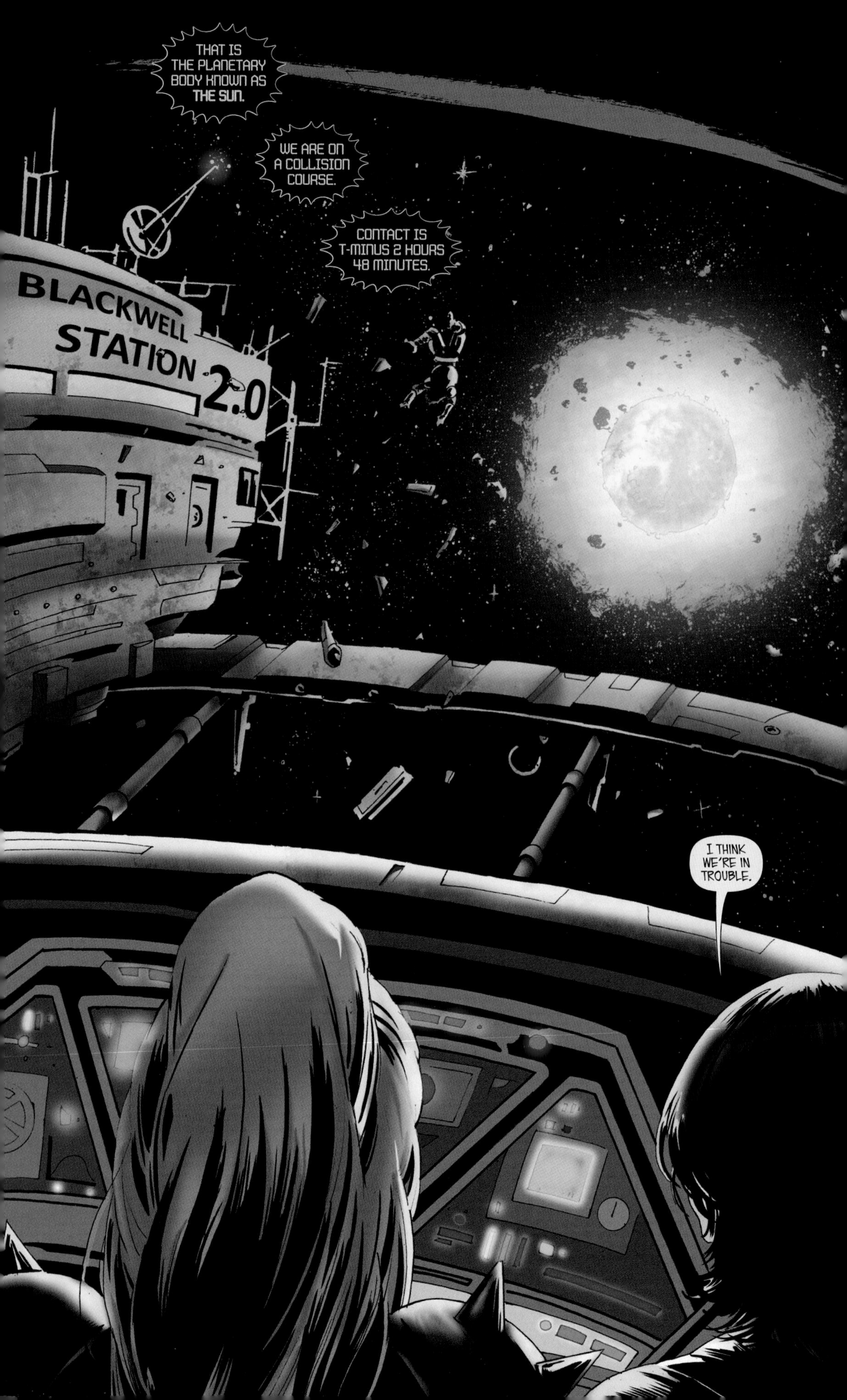
THAT IS THE PLANETARY BODY KNOWN AS THE SUN.
WE ARE ON A COLLISION COURSE.
CONTACT IS T-MINUS 2 HOURS 48 MINUTES.
BLACKWELL STATION 2.0
I THINK WE'RE IN TROUBLE.

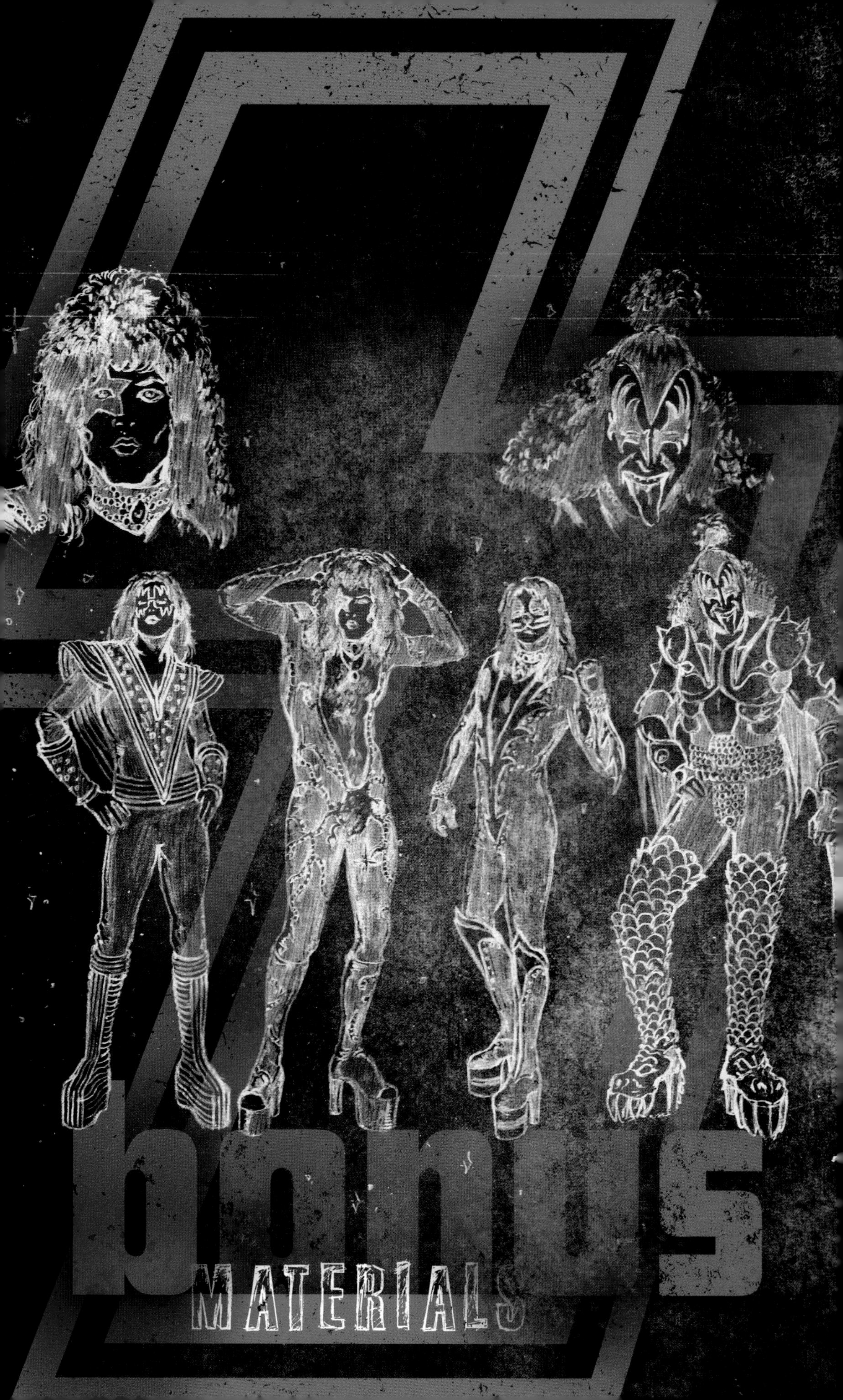
bonus
MATERIALS

KISS COMICS!!
WOW.
I'M A FANBOY!
Always have been one —
since 1958, when I first came
to America and beheld the BRAVE
AND THE BOLD! TOR! THE ATOM!
THE FLASH! AND Atlas Comics and
then, of course MARVEL!
KISS has had a 4 decade
long proud history in Comics!
AND NOW WITH THE DYNAMIC
Team, WE will Go where NO
band has gone before.
I CAN'T WAIT!

GENE SIMMONS

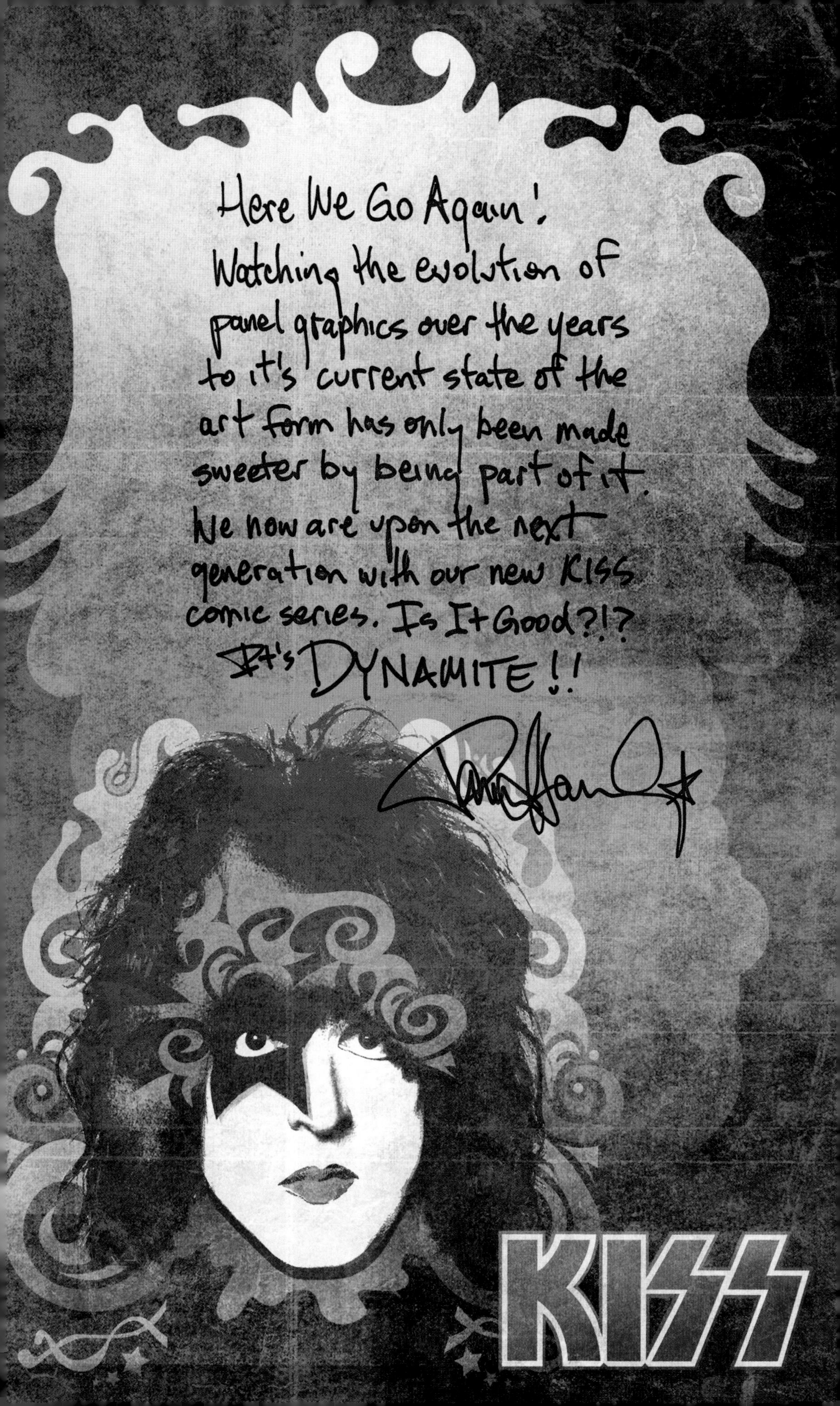
Here We Go Again!
Watching the evolution of
panel graphics over the years
to it's current state of the
art form has only been made
sweeter by being part of it.
We now are upon the next
generation with our new KISS
comic series. Is It Good?!?
It's DYNAMITE!!
KISS

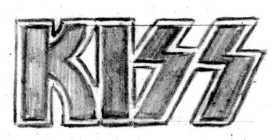

KISS CHARACTER DESIGN

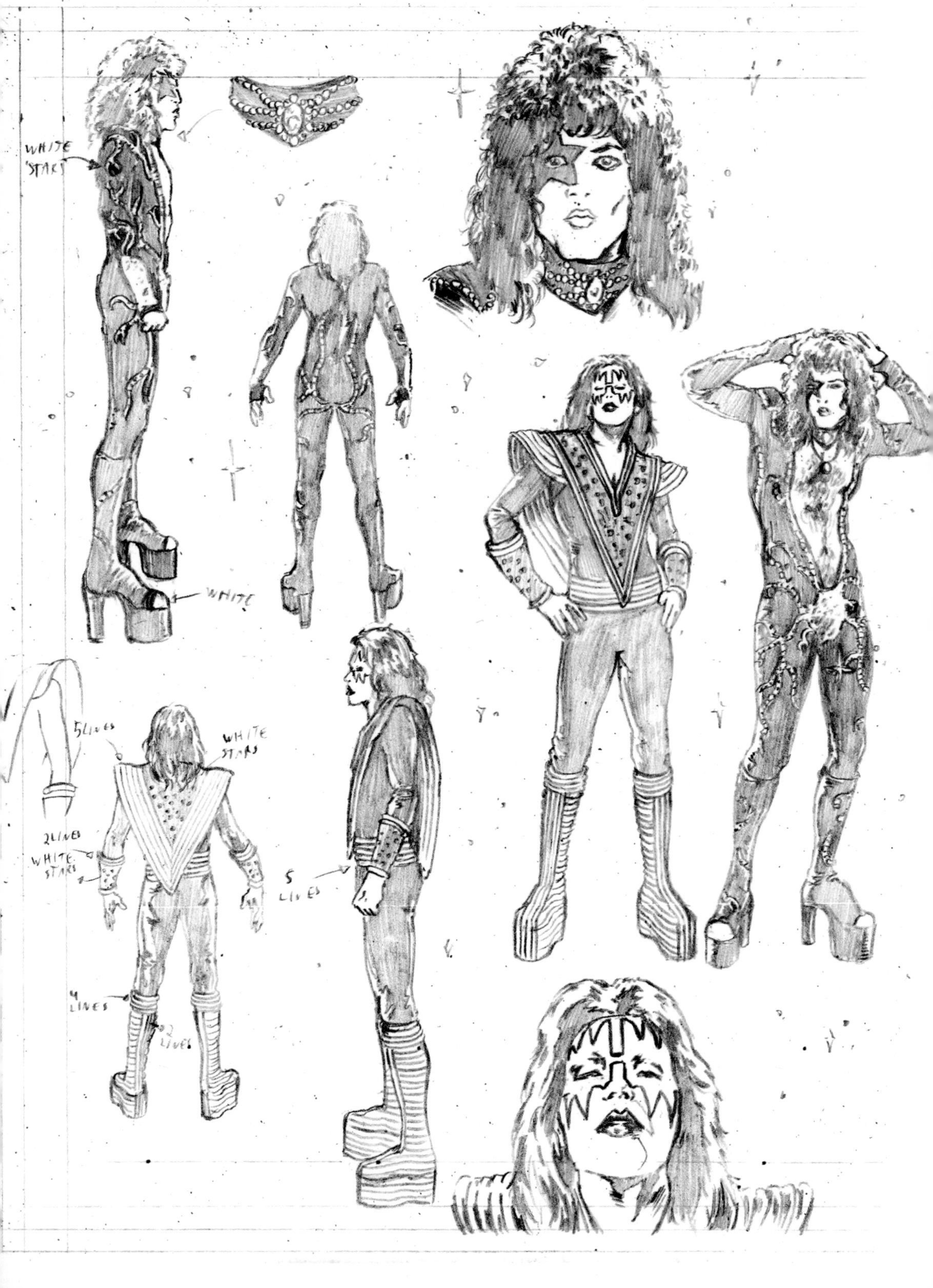

WHITE 'STARS'
WHITE
5 LINES
WHITE STARS
2 LINES
WHITE STARS
5 LINES
4 LINES
2 LINES

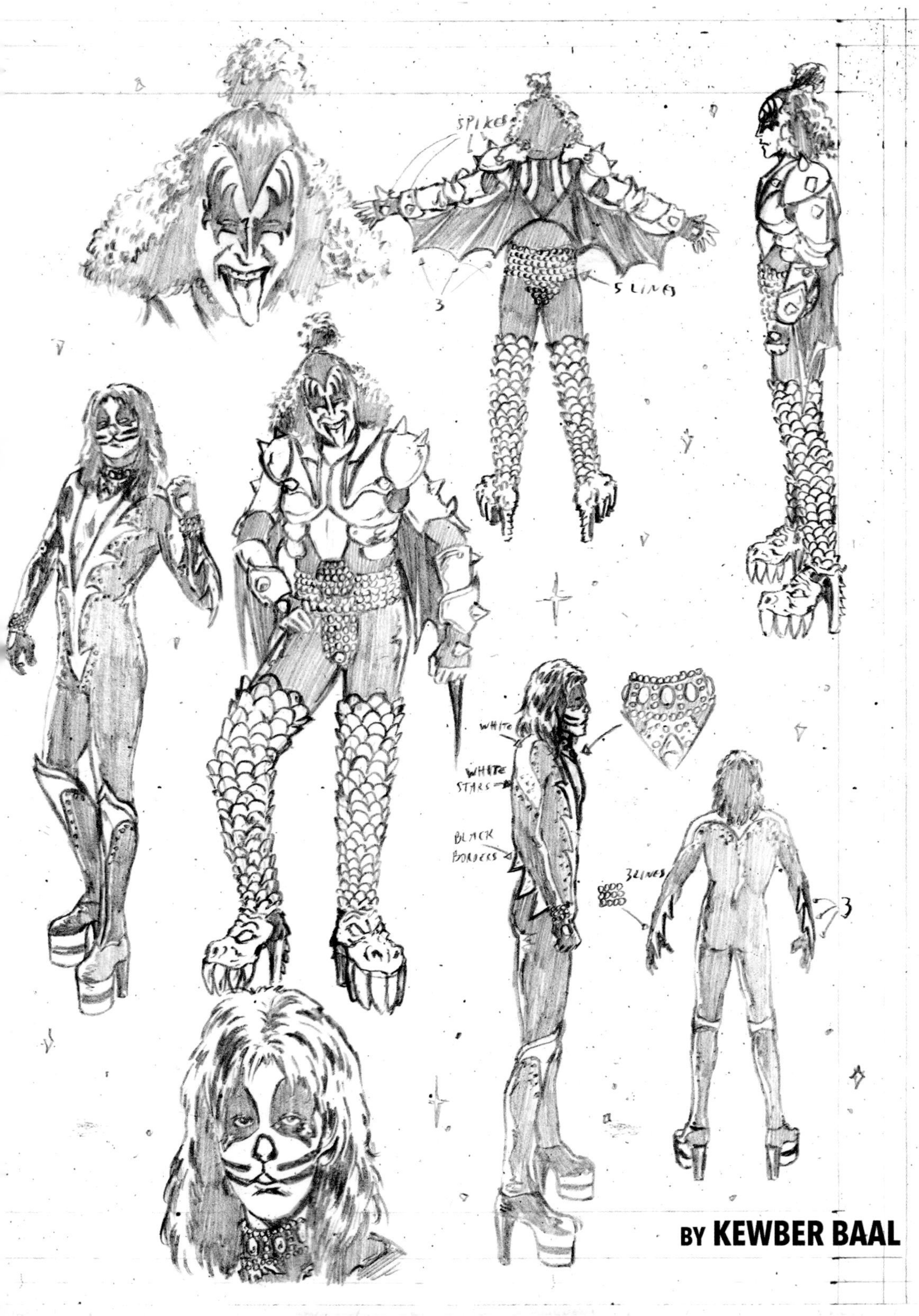
SPIKES
3
5 LINES
WHITE
WHITE STARS
BLACK BORDERS
3 LINES
3

BY KEWBER BAAL

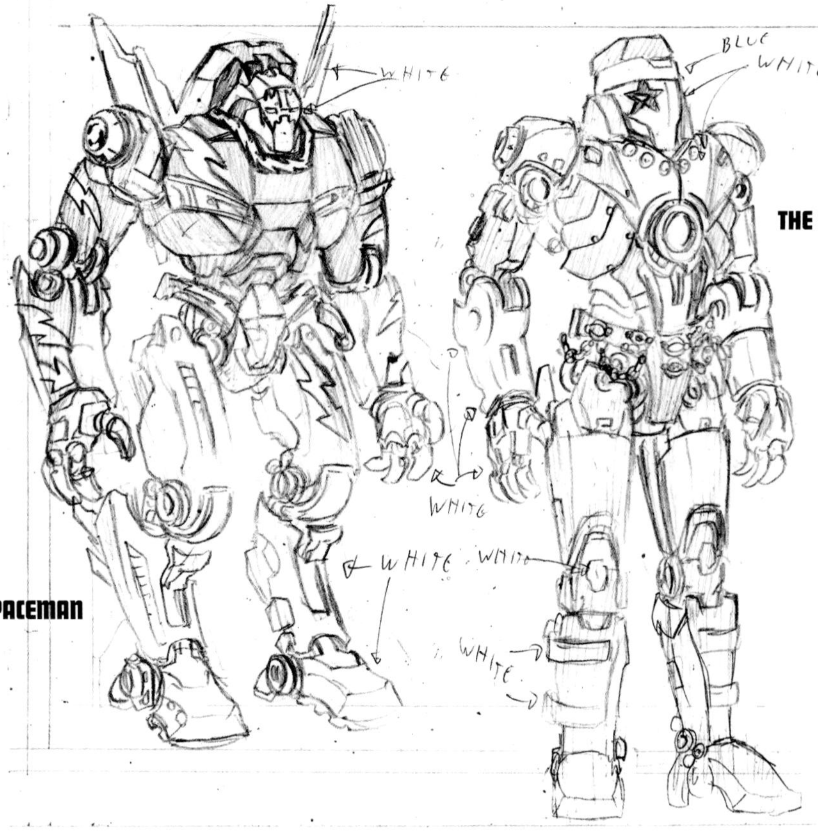
WHITE
BLUE
WHITE
WHITE
WHITE
WHITE
WHITE

THE SPACEMAN

THE STARCHILD

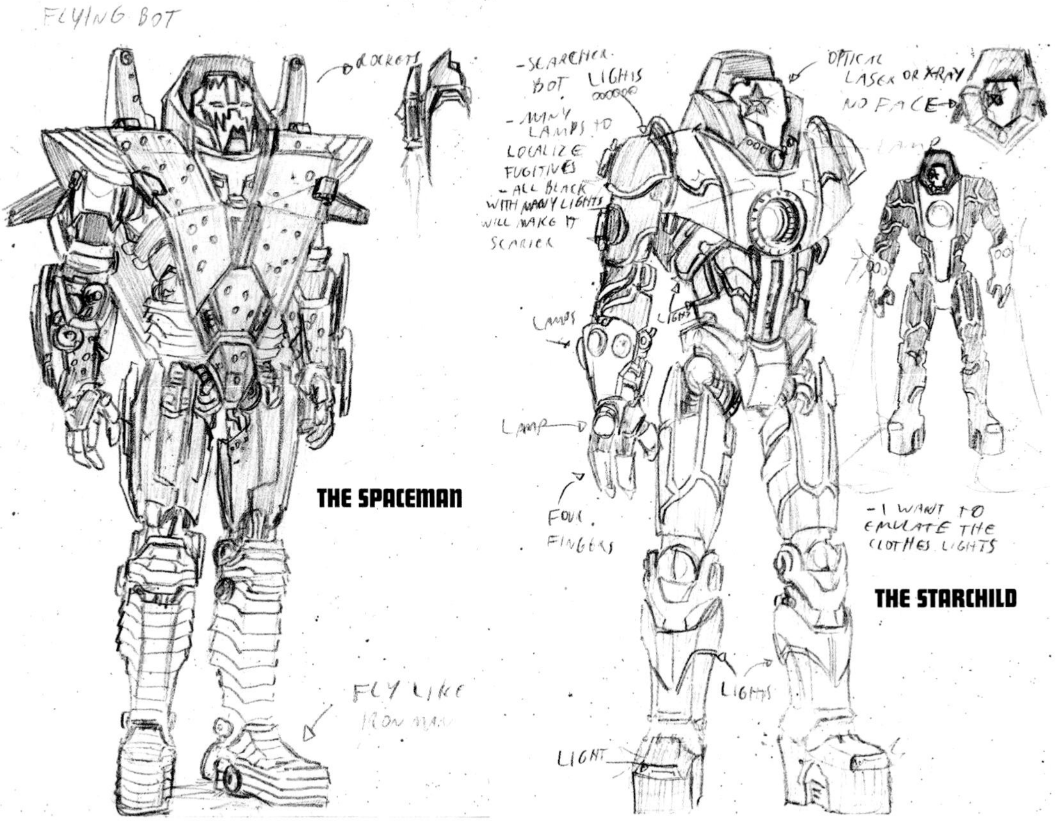
FLYING BOT
ROCKETS
-SEARCHER BOT
LIGHTS
-MANY LAMPS TO LOCALIZE FUGITIVES
-ALL BLACK WITH MANY LIGHTS WILL MAKE IT SCARIER
OPTICAL LASER OR XRAY
NO FACE
LAMP
LIGHTS
LAMPS
LAMP
FOUR FINGERS
-I WANT TO EMULATE THE CLOTHES LIGHTS
LIGHTS
LIGHT
FLY LIKE IRON MAN

THE SPACEMAN

THE STARCHILD

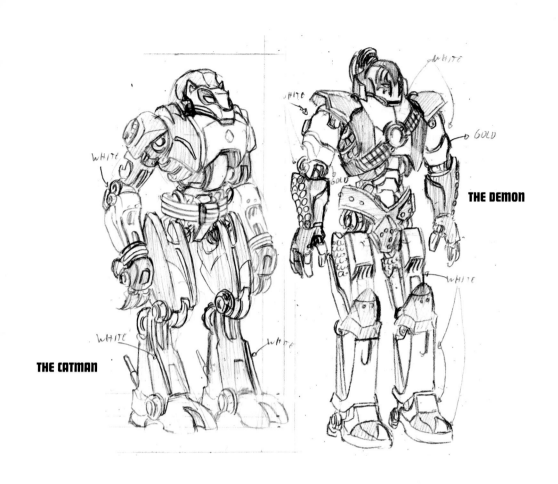

THE CATMAN

WHITE

WHITE

WHITE

WHITE

THE DEMON

WHITE

WHITE

GOLD

GOLD

WHITE

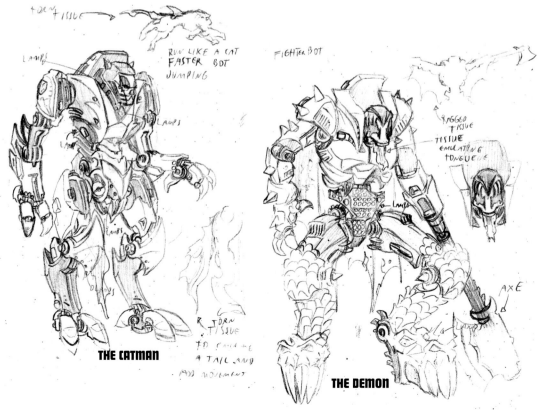

TORN TISSUE

RUN LIKE A CAT
FASTER BOT
JUMPING

LAMPS

LAMPS

LAMPS

LAMPS

LAMPS

FIGHTER BOT

RAGGED
TISSUE

TISSUE
EMULATING
TONGUE

AXE

LAMPS

THE CATMAN

R TORN
TISSUE
TO SIMULATE
A TAIL AND
ADD MOVEMENT

THE DEMON

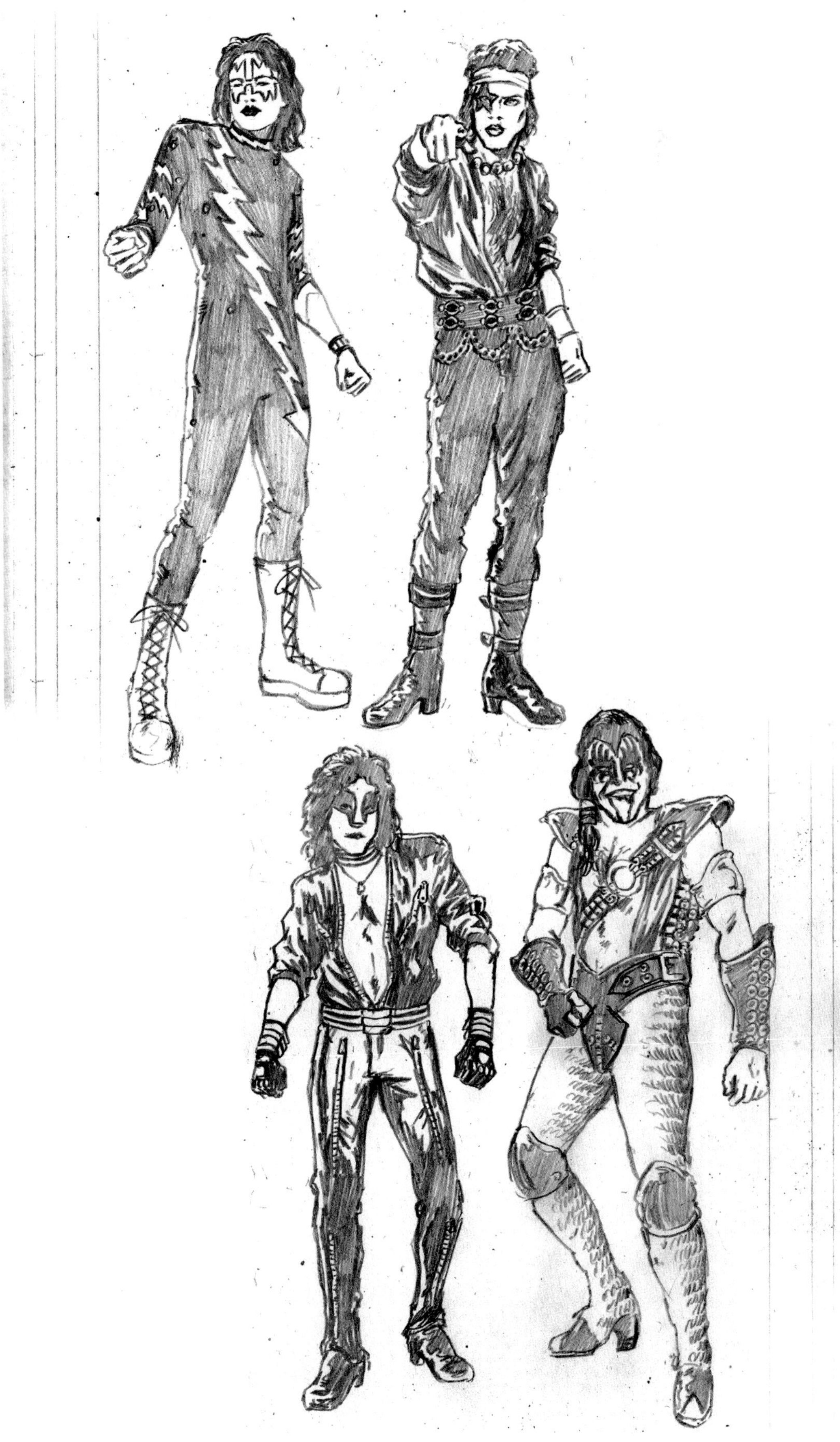

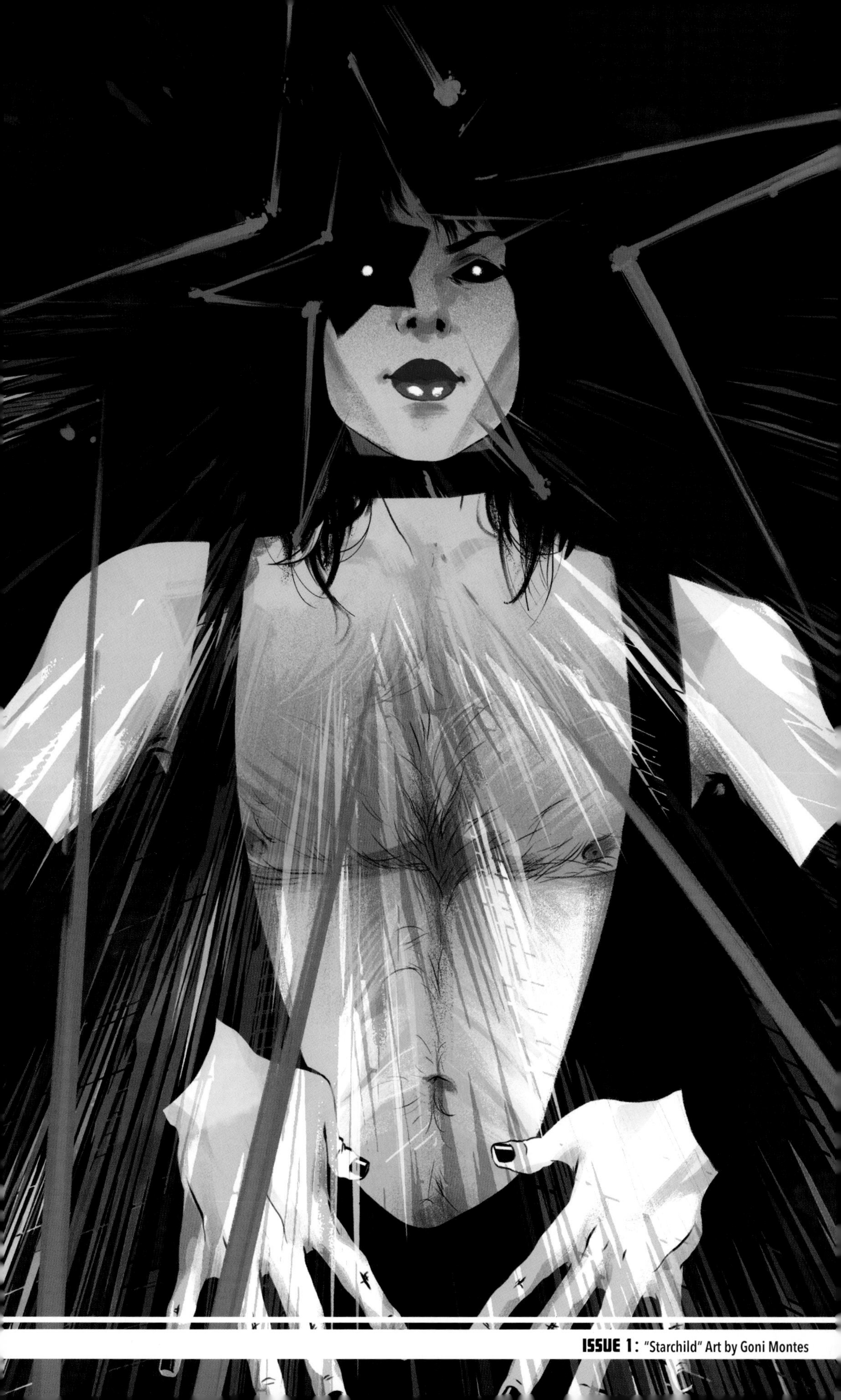

ISSUE 1: "Starchild" Art by Goni Montes

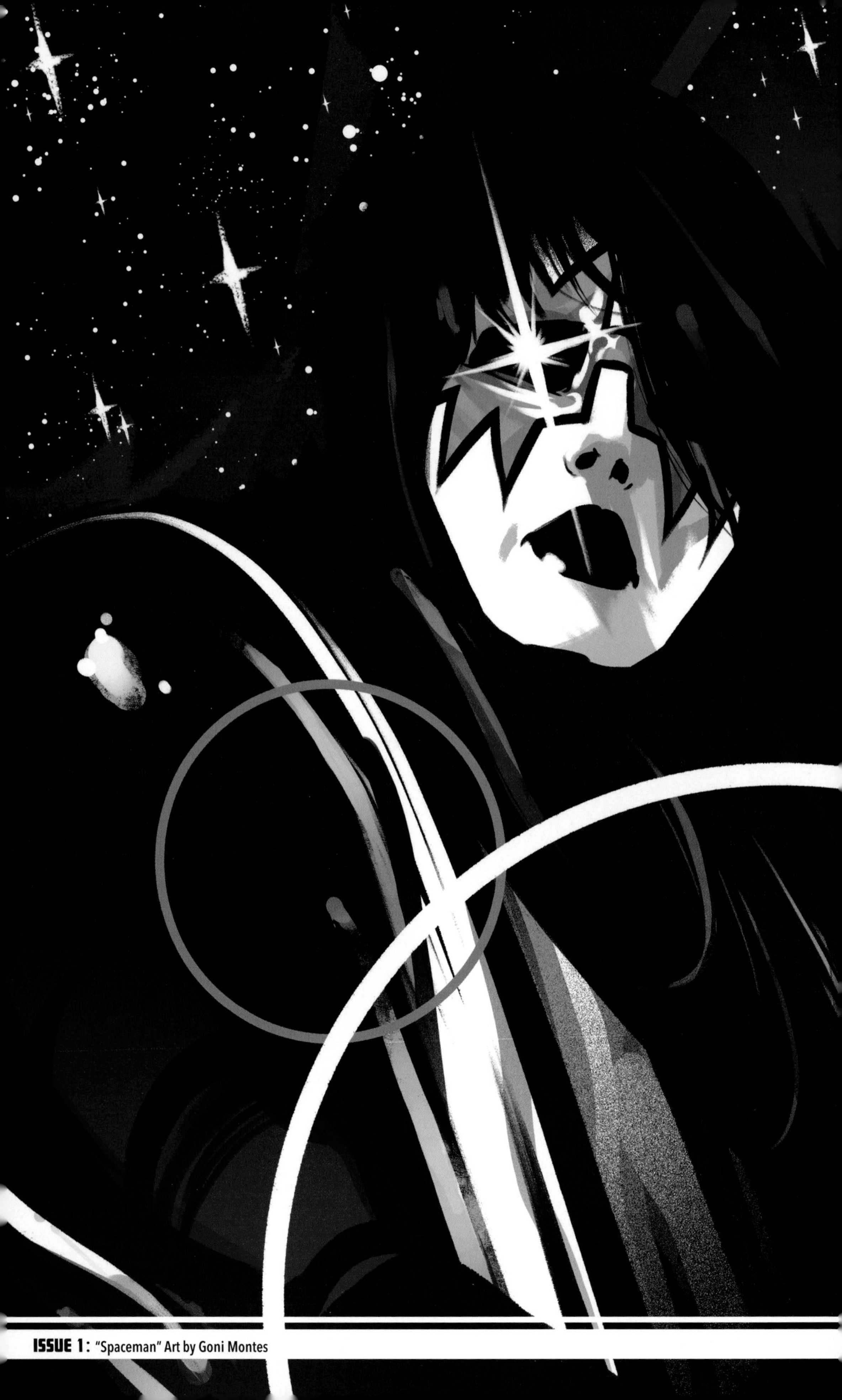

ISSUE 1: "Spaceman" Art by Goni Montes

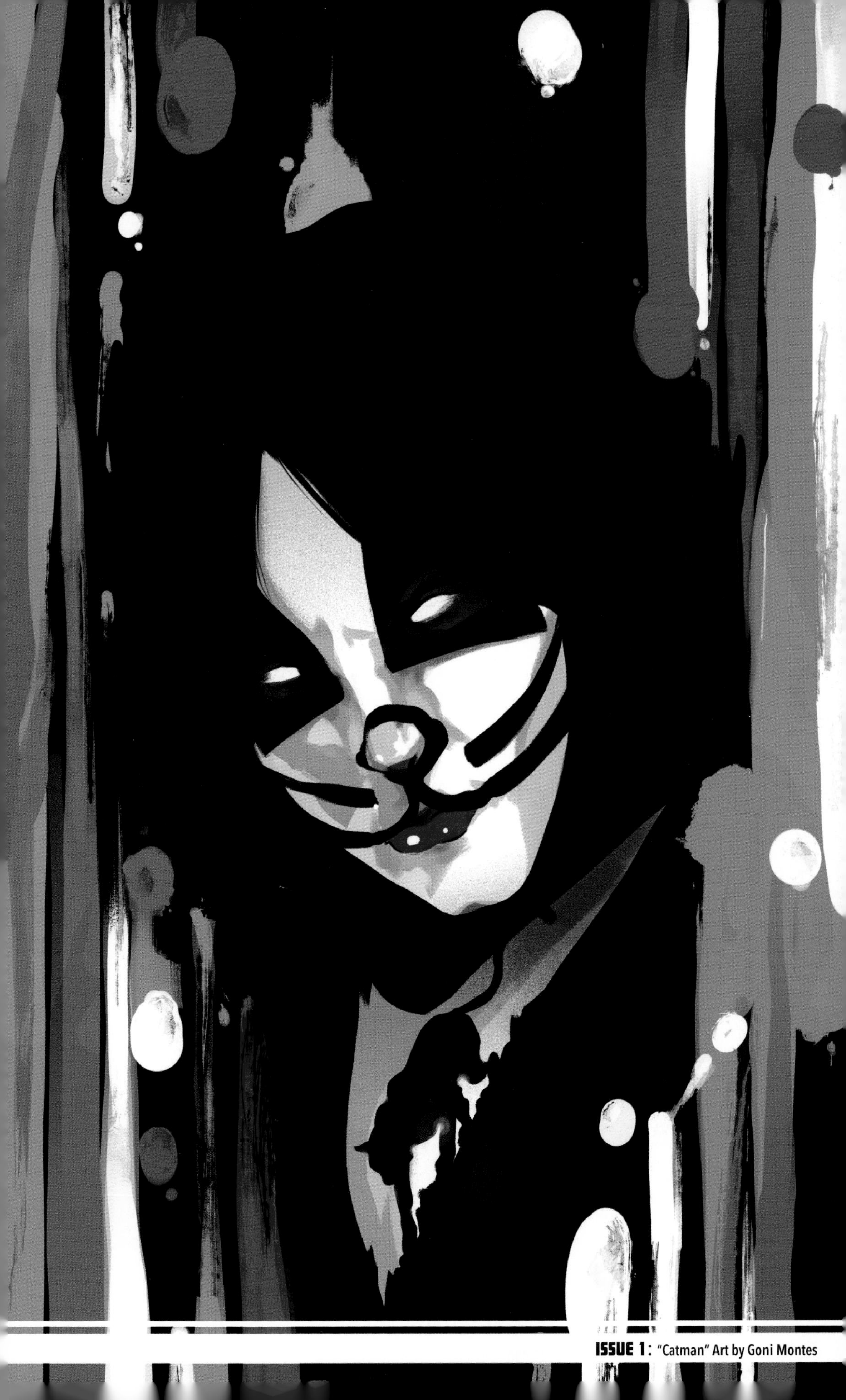

ISSUE 1: "Catman" Art by Goni Montes

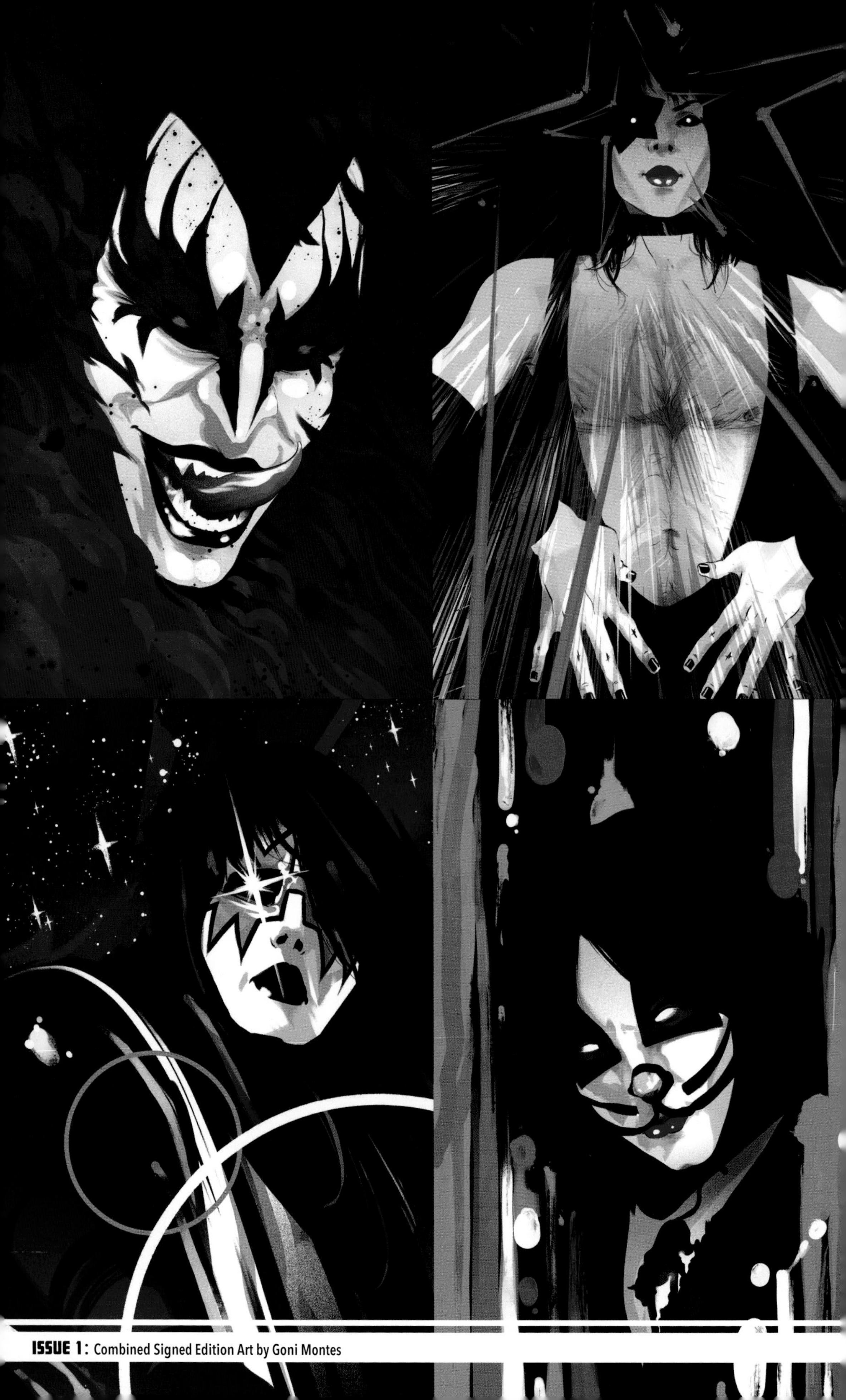

ISSUE 1: Combined Signed Edition Art by Goni Montes

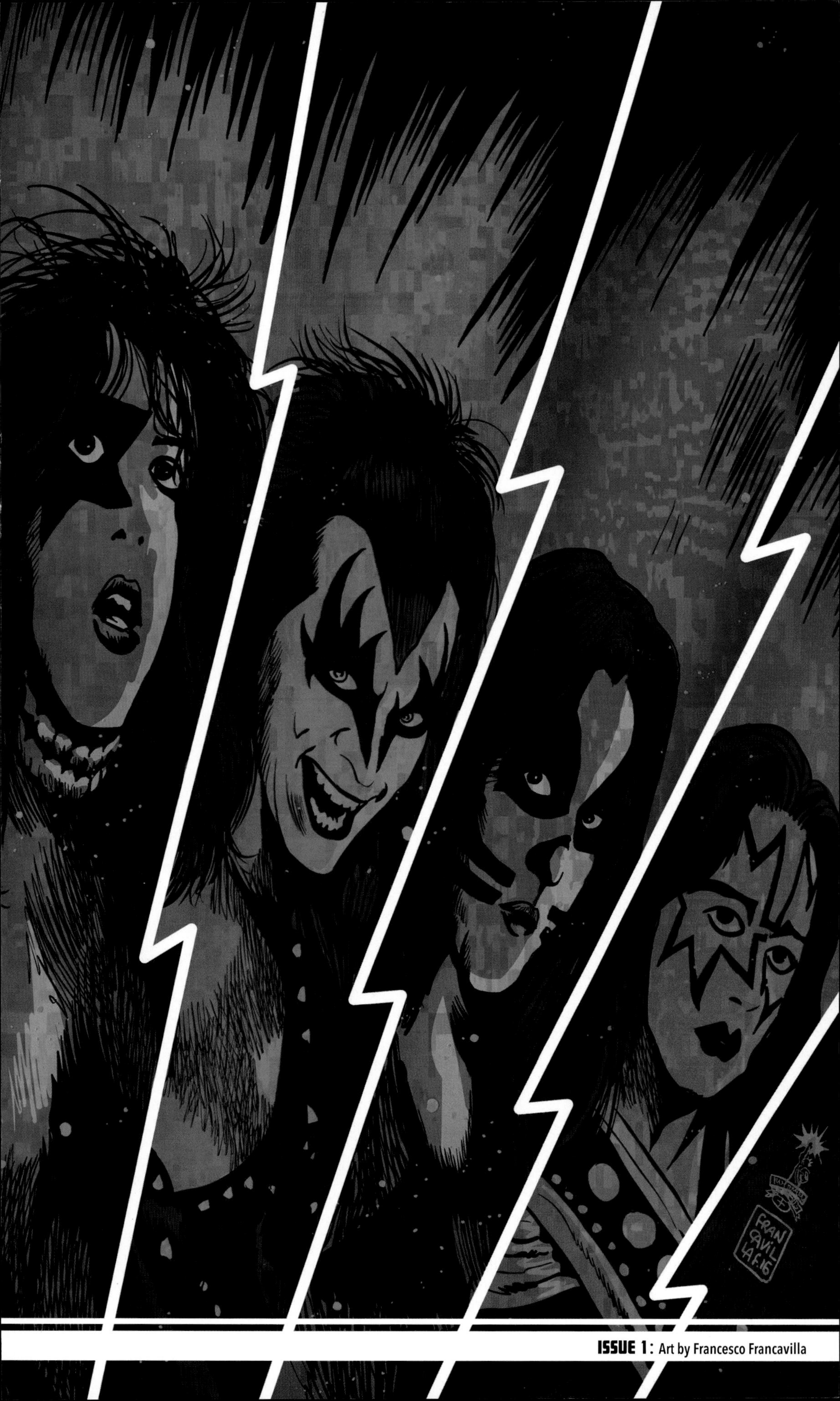
FRAN
CAVIL
LA F. 16

ISSUE 1: Art by Francesco Francavilla

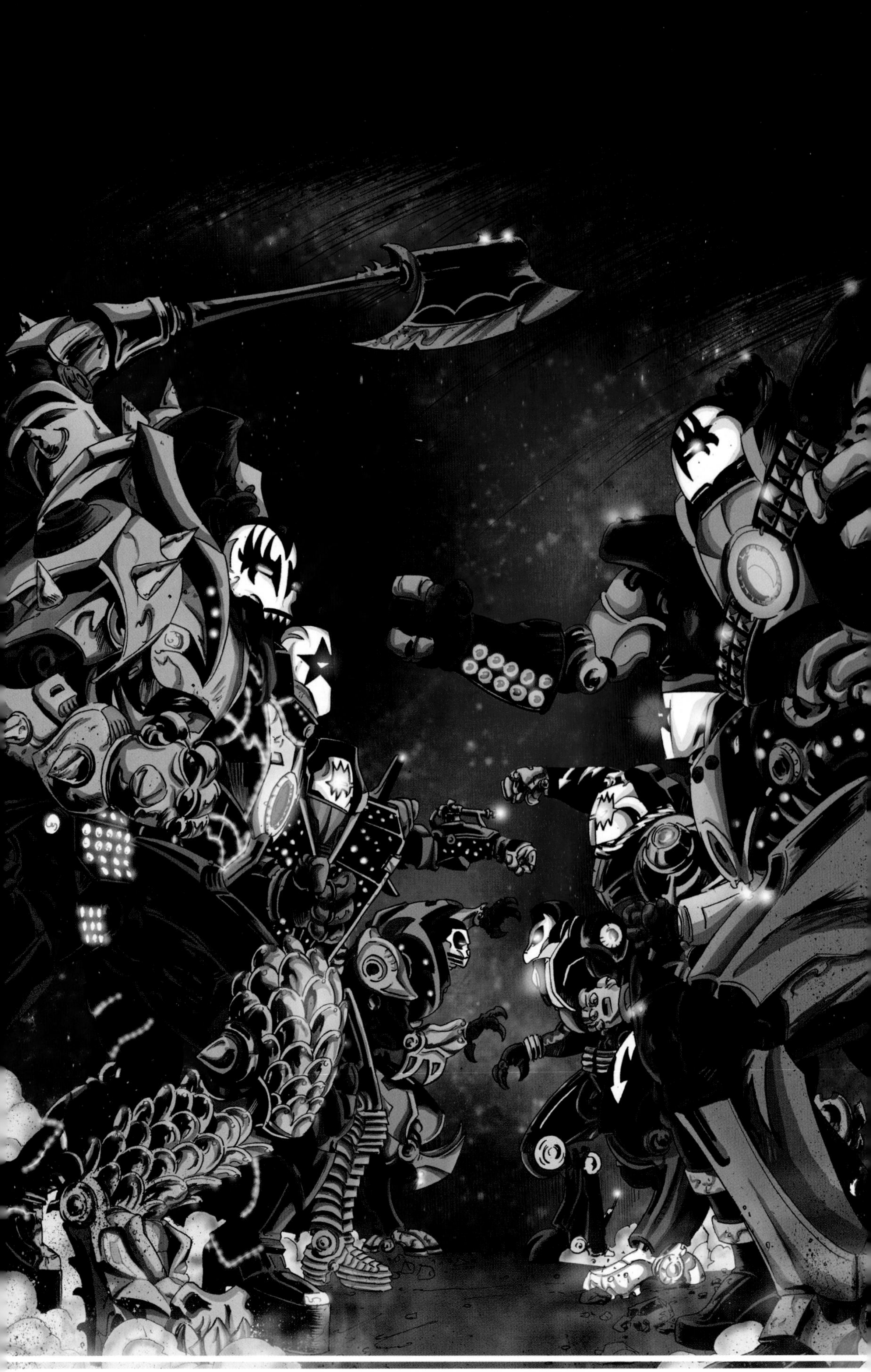

ISSUE 1: Art by Kewber Baal & Schimerys Baal

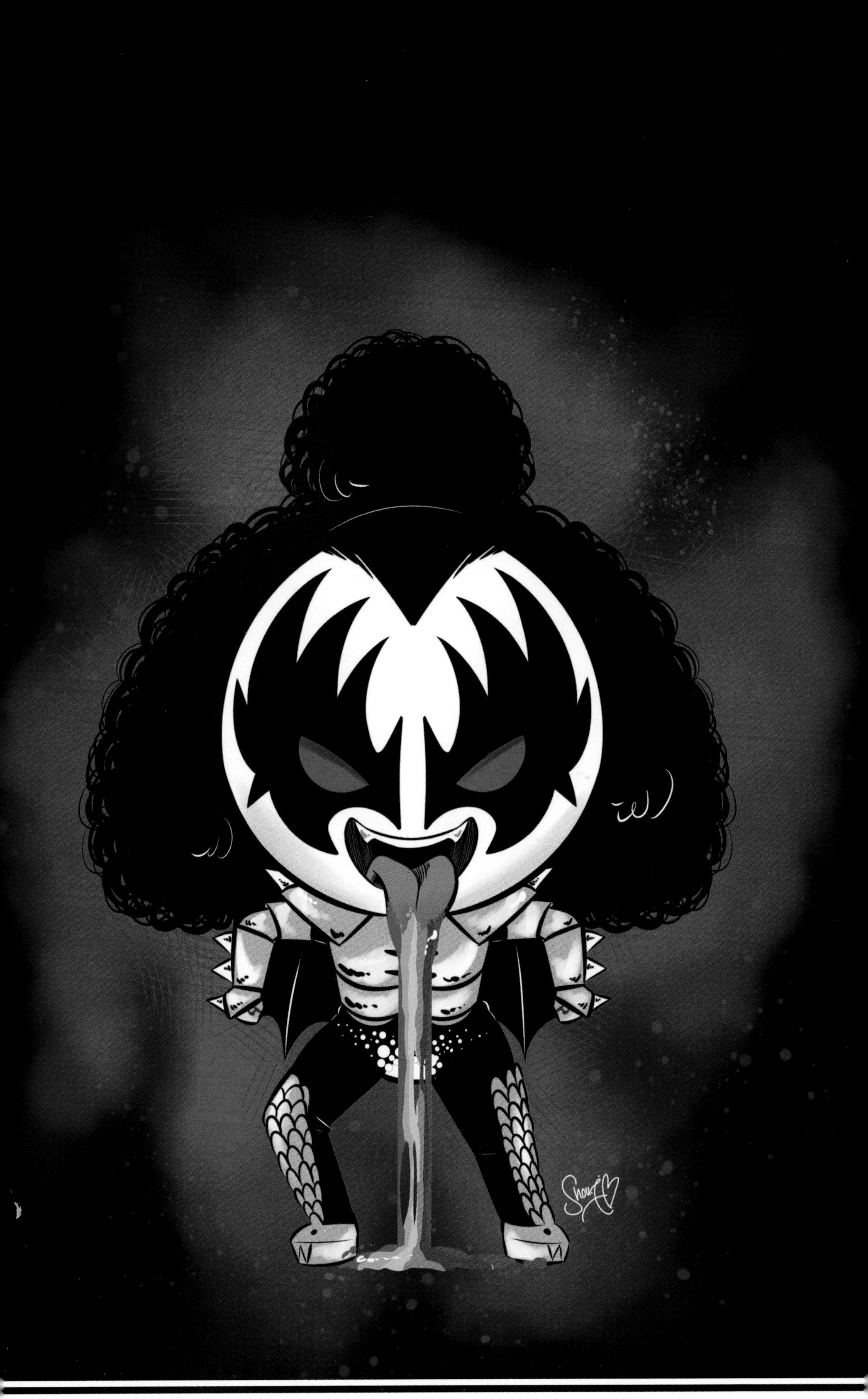
Shouri

ISSUE 1: "Demon Emoji" Art by Shouri

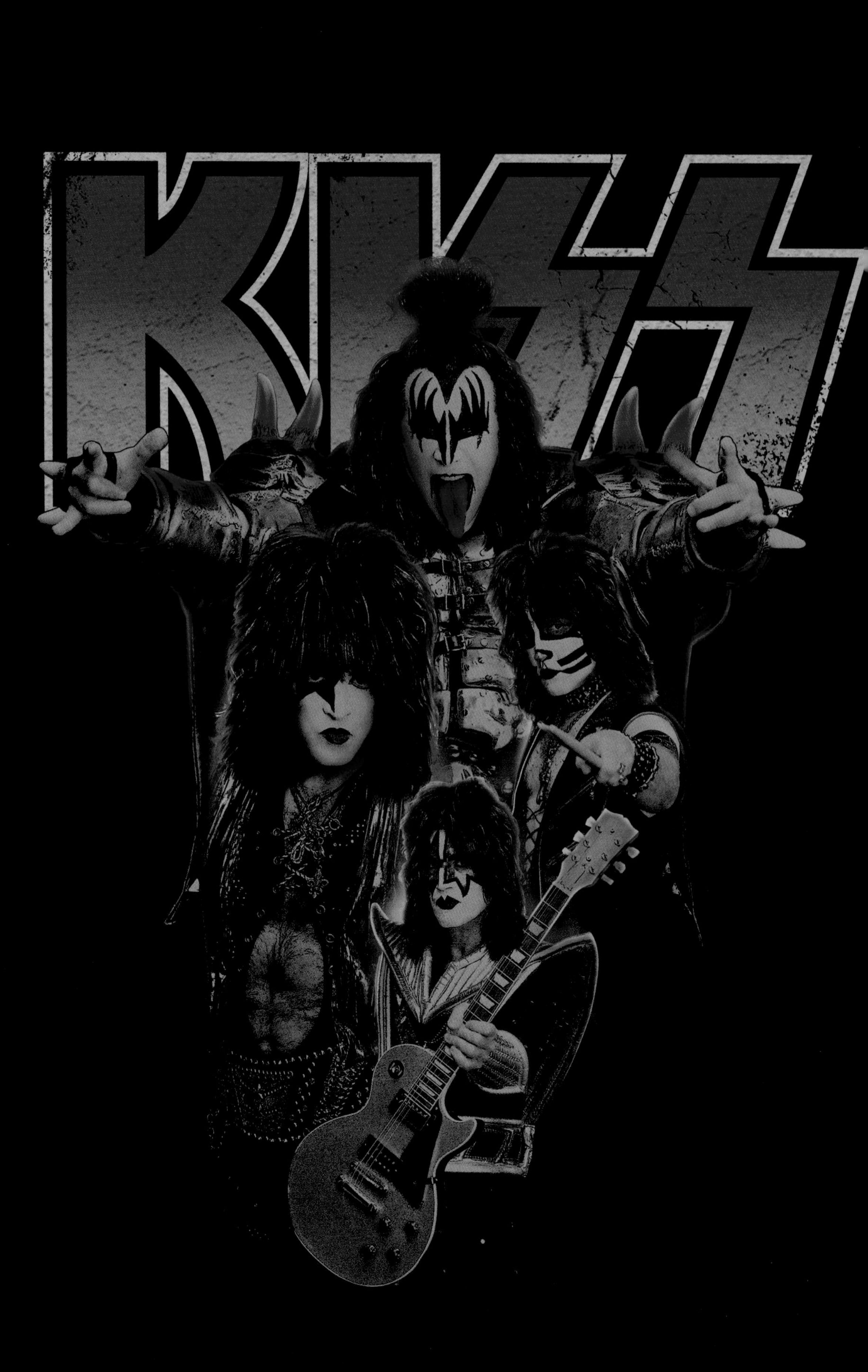
KISS

ISSUE 1: Photo Variant Cover

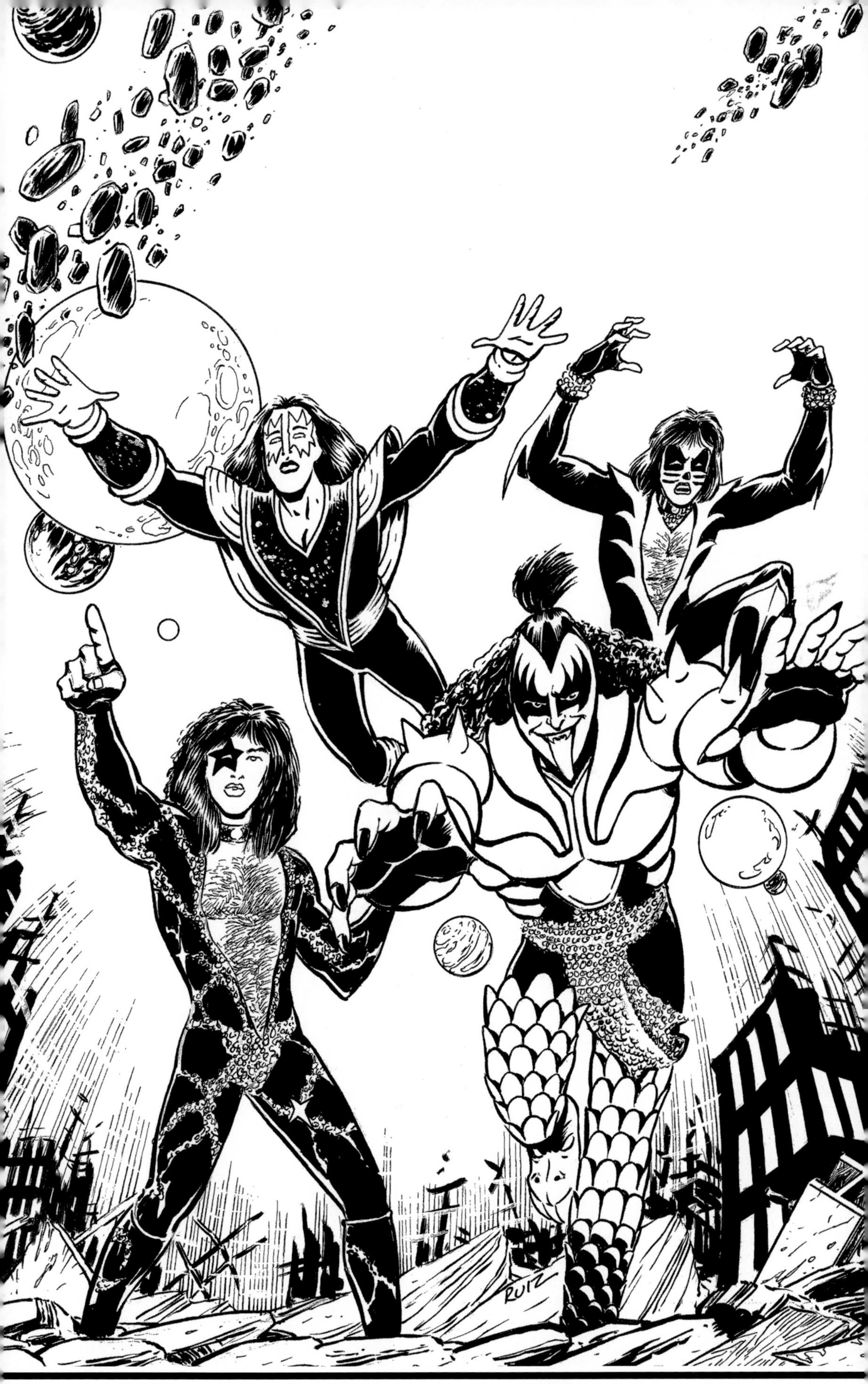
RUIZ

ISSUE 1: Coloring Book Cover Art by Fernando Ruiz

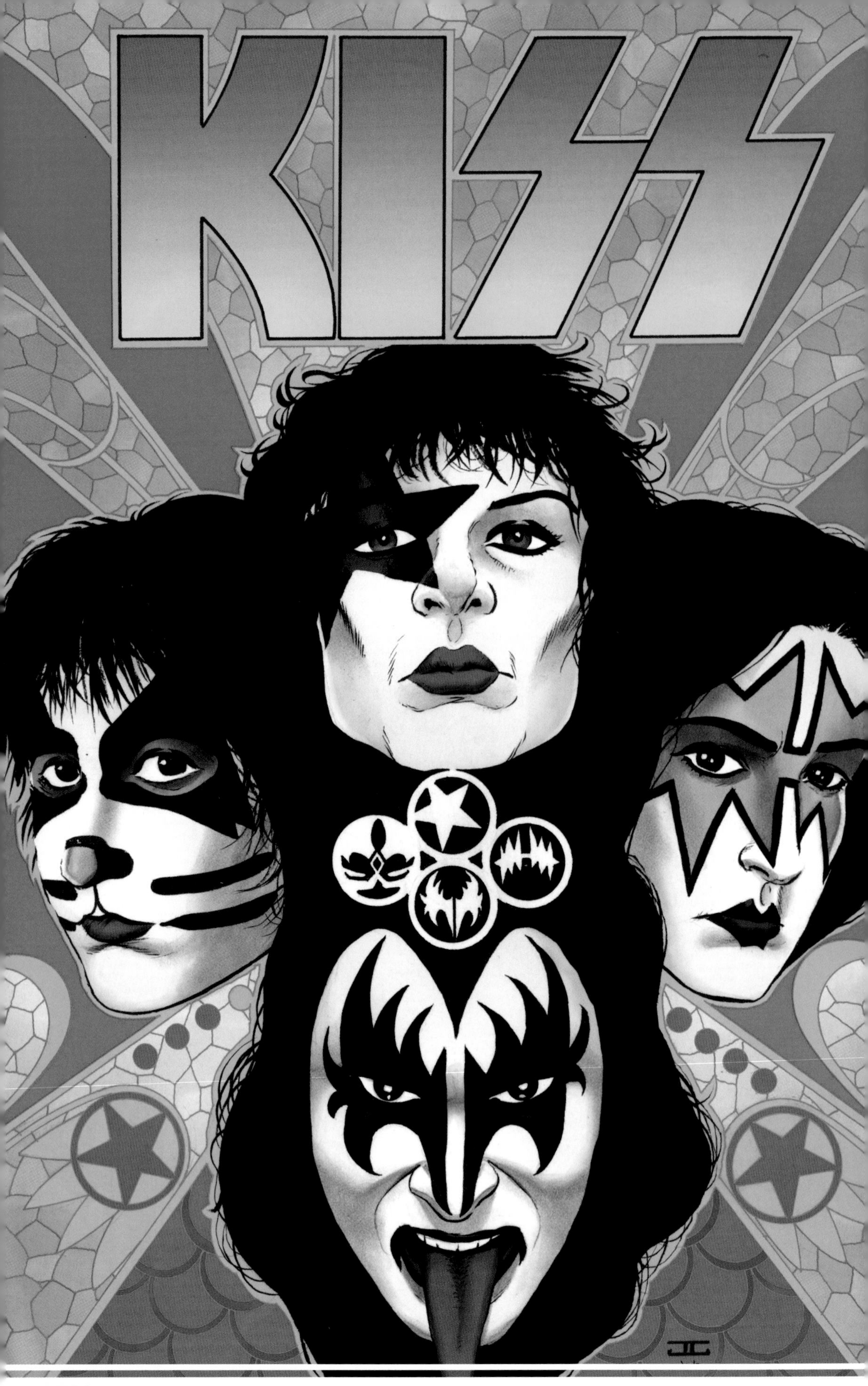
KISS

ISSUE 1: KISS Army Limited Edition Variant Cover Art by John Cassaday & June Chung

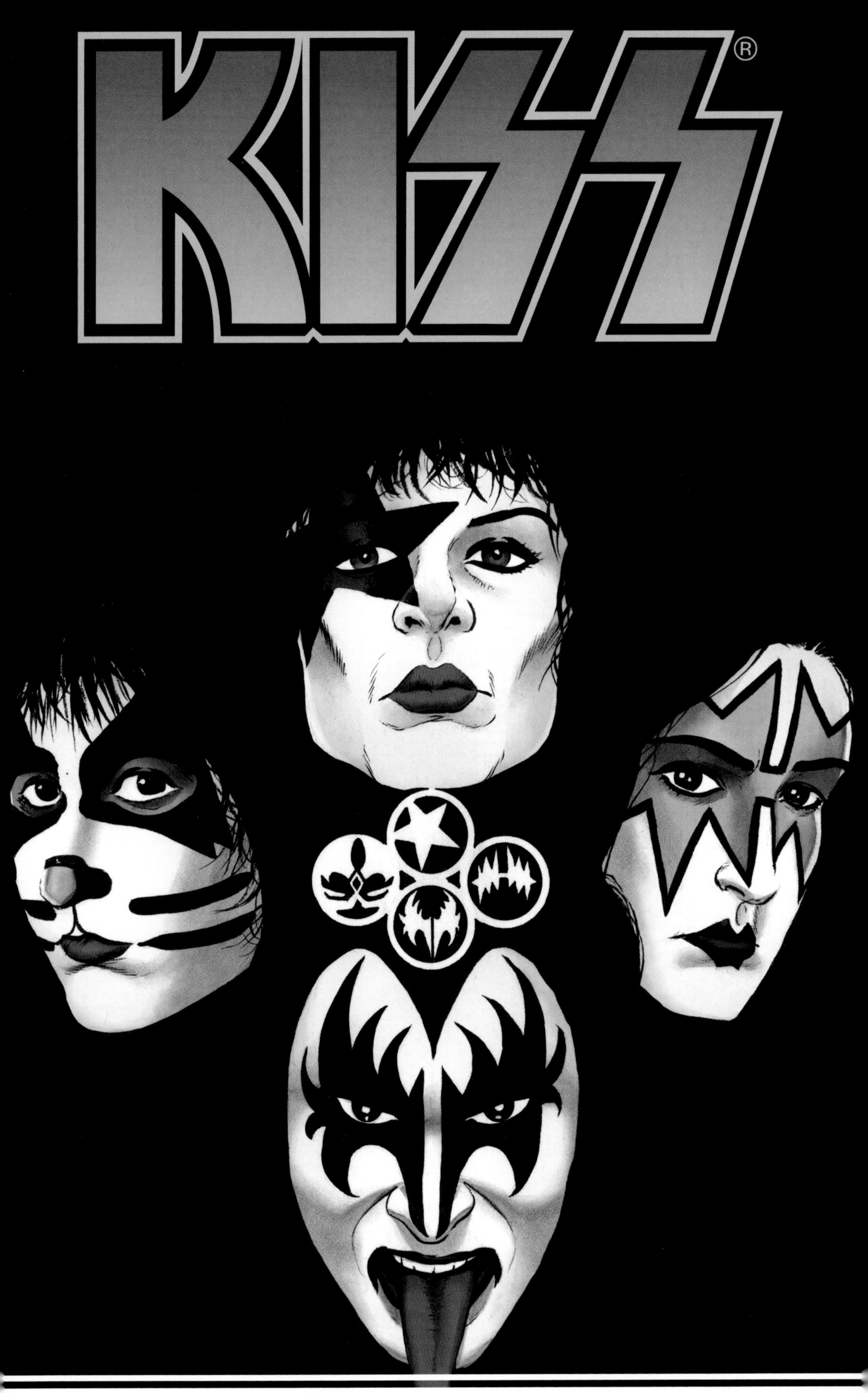
KISS®

ISSUE 1: KISS Army Limited Edition "Black" Variant Cover Art by John Cassaday & June Chung

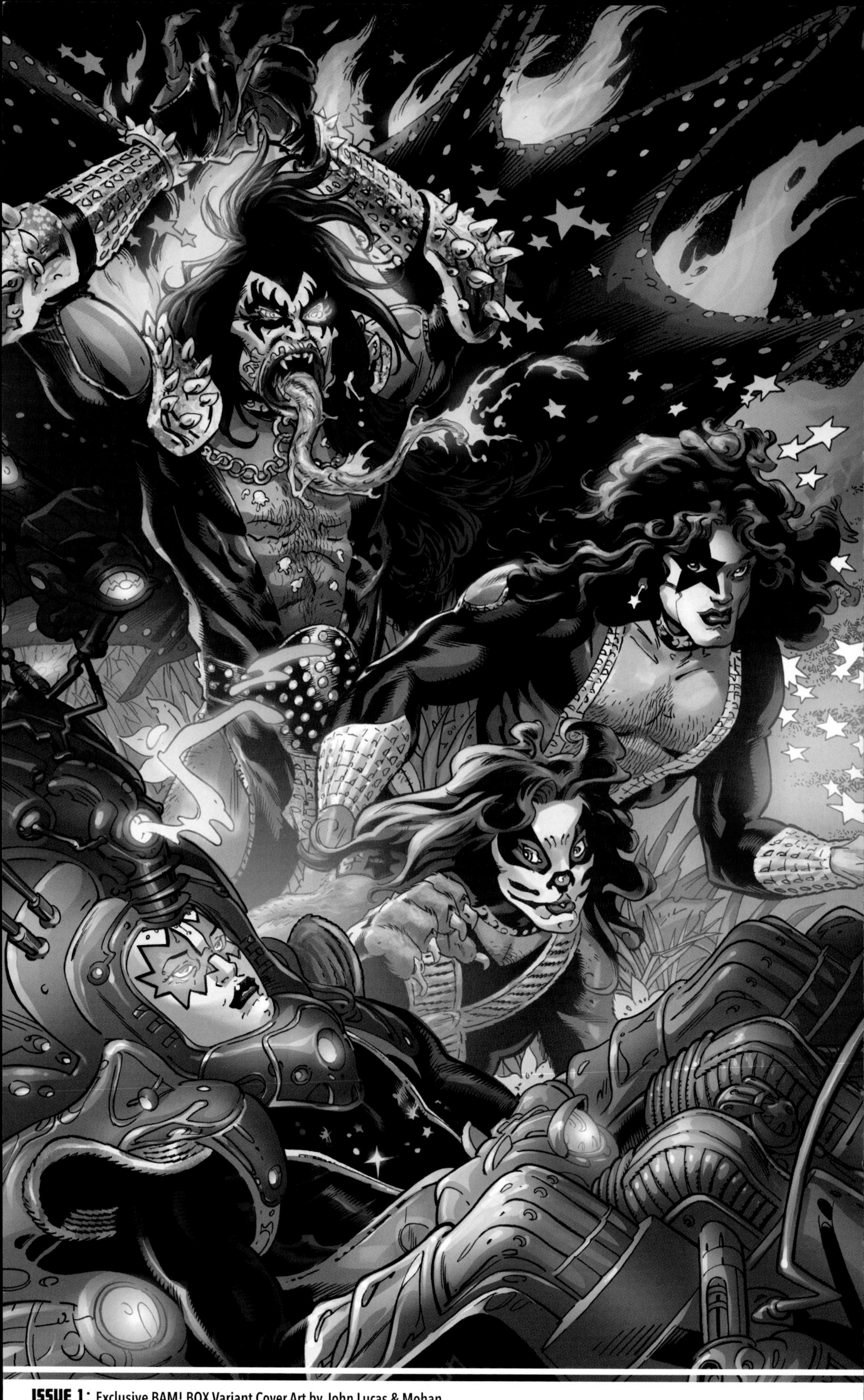

ISSUE 1: Exclusive BAM! BOX Variant Cover Art by John Lucas & Mohan

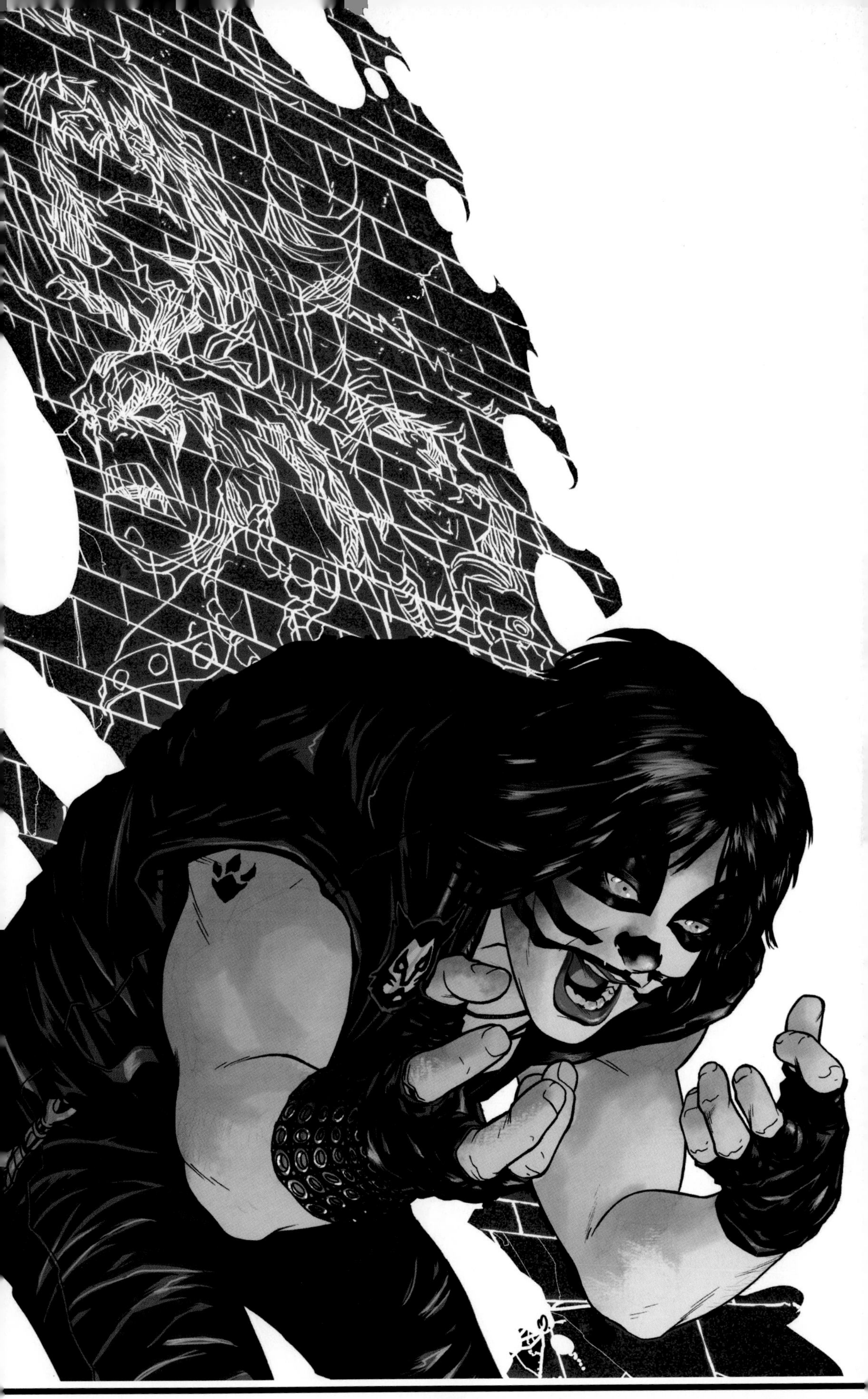

ISSUE 1: Exclusive Black C`at Comics Variant Cover Art by Mike McKone

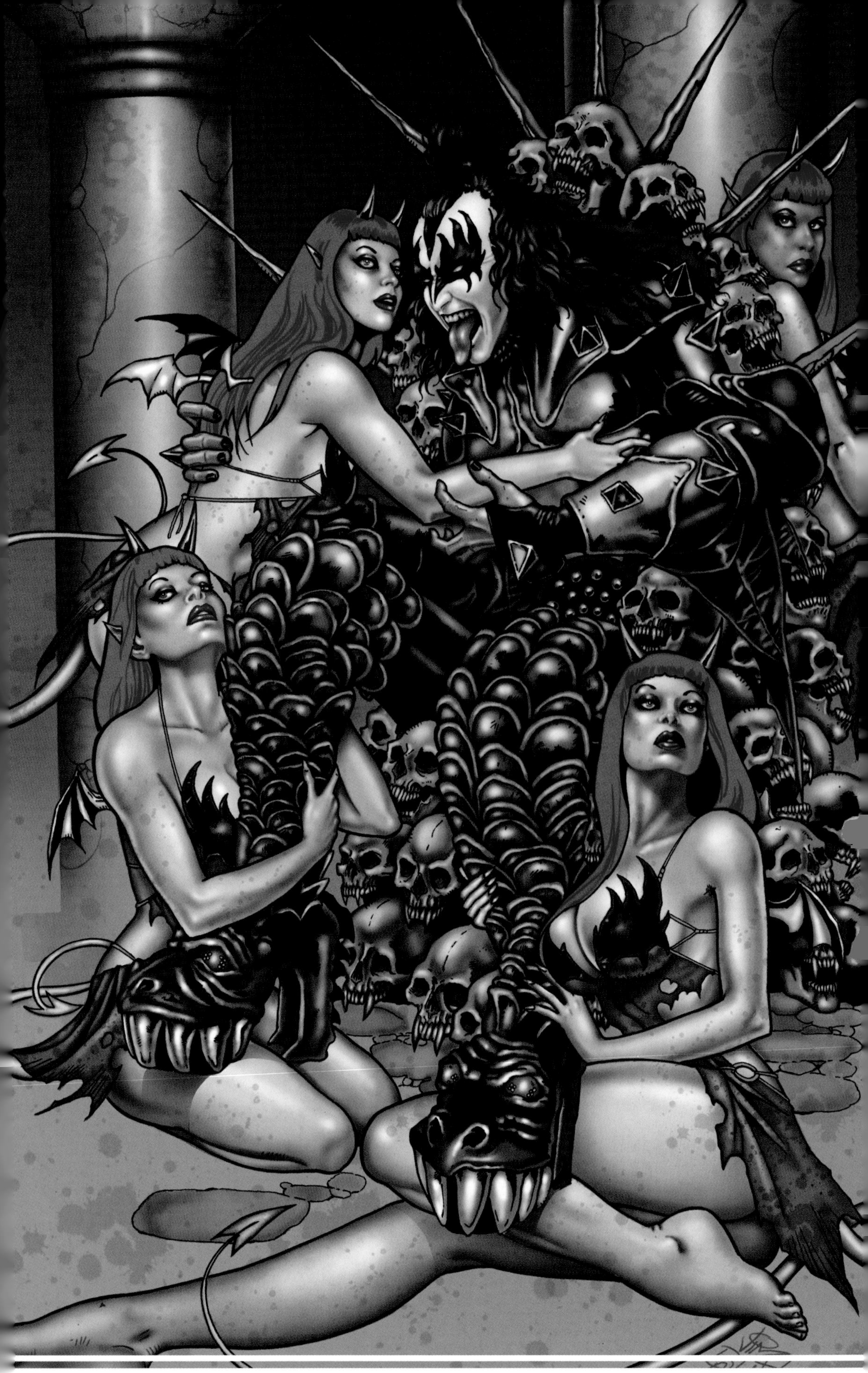

ISSUE 1: Exclusive Midtown Comics Variant Cover Art by Jim Balent

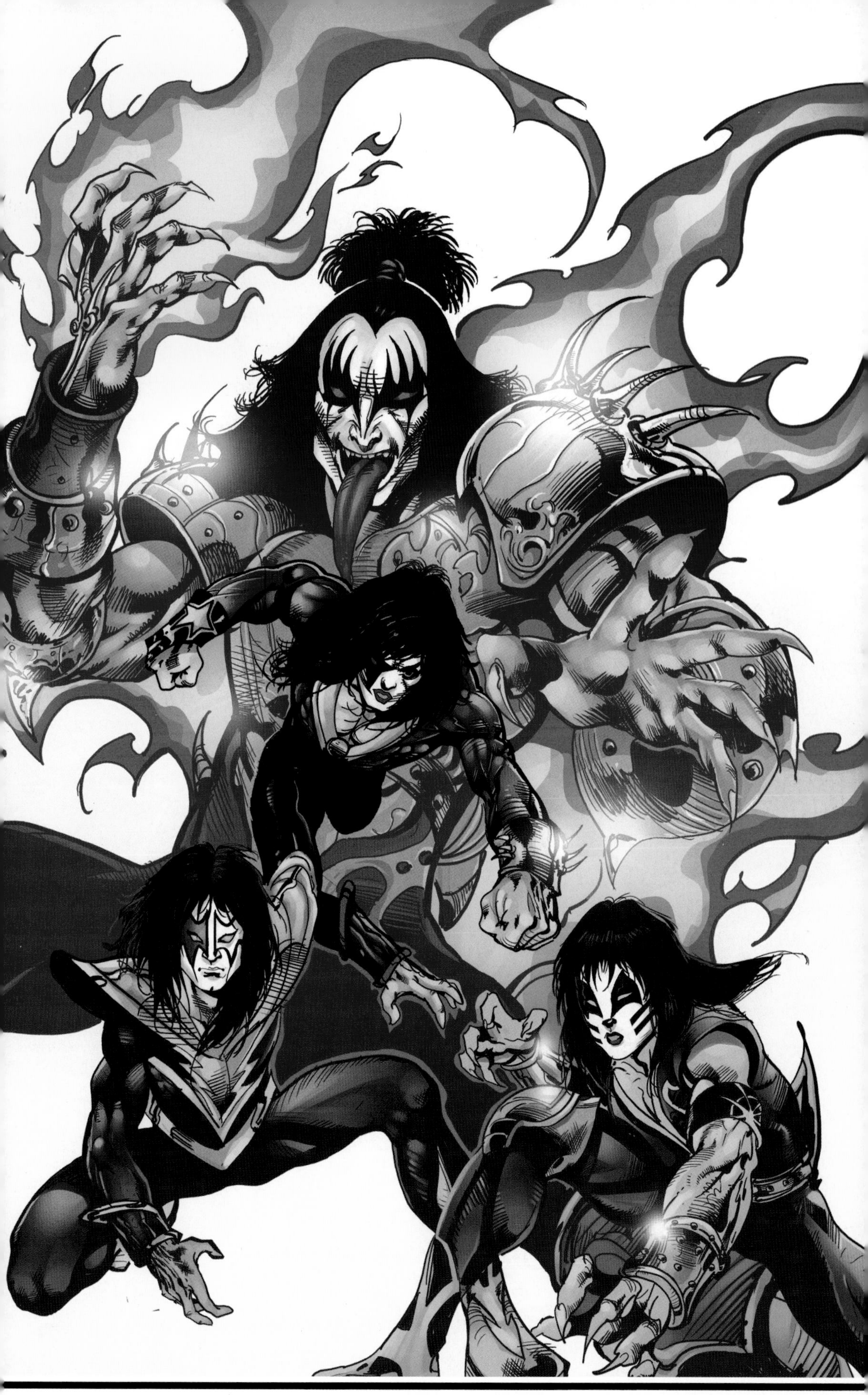

ISSUE 1: Exclusive New Jersey Comic Expo Variant Cover Art by Roberto Castro & Sal Aiala

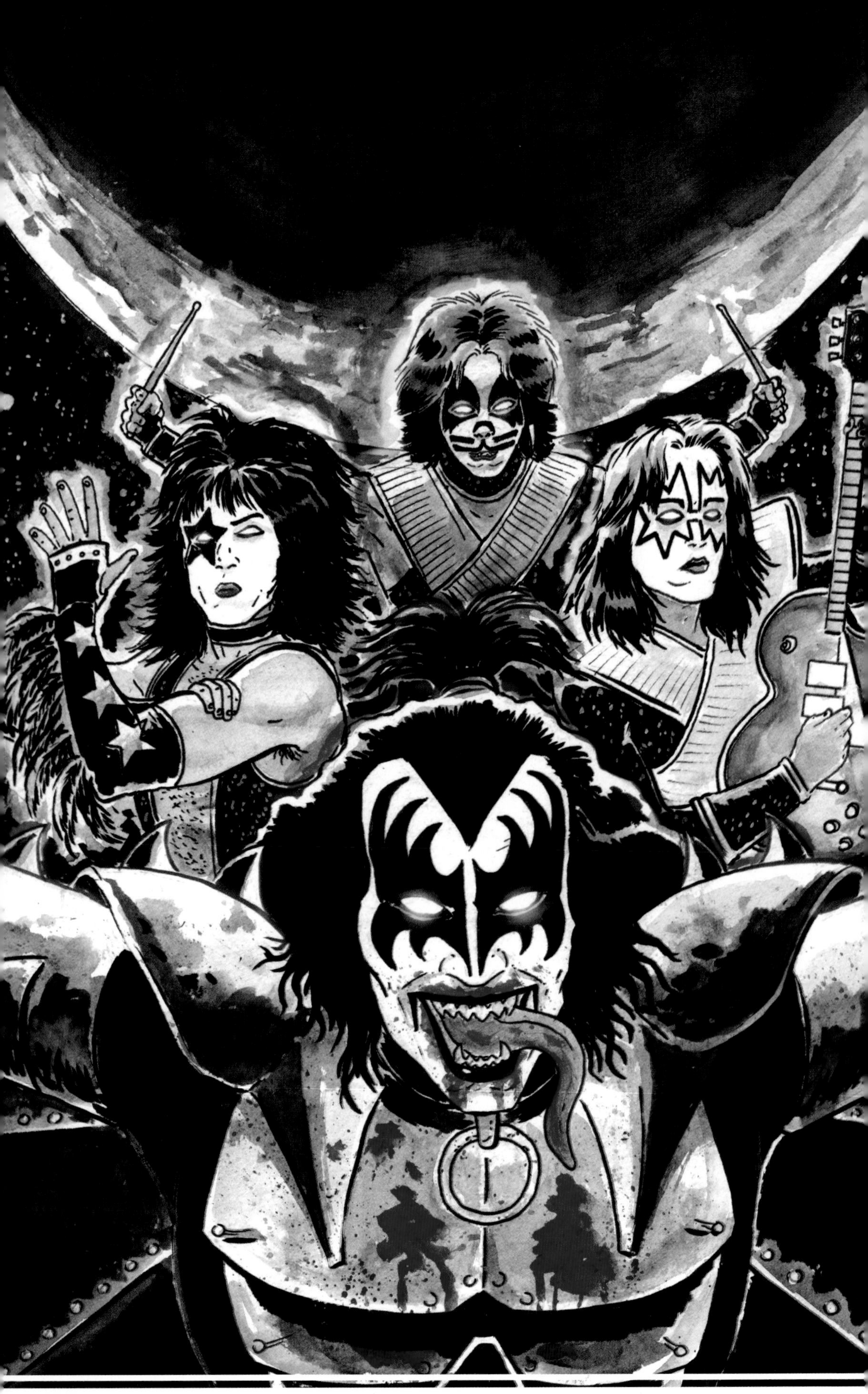

ISSUE 1: Exclusive Twilight Comics Variant Cover Art by Sean Gorman

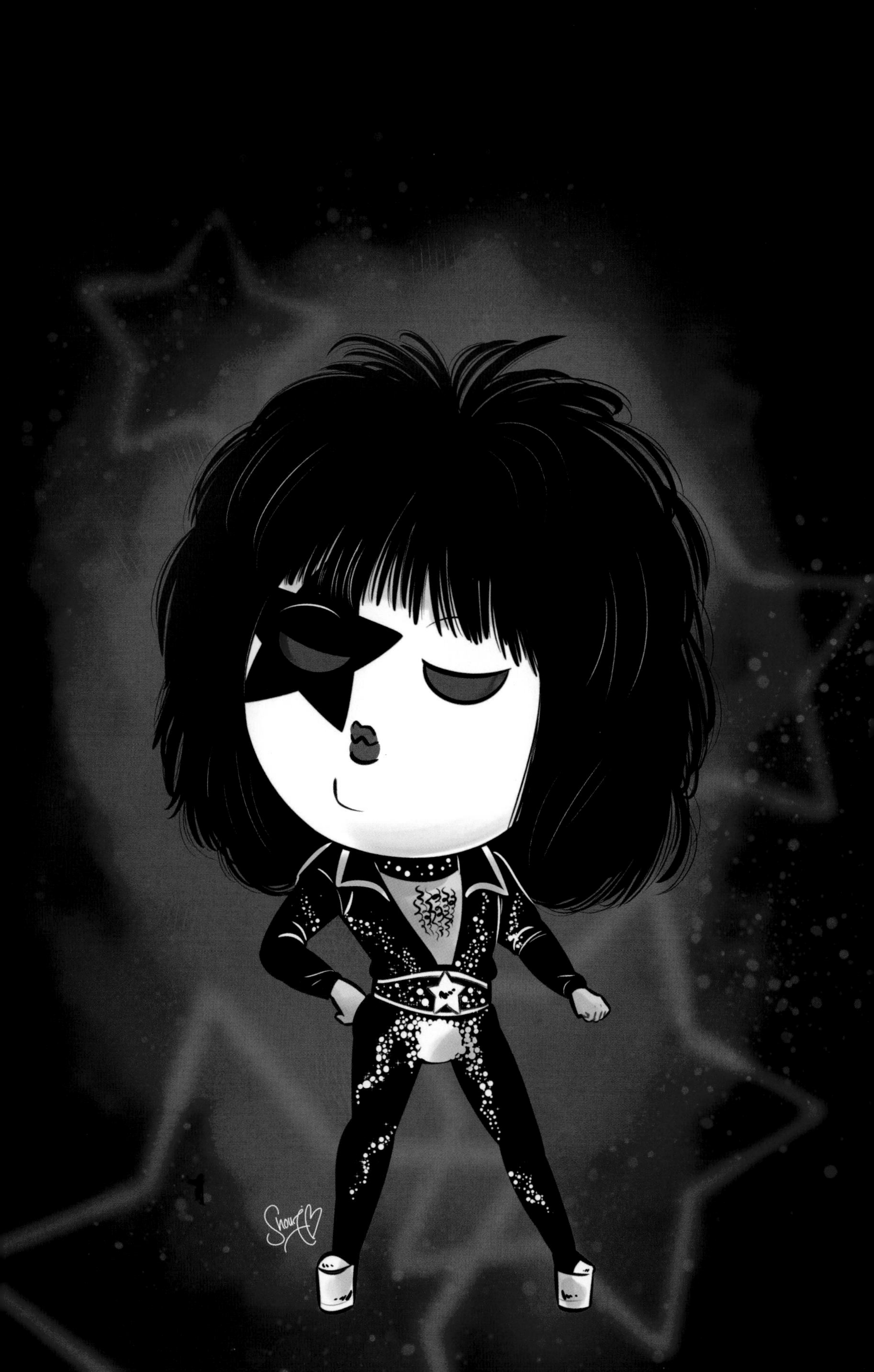

ISSUE 2: "Starchild Emoji" Art by Shouri

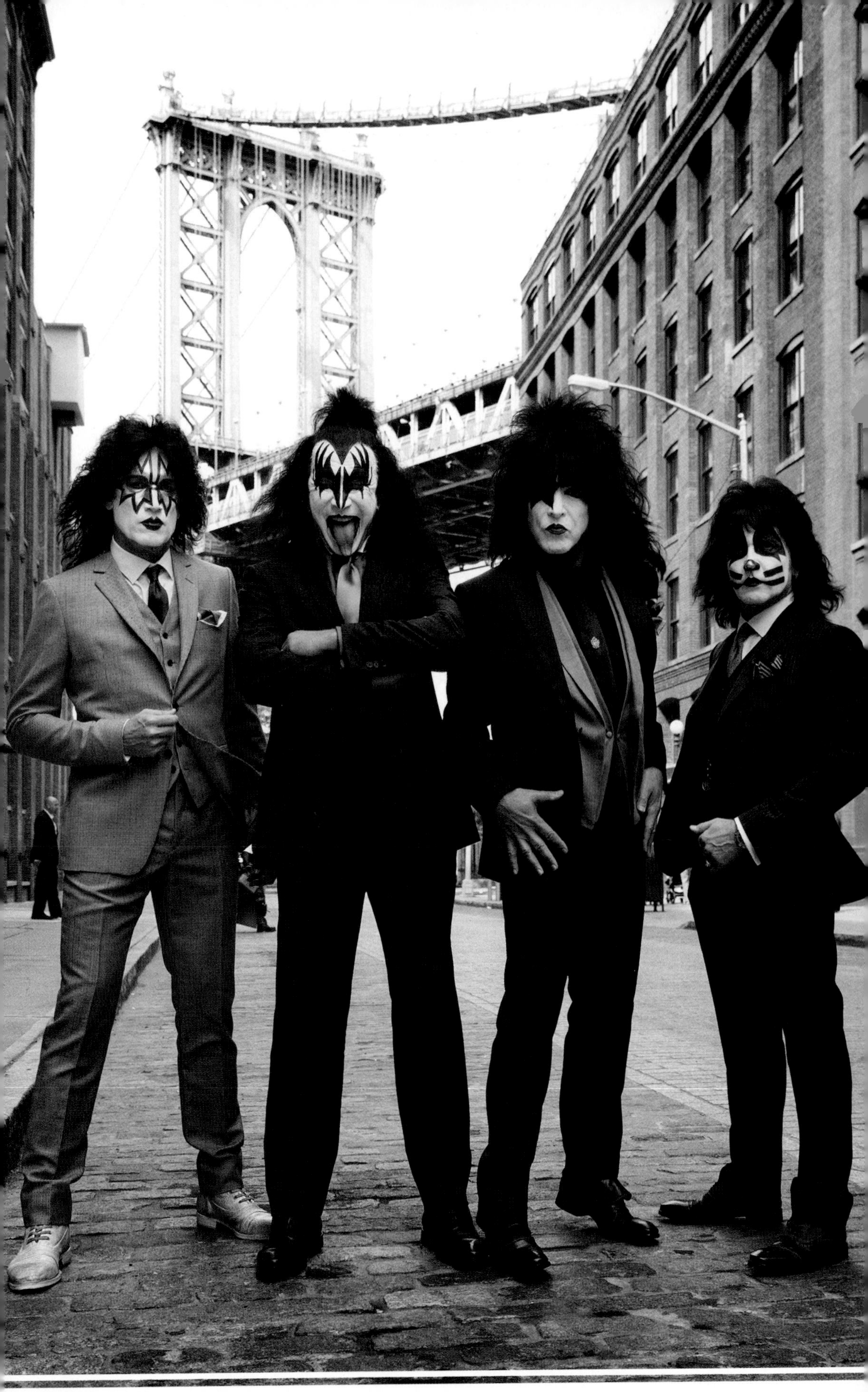

ISSUE 2: Photo Variant Cover

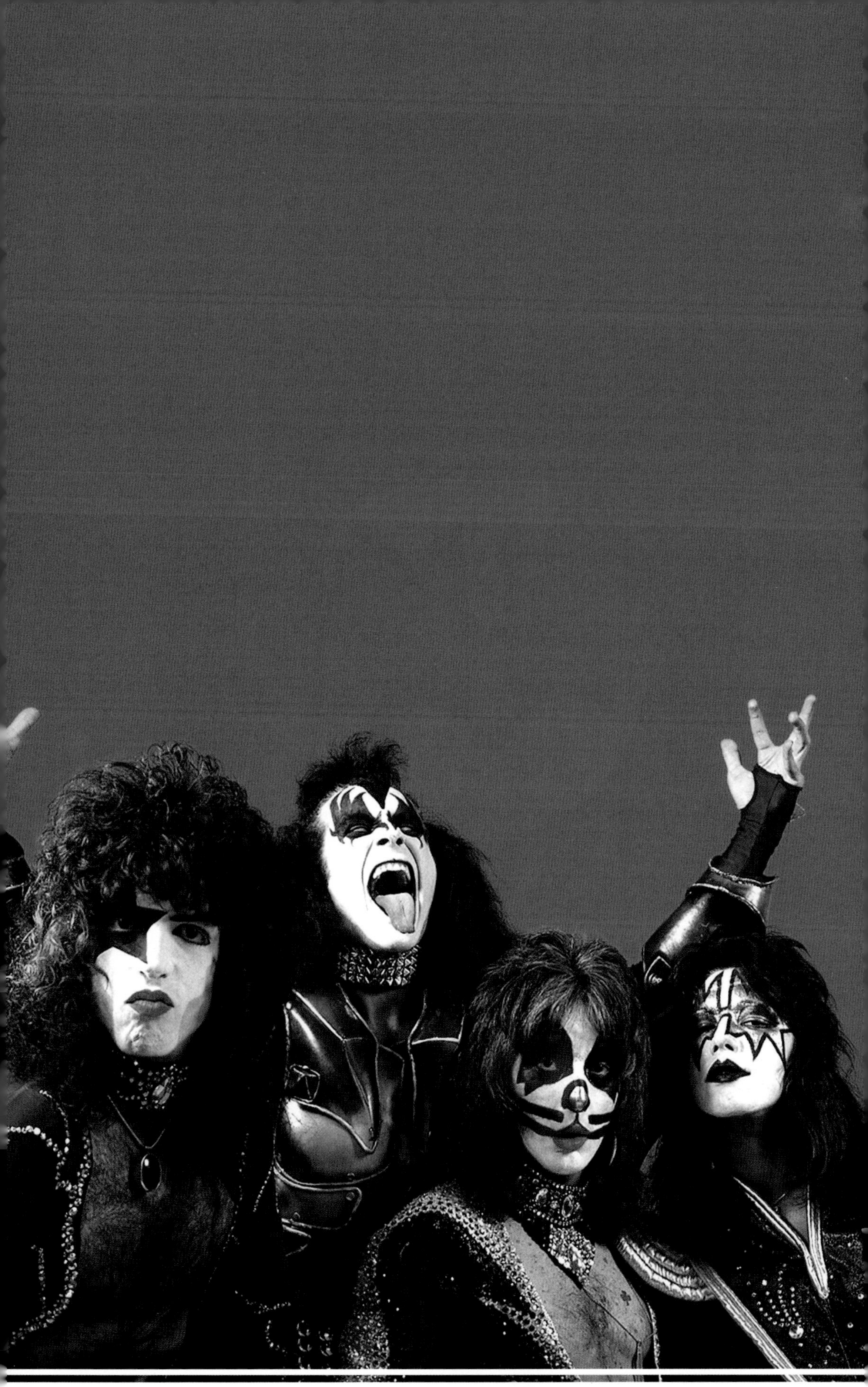

ISSUE 2: KISS Army Limited Edition Photo Variant Cover

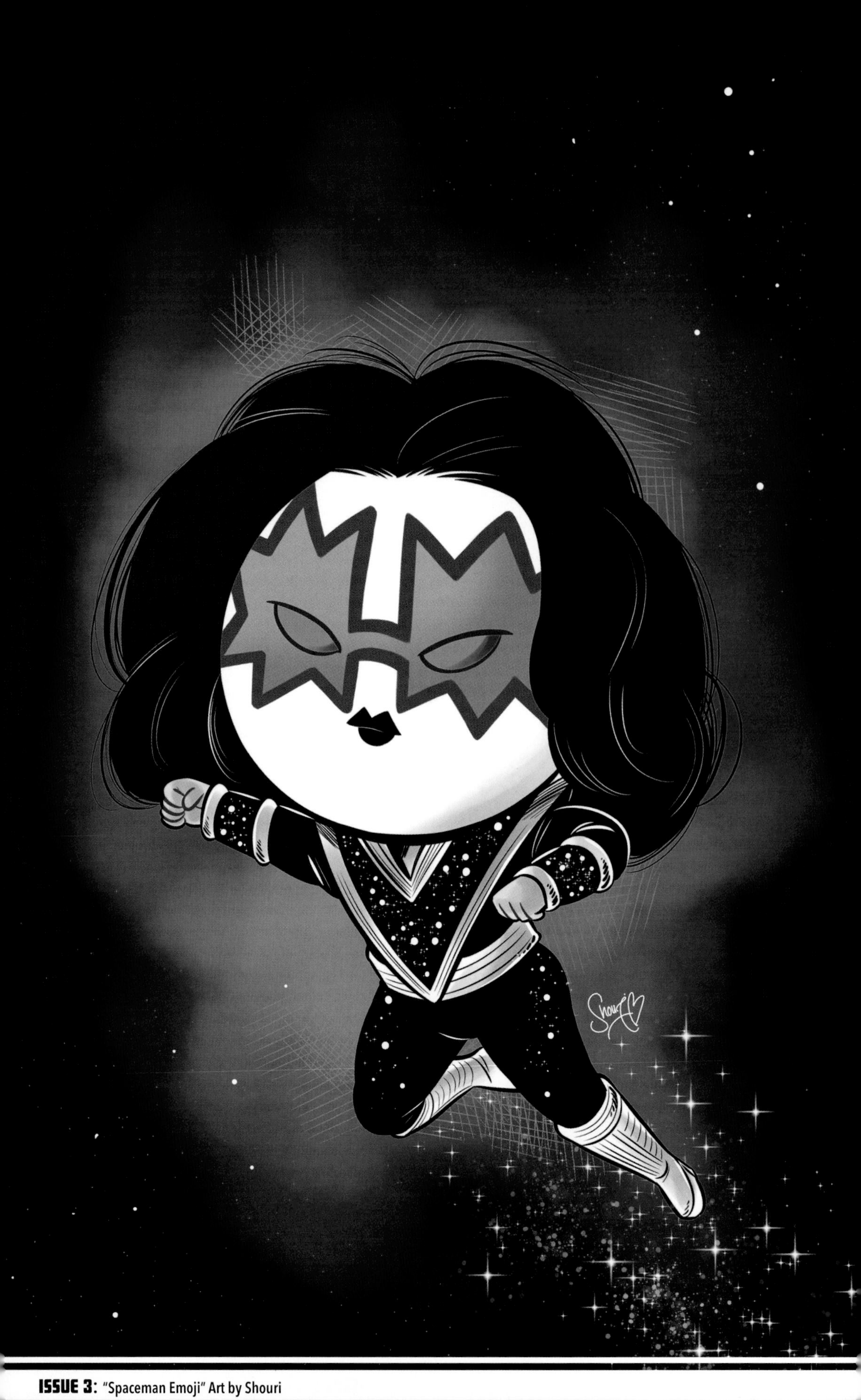
Shouri

ISSUE 3: "Spaceman Emoji" Art by Shouri

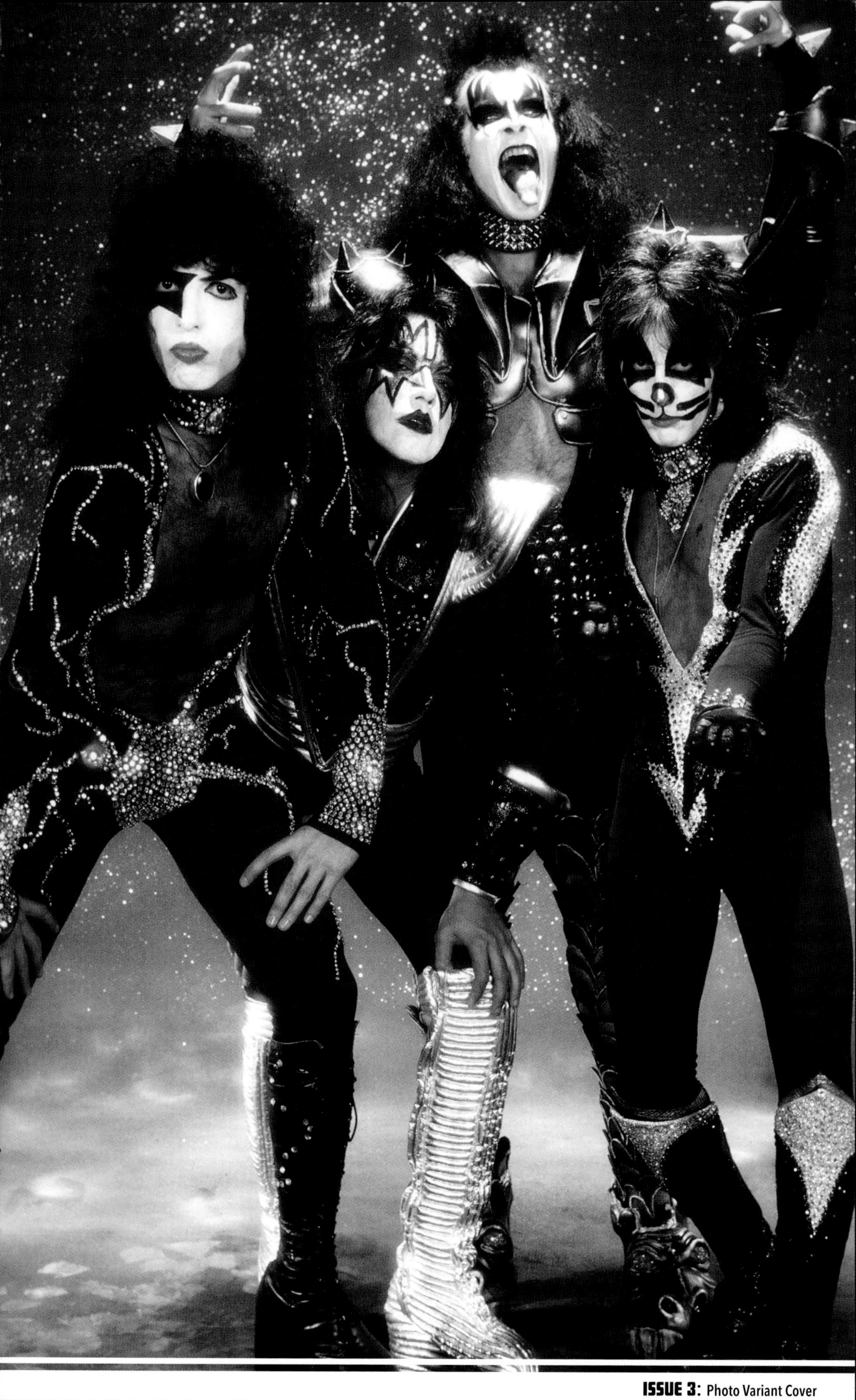

ISSUE 3: Photo Variant Cover

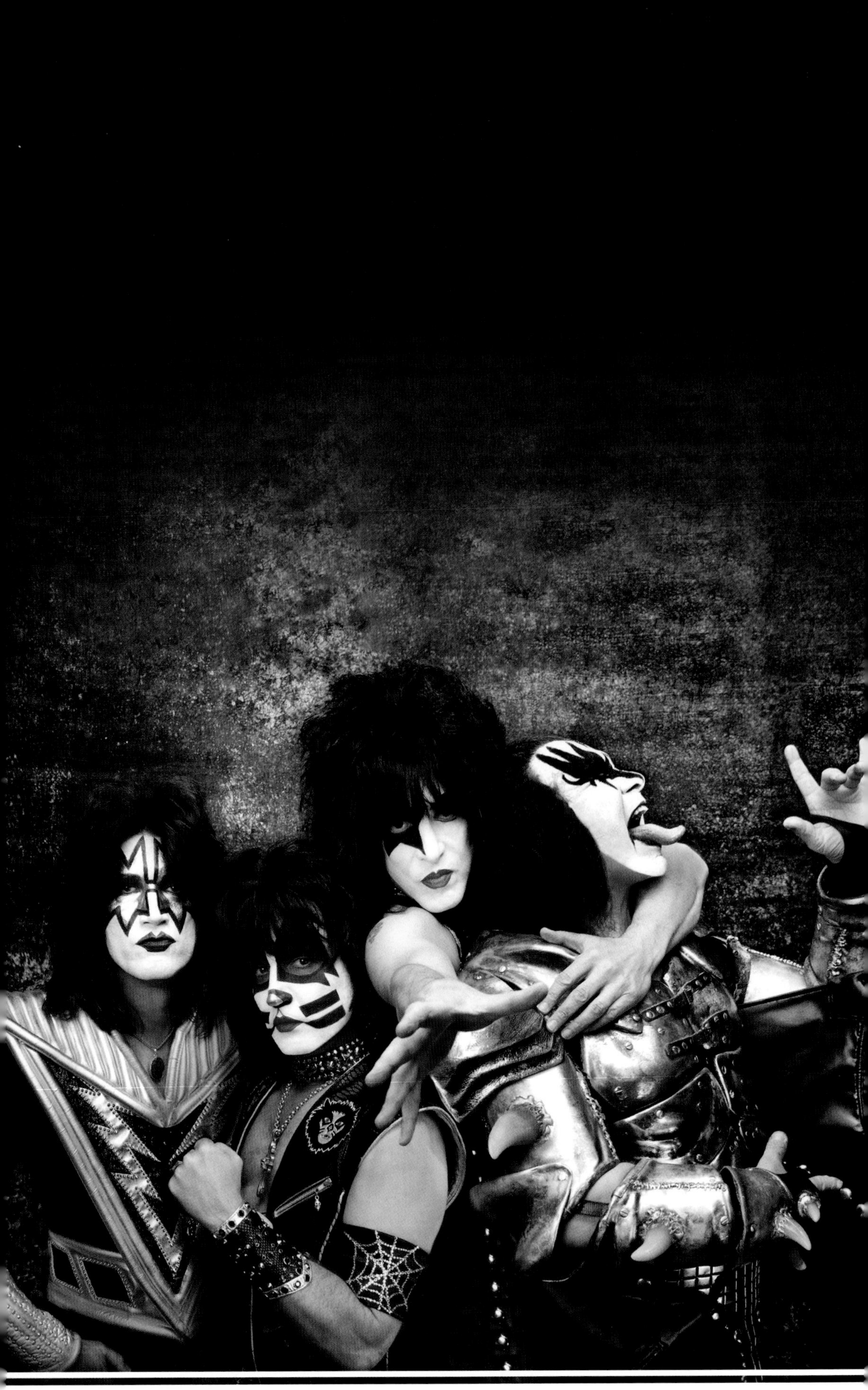

ISSUE 3: KISS Army Limited Edition Photo Variant Cover

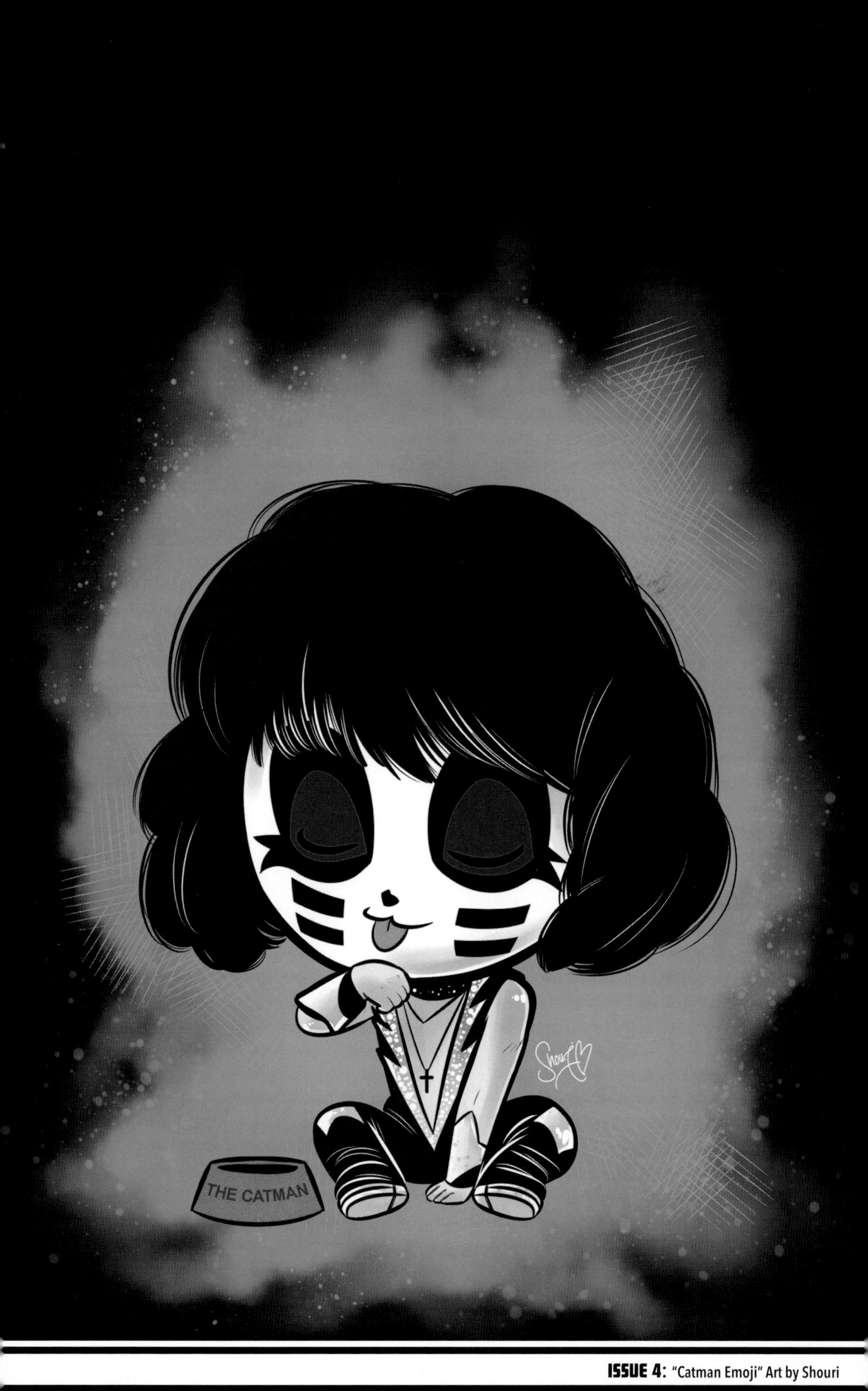
THE CATMAN
Shouri

ISSUE 4: "Catman Emoji" Art by Shouri

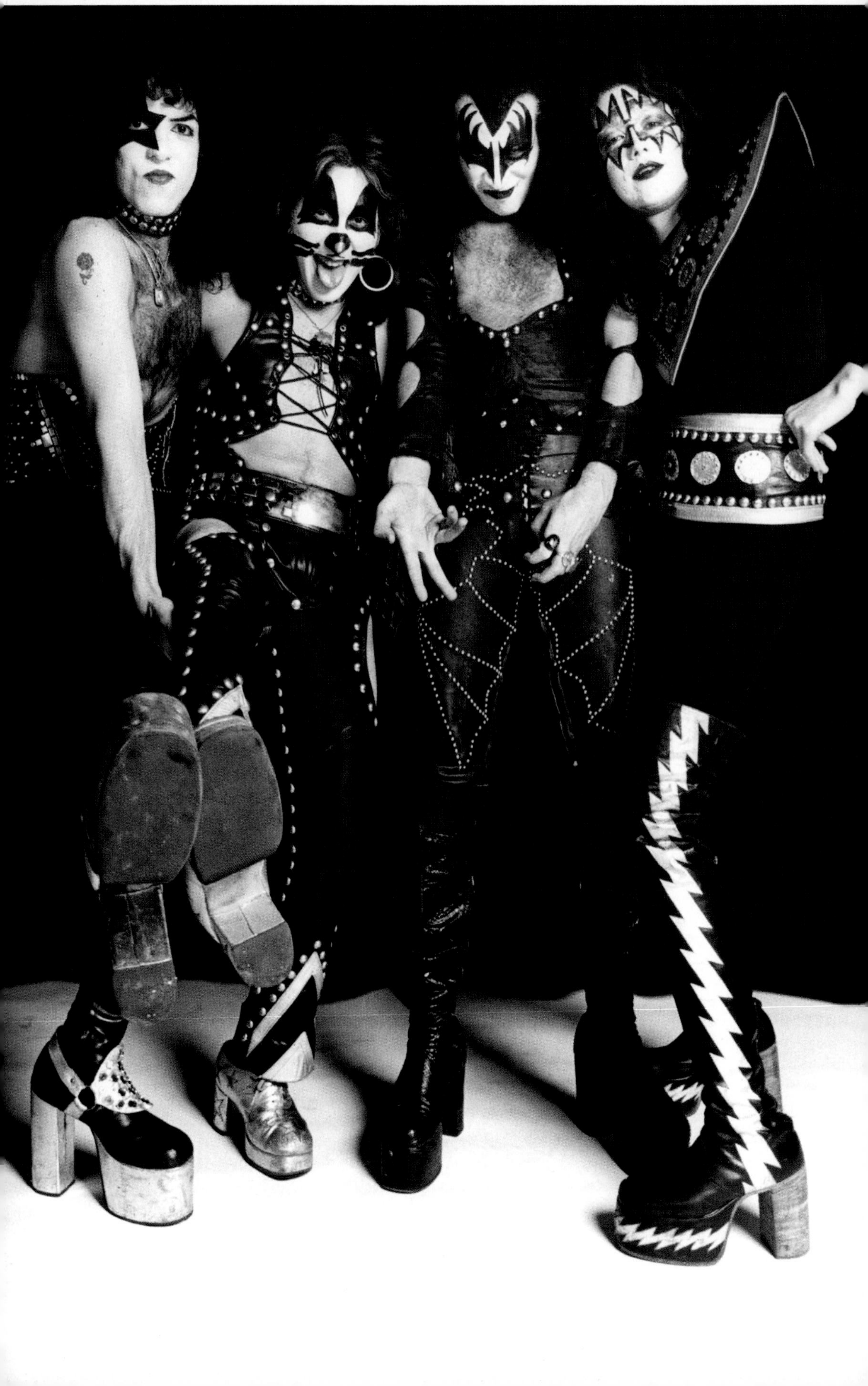

ISSUE 5: "KISS Emoji" Art by Shouri

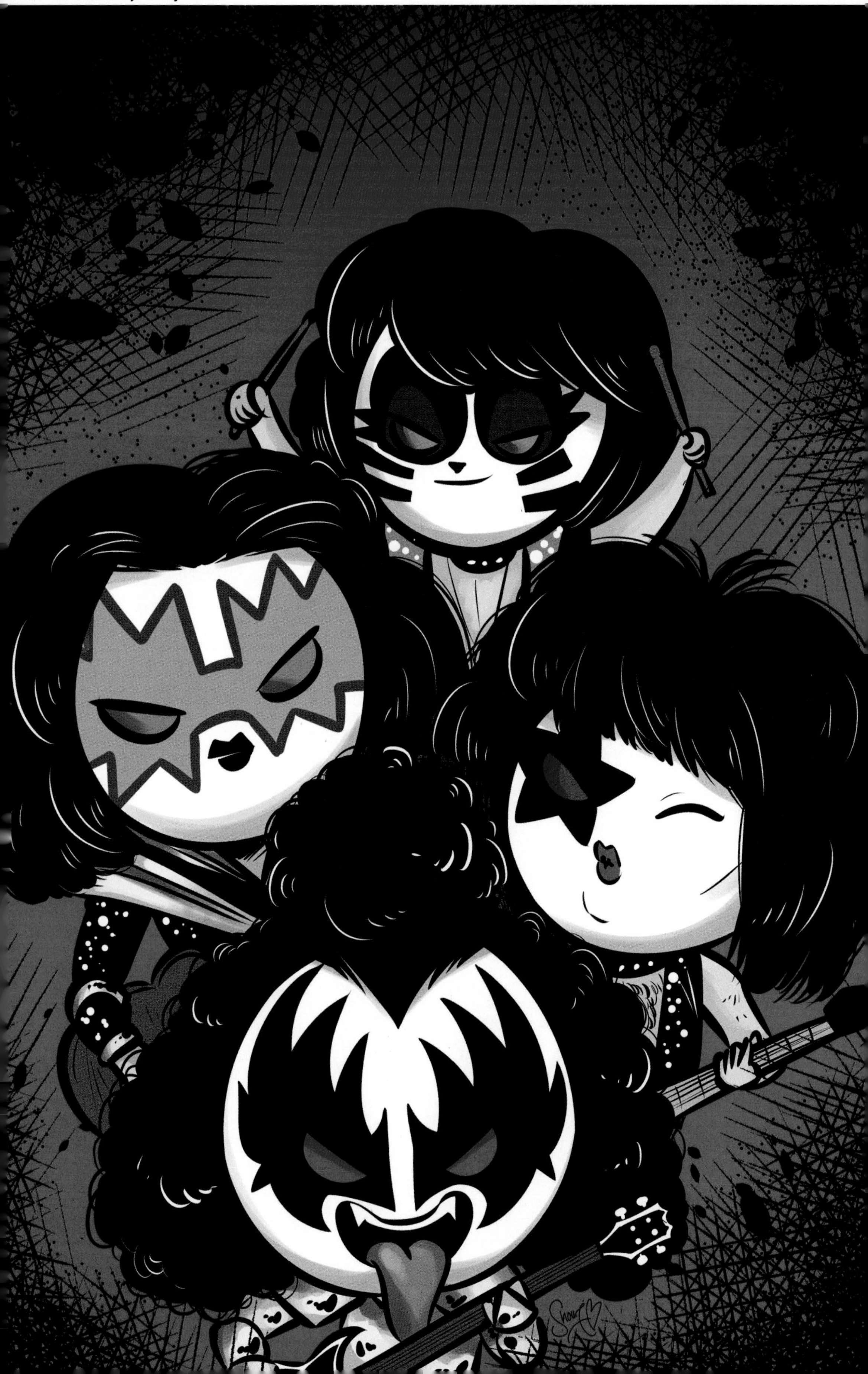

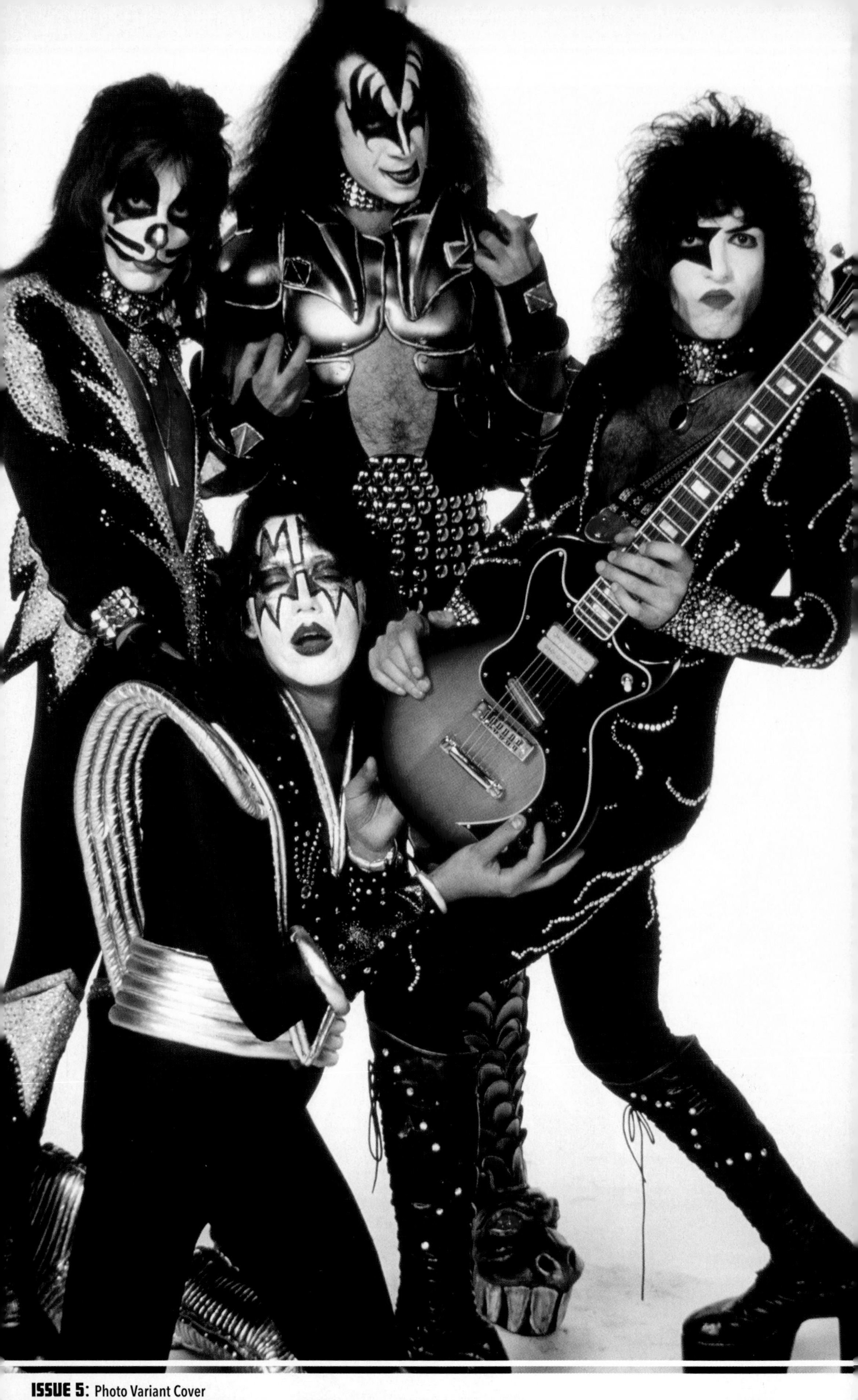

ISSUE 5: Photo Variant Cover

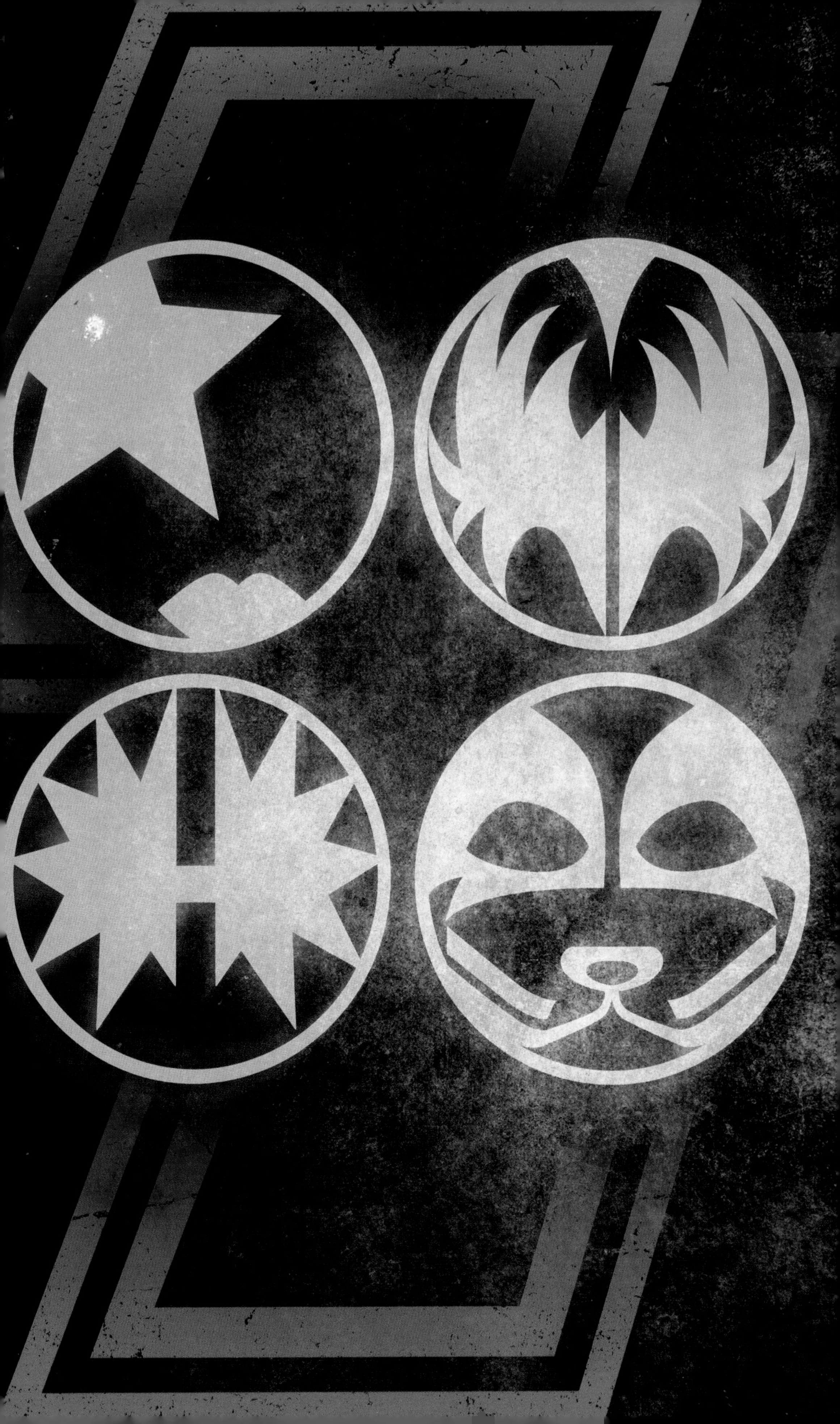

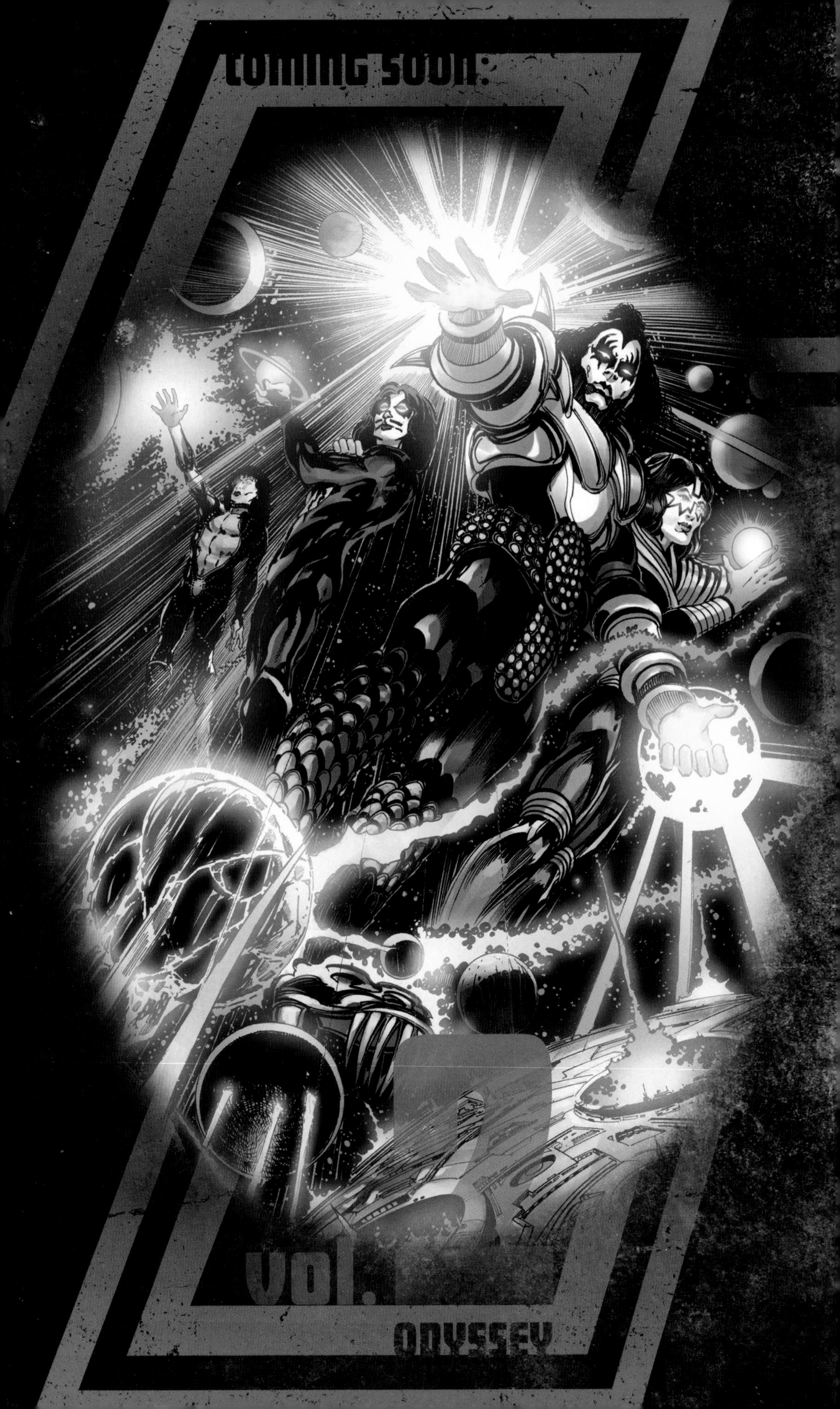
COMING SOON:
VOL.
ODYSSEY